Between Republic
and Market

Between Republic and Market

Globalization and Identity in Contemporary France

SARAH WATERS

continuum

Continuum International Publishing Group
A Bloomsbury Company

50 Bedford Square	80 Maiden Lane
London	New York
WC1B 3DP	NY 10038

www.continuumbooks.com

ISBN: 978-1-4411-2841-6 (hardcover)
978-1-4411-7208-2 (paperback)

Library of Congress Cataloging-in-Publication Data
A catalog record of this title is available from the Library of Congress.

Typeset by Newgen Imaging Systems Pvt Ltd, Chennai, India
Printed and bound in the United States of America

Contents

Acknowledgements

This book has been a long time in the making and at times I thought it would never be finished. My very patient editor at Continuum may well tell you that she shared the same opinion. Needless to say, I am very grateful to all the friends and colleagues who helped me along the way with their support, advice and encouragement. I would like to thank the Faculty of Arts at University of Leeds for granting me a precious period of research leave in 2010–2011, without which this book would never have been completed. I am grateful to all my colleagues in French at University of Leeds, who inevitably took on extra teaching and administration when I took a year's leave. Thanks to those colleagues who read chapters and made comments on the manuscript, including Brian Jenkins, David Looseley, Jim House and Martin O'Shaughnessy. Marie-Claire Antoine at Continuum was a model of patience and efficiency as the book reached its conclusion. Over the years, I have met many political activists in France whose ideas have been a huge source of inspiration to me. These include Bernard Cassen, Pierre Tartatowsky and François Chenais at Attac and Régis Hochart at the Confédération paysanne. Both associations were extremely generous in allowing me to access their archives and internal documentation. Thanks also to my old friend, Marie Lapel who always found time to welcome me at her home during my visits to France. The book draws on research carried out over many years, some of which has appeared in earlier published articles. Chapter 4 draws on an article I published in *French Cultural Studies* (vol. 22, no. 4, November 2011) and an earlier version of Chapter 6 appeared in *French Politics, Culture and Society* (vol. 28, no. 2, Summer 2010). I owe my deepest gratitude to my partner, Jonny and to our two fabulous boys, Cian and Fintan, for their love and wicked sense of humour.

1

Introduction: Republic against market

The onset of the economic crisis of 2008 sparked intense criticism, within many countries across the world, of the failings of a model of globalization that was seen as responsible for the wholesale collapse of the world economy. Many of those who had once championed free market economics now seemed to become its fiercest critics, calling for a radical overhaul of the economic system, a return to state interventionism, tougher market regulation and new financial controls. This sense of disillusionment was widespread within public opinion, the media and political life and was summed up by one observer in the following terms: 'Laissez-faire is out and activist governments are in; deregulation has become a four-letter word and the cry for more government control of the financial sector is universal' (Naím, 2009: 30).[1] In France too, the crisis triggered a fresh wave of criticism that called into question the basic tenets of neo-liberal economics. For many on the Left, this crisis vindicated what they had said all along about the dangers of 'jungle' capitalism and had brought an end to 'the most savage and irrational phase of neo-liberal capitalism' (Ramonet, 2009: 140). Hence, there was 'grim satisfaction' that a profoundly unequal economic system had come crashing to its knees and while 'leftist France gloats at capitalism's failings' there were also deeply felt concerns about the social consequences of this collapse (Vandore, 2008). Meanwhile on the Right, the crisis seemed to reaffirm long-standing criticisms of an Anglo-Saxon model that had weakened traditional forms of order, community and authority. For instance, Nicolas Sarkozy inveighed against 'Anglo-Saxon Europe, that of the big market' and reasserted France's mission to lead the world out of the present crisis and to become a beacon for a new enlightened capitalism 'so that France becomes the soul of the new rebirth that the world needs' (Sarkozy, 2008a). At the same time, the crisis prompted a renewed activism by leftist intellectuals who produced an 'unprecedented outpouring' of new books, newspaper articles and manifestos on the theme of the crisis (Wieder, 2010). In September 2010, notably, over 700 French economists signed a widely publicized manifesto for 'an alternative economic and social strategy' for Europe in the wake of the economic crisis which, they argued, had proven the disastrous consequences of neo-liberalism for the world.[2]

Yet in France, this criticism was not a response to recent economic events, but reflected arguments that had been consistently and forcefully made over the preceding 20 years. During this period, France had been at the forefront of a movement of opposition to globalization that mobilized on a national and international stage, so that for many activists 'the Hexagon has often been perceived across the world as the model to follow' (Pleyers, 2003: 141). The purpose of this book is to examine the nature and causes of French opposition to globalization during this period. Why did France seem to produce greater opposition to globalization than anywhere else? How was this opposition articulated and expressed? To consider these questions is to look in on a nation that is struggling to redefine itself and the terms of its political identity in a changing globalized world.

While all European nations have experienced globalization, it is in France that this produced its deepest tensions and generated its greatest resistance. Nowhere else did globalization spark such a scale of social protest, public malaise, political opposition and intellectual self-enquiry. An official report carried out at the request of Nicolas Sarkozy summed up French attitudes to globalization in the following terms: 'For over 15 years at least, the French attitude towards globalization has been characterized by persistent mistrust and by a constant pessimism of the French towards their future, their country and the future of their children' (Védrine, 2007: 13). Repeated opinion polls demonstrate that globalization in France remains a source of deep-seated anxiety, fear and malaise and globalization is blamed for a range of ills from national decline to fading international prestige, from loss of cultural identity to increased economic vulnerability. A 2010 Eurobarometer public opinion survey of the 27 member states of the European Union, showed that France has higher levels of mistrust towards globalization than almost any other country. Such hostility intensified after the economic crisis with a loss of confidence in the role of international institutions and France was shown to have the third lowest level of trust in the European Union of all 27 countries, at 39 per cent (above Germany at 37 per cent and the UK at 20 per cent) (European Commission, 2010).

Such grievances were forcefully expressed through social protest in the streets and since the public sector strikes of 1995, described as 'the first revolt against globalization', this has become the single most important source of conflict in France, triggering an ongoing cycle of protest including the 2005 demonstrations against the European Constitutional Treaty, the 2006 demonstrations against the right-wing government's youth employment bill (Contrat première embauche), the 2009 trade union strikes and the 2010 demonstrations against Nicolas Sarkozy's pension reform (Izraelewicz, 1995). During this period, globalization became 'the new face of the enemy' as protestors focussed their anger less on the political decisions of the French government, but on 'financial markets' that were seen to reduce the state to a mere pawn in an economic game that was outside its control (Mouchard, 2005: 5). Hence those who took part in the 2010 demonstrations against pension reform argued that the real target of their protest was a neo-liberal onslaught that was undermining solidarity within French society and preventing the state from fulfilling its duties towards its citizens (Aguiton et al., 2011). Such protest was not confined to the domestic scene and France has been at the centre of a movement of opposition to neo-liberalism that has mobilized across an international stage and which French activists refer to as *altermondialisme*. French protest groupings such as Attac and the Confédération paysanne helped to spawn an international movement of opposition that brought together activists from across the world. Originally created in order to promote a 'Tobin tax' on international financial transactions, Attac was until recently an influential international grouping with affiliated organizations in nearly forty countries. Meanwhile, José Bové's Confédération paysanne has been at the centre of an international peasant movement that mobilizes farmers and citizens more widely, in a campaign for an alternative economic order that challenges both the economic and symbolic dimensions of globalization.

Such protest has been vigorously endorsed by French intellectuals who, during this period, mobilized on a scale not seen since the 1960s. Since 1995 France has been marked by 'a return of intellectual engagement' after a prolonged period of apparent inactivity and quiescence (Sommier, 2003: 151). Impelled by a deep-seated outrage against what they saw as a profoundly unjust economic order, they wrote books and newspaper articles, took to the streets, formed petition movements and created new intellectual clubs and think tanks. This period was marked by the rise of the 'radical intellectual' who increasingly challenged the mainstream Left and called for the creation of new leftist popular movements (Noiriel, 2005). Leading leftist thinkers such as Pierre Bourdieu, Cornelius Castoriadis, Ignacio Ramonet, Viviane Forrester, Susan George and Alain Badiou became the figureheads of a new anti-liberal critique that denounced globalization and called for radical reform. At the same time, there was a proliferation of intellectual clubs and think tanks (Attac, Raisons d'agir, Pénombre, Fondation Copernic, Acrimed and Fondation Voltaire) that sought to construct a new analytical framework for left-wing opposition. Drawing on their own intellectual resources, French thinkers aimed to produce a 'counter-expertise' that would challenge the tenets of neo-liberalism and legitimize demands for radical social change. Similarly, the leftist intellectual press experienced an exponential success during this period, with newspapers such as *Le Monde diplomatique* doubling its sales to the French public.

In international settings, such as the European Union, G20 or the World Economic Forum, French political leaders on both the Left and Right acted as a voice of opposition to a dominant neo-liberal doctrine. At a time when many governments accepted neo-liberal policies unquestioningly, France was one of the few countries to challenge this model and to question its benefits for society. Hence Lionel Jospin, when he was Prime Minister of the Plural Left government (1997–2002), warned about the dangers of a 'casino economy' and argued that the world economy needed to be 'tamed', 'mastered' and 'civilized' in the interests of France and of all humanity. He believed that France had a central role to play in reordering the world system around democratic and humanist values which might lead to 'the blossoming of a new universalism' (Jospin, 2002a: 10). Meanwhile, Jacques Chirac during his two consecutive terms as president (1995–2002 and 2002–2007) sought to 'humanize' globalization and create a world economic order which placed the interests of people before profit. In his diplomatic visits to foreign leaders, he increasingly spoke of the need for a 'globalization for everyone' and for a world order rooted in universalist principles. Finally, Nicolas Sarkozy when he became president in 2007 reaffirmed a well-versed French stance, seeing himself as the pioneer of a 'moral capitalism' that would restore European values and principles to the heart of the world economic order. In the period since the economic crisis, Sarkozy went further than any other European leader in his demands for tough financial regulation and structural reform. While coming to power on a campaign of ultra-liberalism, Sarkozy, in the wake of the economic crisis, called for a 'new social regulation' of capitalism and sought to place the social question at the centre of the G20 summit which took place in November 2011 in Cannes.

Recent studies in the social sciences have explored France's difficult relationship with globalization and looked at the nature of such vehement opposition (Touraine, 1996, 2001, 2010; Gordon & Meunier, 2001; Bavarez, 2003, 2009; Smith, 2004; Arthuis, 2007; Dockès, 2007; Sylvestre, 2008). Some suggest that globalization has become 'the great fear of the 21st century' and that France has become paralysed by a state of stagnation and immobilism (Dockès, 2007: 15). For others, France has lost its foothold in a post–Cold War order and is headed for steep and irreversible decline

(Bavarez, 2003, 2009; Zemmour, 2010; Chevènement, 2011). Yet these studies (written mainly by economists, economic historians or trade policy specialists) tend to treat France's relationship with globalization as an economic problem alone, one that concerns the structures and mechanisms of the French economy. If France had such difficulties with globalization, according to this view, this was because its economic structures were insufficiently adapted to the requirements of an international economy and were impervious to change. They each portray a France that is encumbered by statist institutions and obsolete structures and that is desperately in need of reform. French opposition, in their view, was driven by corporatist interests and a desire to cling onto the 'generous' privileges afforded by the French welfare system. In the trade off between the costs and benefits of market integration, these authors argue, the French preferred to safeguard their own social model and to resist change. As globalization is seen in these studies primarily as an economic or structural problem, the solution to this problem is also seen to lie in the economic domain, in a better 'adaptation' of the French economy, policy adjustment and structural reform. If only France would reform its structures, open up its economy and reduce its public deficit, it would soon reap all the benefits of global capitalism. Faced with the prospect of cheap imports, economic productivity and increased growth, many believe that all sources of discontent would soon melt away. This economistic perspective is widely shared by political leaders, intellectuals and economists alike and helped to give rise, over the past 20 years, to a consensual political viewpoint or *pensée unique*, which saw economic reform as the only path open to France. It helped to pave the way for Nicolas Sarkozy's reformist campaign and his promise for a 'clean break' with the past and for sweeping economic reforms. Indeed, some of the key proponents of this economistic viewpoint threw their weight behind Sarkozy during the 2007 presidential elections and supported his demands for radical reform. We will see that French political leaders have been characterized by a highly contradictory stance in relation to globalization that consists of both virulently denouncing it, while actively pursuing policies of economic liberalization and structural reform in order to integrate France more fully into a global economy.

I argue in this book that French opposition to globalization transcends economic matters alone and also concerns more complex, deeply rooted and irreducible questions of identity. At stake are not only issues of economic calculus, market competition or trade advantage, but rather, the fundamental means by which the French define themselves and their place in the world. If the French resist globalization so virulently, this is because they often believe they are defending a whole way of life, or 'civilization' with its roots in the French Revolution, defined by social gains or *acquis* and by immutable collective principles. Their opposition is articulated, not in terms of material or economic advantages alone, but in relation to ideological principles, political traditions, collective institutions and universalist goals. Globalization in the French public sphere is rarely perceived or represented in terms of a piecemeal economic adjustment or market reform. In recent French books on globalization by leading public intellectuals, a language of economic rationalism is eschewed in favour of more compelling metaphors of 'dictatorship', 'tyranny', 'barbarism' or 'chaos'. Such books have found a deep-seated resonance within public opinion and helped to shape wider French perceptions of globalization as a profound and all-encompassing threat. Since globalization was seen to threaten democracy itself, the only recourse available to the French people was one of mass resistance. The theme of 'resistance' is increasingly invoked in order to convey the dangers represented by globalization and the urgency of popular mobilization against it. Just as during World War II, when many engaged in resistance against the Nazi regime, so many now believe that it is necessary to engage in a new phase of resistance against the 'dictatorship of the markets'. Hence, the former resistance hero, Stéphane Hessel's book *Indignez-Vous* (*A Time for Outrage*, 2010) in which he calls for the spirit of the resistance to be revived at a time of globalization and appeals to young people to mobilize against it, was one of France's best-selling books in 2010.

If globalization has provoked greater opposition in France than elsewhere, this is because it is here that it seems to come most sharply into conflict with the symbols and structures of political identity. Globalization has been experienced in France not as a market adjustment, but as an assault on the Republic and as a clash between two opposing universes whose differences seem irreconcilable. In the French case, globalization turned the whole pattern of identity upside down, challenging the very foundations on which Frenchness is based. Recent studies by leading international scholars emphasize the profound implications of globalization for identity. They tend to see globalization as a process that transcends the economic sphere alone and that penetrates into every aspect of social, political and cultural life. In their best-selling book, *Empire* (2000), neo-Marxist scholars, Antonio Negri and Michael Hardt describe globalization as the rise of a new hegemonic and deterritorialized system of power that is progressively extending its control over the whole planet. Unlike older forms of imperial rule, Empire is not limited to particular institutions or territories, but intrudes on every aspect of personal life, producing new forms of domination and transforming the human condition itself. For the American conservative political scientist Samuel Huntington, in his controversial book, *The Clash of Civilisations* (1996), globalization has exacerbated conflict between cultures, not on the basis of competing economic interests, but along broad civilizational lines. He sees a post–Cold War order defined by a kind of conflict between different cultures whose differences are 'real and basic'. For him, conflict in a globalized world transcends the economic domain and involves more fundamental and deeply rooted questions of tradition, belief, ideology, community and belonging. Similarly, for the prominent sociologist, Zygmunt Bauman in *Liquid Fear* (2006), globalization is a cataclysmic force that destroys social and political relationships and leaves individuals alone to face all the dangers and uncertainties of a globalized world. He defines our contemporary globalized age by a state of existential anxiety or 'liquid fear' as people become dislocated from the bonds that tie them to community and place and assailed by unimaginable fears. Globalization has prompted a search for belonging and rootedness, a search which is ultimately futile, as all forms of social relationship have been destroyed. While coming from very different political and disciplinary perspectives, these international scholars all emphasize the profound implications of globalization for questions of identity, political culture, ideological beliefs and belonging.

However, the impact of globalization in any one place is likely to depend on a complex interaction between international processes of economic restructuring and nationally defined structures, values and traditions. Whereas in some countries, with a different political culture, globalization was perceived as a simple market expansion, in France it was experienced as an attack on the essence of democracy itself. Here globalization seemed to call into question key dimensions of what it meant to be French and the relationship of the French people to their history, ideological values and institutions. Globalization can be seen to challenge French identity in a number of fundamental ways. Firstly, it undermines the role of the French state and therefore a key component of identity. Globalization is seen by many to represent a 'dictature des marchés' that empowers unelected international institutions (European Union, International Monetary Fund, World Trade Organization) and multinational corporations at the expense of representative government. The ratification of the Lisbon Treaty by the French government on 8 February 2008, which significantly reinforced the decision-making powers of the European Union to the detriment of national governments, has been seen by many as a further step in the demise of a French model centred on state sovereignty and independence.

Secondly, globalization challenges the foundational values on which the French Republic is built and which continue to define the terms of identity today. If globalization has provoked such deep-seated reaction in France, this is because it transcends economic interests alone and is seen to violate values that are held as sacred and universal, to contravene an entire 'religion of humanity' that provides the cornerstone on which French society is built

(Peillon, 2008: 152). Opposition to globalization is expressed not in a language of trade or economics but by appealing to abstract ideological principles that are deemed to be valid for all peoples and all times. Hence political leaders from Left to Right denounce globalization in the name of values of equality, solidarity and justice which are seen as the foundational values of French and European civilization.

Thirdly, globalization diminishes France's stature in the world and its self-image as a beacon of universalism and a model for other nations to follow. Debates about globalization are suffused with fears about French decline, loss of stature and fading prestige on an international stage. This debate, launched by the right-wing economist Nicolas Bavarez in his 2003 book *La France qui tombe* (*France in Free-fall*), has continued unabated ever since and has been articulated more recently in books by Eric Zemmour and Jean-Pierre Chevènement (Zemmour, 2010; Chevènement, 2011). These 'déclinologues' point to a France that has lost its political and cultural influence in the world and hence an essential part of its collective self. Since the onset of the 2008 economic crisis, concerns about American 'hyperpower' have been displaced, for many, by fears of the rising economic power of China and India and of a new threat to French integrity in the form of a 'globalization of Islam' (Juvin, 2010; Zemmour, 2010).

Fourthly, globalization threatens the French social model and a relationship between state and citizen that is seen to provide the foundation for national cohesion. Originating in the principles defined by the French Revolution and the Third Republic concept of 'solidarity' and institutionalized by the *Etat Providence,* created in the aftermath of World War II, the French social model is intrinsic to national identity and to a sense of Frenchness itself (Audier, 2010). In France, identity is bound with a conception of the state that protects its citizens, that redistributes wealth and that guarantees equality. This explains why French political leaders have anchored their ongoing neo-liberal reforms in a discourse which appeals to a social state and why economic liberalization has been accompanied by high levels of social spending. Likewise, protest against globalization is expressed not in terms of sectional economic interests, but as the defence of an entire social model with its roots in the French Revolution and in principles defined over two centuries. Hence, the 2010 protest against pension reform was articulated in terms of the principle of solidarity and a defence of France's social model and therefore of a precious legacy of national tradition.

Fifthly, globalization challenges French cultural identity and has long been equated with an Americanization of French culture and with cultural loss. It has been widely documented that France has gone further than any other European country in its efforts to protect, subsidize and promote national culture in the face of homogenizing globalizing forces. France championed the notion of 'cultural diversity' and the idea that cultural products should be exempt from rules on free trade and this notion was incarnated by the UNESCO Convention in 2005.

The purpose of this book is to examine how France's political identity has been renegotiated at a time a globalization. What has French identity come to signify in today's globalized world? Does this identity look backwards towards an idealized national past or have there been efforts to construct new and alternative forms of that identity that transcend national boundaries? If globalization challenged French identity, it also led to a profound reassertion of identity, with a renewed search for symbols and repositories of national unity, cohesion and belonging. France's preoccupation with its own identity and self-image is hardly new and such concerns have surfaced periodically throughout the twentieth century, particularly during periods of national crisis. Yet, many agree that today this concern with identity has been elevated to the status of a national obsession. In this book, I will draw on a constructivist approach that sees identity as something that is constantly reinvented in response to changing contingencies and needs over time. A constructivist approach, as developed by French scholars, emphasizes three core aspects of identity (Thiesse, 2001; Noiriel, 2007; Citron, 2008). First, identity is a construct that is created, fabricated and invented in response to specific needs. A constructivist approach emphasizes the instrumental uses to which identity is put and in particular, the way in which history can be manipulated in order to serve political ends in the present. Second, identity is a fluid and changing concept that tends to become important at times of profound transformation or external threat, when the boundaries of a community or nation seem to be vulnerable. At such times, identity becomes a means to reaffirm symbolically the boundaries of the community and to rebuild forms of belonging, community and rootedness. Third, identity is dialectical in nature and is always defined in relation to a perceived enemy or Other. Identity is not created in a void, but requires an Other to constitute itself, as it counterposes the specific features of 'Us' against those of an external 'them'.

French identity, at a time of globalization, has been reconfigured in a variety of ways, some of which invoke an idealized rural past, an illustrious national history or images of colonial grandeur and others that point to an *altermondialisme* that transcends the boundaries of France alone and emphasizes the irreducible rights and freedoms of all human beings. Nowhere is this reassertion of identity more evident that in the rise of the Republic as a unifying symbol of the nation and of Frenchness itself. Scholars have recently highlighted the resurgence of the Republic as a symbol of national identity at a time of globalization and this is a symbol that mobilizes support across party lines and within all sections of society (Spitz, 2005; Sieffert, 2006; Bernstein, 2007; Ferrand, 2007; Peillon, 2008; Rozès, 2009; Audier, 2010). For Stéphane Rozès, the Republic today provides a 'national imaginary', a repository for meaning and identification in the face of the uncertainties and upheaval of the market. It provides a refuge from harsh economic realities, conjuring up an idealized world in which identity remains strong, tradition is preserved, social bonds are restored and in which a benevolent state still casts its eye over the people (Rozès, 2009). Through the symbol of the Republic, the French can imagine a world in which the state retains its authority and in which France still has a universalist mission to fulfil in the world. This is a reverse mirror image of contemporary realities and seems to offer an antidote to all the perceived evils of today's globalizing world.

It is in relation to the Republic, to its foundational values and to its institutional model that French opposition to globalization has often been articulated and expressed. Yet this revived republican identity has had contradictory effects on France's relationship with the outside world. On the one hand, it provided a countermodel with which to challenge political developments, to contest neo-liberal doctrine and to make demands for progressive social change. Over the past 20 years, France has been at the forefront of a movement of opposition to globalization that has mobilized on a national and international stage. Hence it was French and Brazilian activists who launched the first World Social Forum in Porto Alegre, Brazil in 2001, which has since become a critical site for international opposition to neo-liberalism. France was the first country to introduce a tax on international financial transactions, the 'Tobin tax' well before it became politically acceptable for European leaders to speak about a 'Robin Hood' tax. Jacques Chirac was responsible for launching the Landau report, which set out a range of new funding mechanisms designed to redistribute wealth from the world economy to poorer countries and which was presented to the World Economic Forum in 2005. On the basis of this report, France was the first country to introduce a taxation on airline tickets on 1 July 2006, which was designed to generate funding to provide HIV medicines to African countries.[3] Similarly, the international development agency, Unitaid, created under France and Brazil's initiative in September 2006, has played a critical role in generating funding from international sources for development aid. Yet beyond these specific measures, France has helped to shape the process of globalization itself, creating an alternative model of 'mondialisation maîtrisée' or 'mastered globalization' based on regulatory controls, worldwide rules and democratic principles. Rawi Abdelal and Sophie Meunier (2010) show how the world economy, over the past 20 years, has been dominated by two opposing models of globalization, the one based on American neo-liberalism and the other, on French-inspired 'mastered globalisation'.

They suggest that in the wake of the economic crisis which discredited an American neo-liberal model, this alternative French model could gain fresh legitimacy and help to pave the way towards a renewed world economy.

On the other hand, France's relationship with globalization has been circumscribed by a republican identity that sees France at the centre of the universe and as a model for other nations to follow. If French leaders called for an alternative world order, this was an order with France at its very centre, restored to its rightful place as a leader of other nations and displacing the United States as the first nation on the world stage. French criticisms of globalization are often inseparable from wider assumptions about France's natural vocation in the world as a pioneer of universalism with a duty to intervene beyond its own borders. Progressive demands for market regulation and state controls are often inextricably bound up with nationalist claims for renewed French influence in the world. Hence, both Jospin and Chirac asserted France's historic vocation to project universalist values on the world stage. Similarly, Nicolas Sarkozy defined France's relationship with globalization in terms of a 'civilizing project' in which France would once again radiate its democratic ideals and show other nations the way. He believed that just as in the past, France's role was to lead other nations out of darkness, to spread the fruits of French civilization and to lift humanity towards progress and enlightenment. Since the 2008 crisis, this republican nationalism has assumed a renewed vigour and self-righteousness. Many in France believe that the crisis has vindicated long-standing French criticisms of a flawed American model and has confirmed France's natural vocation as a leader on the world stage. Some argue that the solution to the manifold problems that beset France and the world is a 'revived Republic' that would spread its message outwards, reassert democratic and humanist values and heal all of humanity's ills (Ferrand, 2007). French opposition to globalization, although a powerful force for contestation, is bound up with myths of national grandeur and a sense of entitlement and this tends to obscure reality and create a blinkered and narcissistic vision of the world.

Chapter 2, 'Globalization and French Identity', examines the complex relationship between international processes of economic restructuring and nationally defined traditions, values and institutions in France, looking at the implications of this relationship for identity. I begin by looking at the different ways in which globalization challenges France, considering in particular, the role of the state, ideological values, the French social model, international status and cultural identity. I go on to look at recent studies of France's relationship with globalization which tend to focus on the economic dimension of this relationship. Drawing on theories of globalization by leading international scholars including Michael Hardt and Antonio Negri, Samuel Huntington and

Zygmunt Bauman, I argue that globalization in France has had a profound impact on questions of identity, belonging and rootedness. But what do we mean by French identity? The chapter goes on to examine theories of French identity, from traditional essentialist conceptions to more recent constructivist approaches. I argue that a constructivist approach helps us better understand the dynamic relationship between globalization and French political identity. A concluding section examines the specific challenges that globalization poses for the French republican model.

Chapter 3, 'Political Leaders: A New Civilizing Mission', examines the highly contradictory relationship between political leaders and globalization by looking at the discourse of three leaders: Lionel Jospin, Jacques Chirac and Nicolas Sarkozy. While these leaders were responsible for a wholesale liberalization of the French economy, their political discourse appealed to symbols of tradition, continuity and stability. In the face of globalization, these leaders revived a colonialist language that portrayed a France at the centre of the world with a great universalist mission to fulfil. Paradoxically, this appeal to republican identity and to colonial myths became a critical discursive means to further the goals of economic liberalization itself. In particular, it allowed political leaders to anchor economic transformations in a bedrock of continuity and in an image of the Republic as a steadfast and authoritative institution at the helm of a great project of universalist transformation.

Chapter 4, 'French Intellectuals: A War of Worlds', examines French intellectual opposition to globalization in the period since 1995. Focusing on a number of best-selling books from this period, the chapter argues that French intellectuals shared a civilizational perspective of globalization, seeing this not as a piecemeal market process or economic reform, but as a profound and all-encompassing threat. This civilizational perspective had contradictory effects on the nature of their opposition. On the one hand, French thinkers helped to challenge neo-liberal theory by politicizing globalization and by inscribing this within a specific political and ideological context at national level. On the other, they exaggerated the cultural determinants of globalization, seeing this as a product of a predetermined Anglo-Saxon type. While French intellectuals challenged the economic determinism of neo-liberal theory, they tended to replace this with their own form of cultural determinism that reduced complex economic processes to a manifestation of cultural predisposition. A final section of the chapter examines French intellectual debates on the economic crisis. I argue that while recent books provide a radical critique of the economic crisis, they also tend to demonize the United States and to obscure the specific role of French leaders in creating the conditions for economic crisis in Europe.

Chapter 5, 'A l'Attac. A New Political Identity for the Left', examines the role of Attac, the French protest grouping that has been at the centre of national and international opposition to globalization. The chapter argues that Attac has played a critical role in forging a new post-Marxist framework for leftist opposition that is attuned to a modified international context of globalization. It has helped to create a new political identity for the Left, one that bridges national frontiers and emphasizes the basic solidarity of all human beings. Yet its political discourse has been circumscribed by an underlying republicanism that views the world through a narrow nationalist prism.

Chapter 6, 'Agriculture and Identity: The Confédération paysanne', examines the way in which this protest grouping transformed itself from a narrow farming union on the margins of French society into a powerful symbol of opposition to globalization with widespread support across public opinion. The chapter argues that the Confédération's popular success was based not on its institutional or political resources, but on its symbolic power and in particular its capacity to transform peasant farming into a symbol of identity at a time of globalizing transformation. The final chapter 'Conclusion' considers some of the consequences of France's identity-based response to globalization, looking at both its positive effects, in challenging a dominant neo-liberal doctrine at international level and its negative effects, in fuelling a republican nationalism that is inward-looking and chauvinistic.

Notes

1 In Britain, the economic crisis triggered a revival of interest in Marxism on the Left with books published in 2010 by leading Marxist political economists including Chris Harman's *Zombie Capitalism* (London: Bookmarks, 2009); David Harvey, *The Enigma of Capital* (London: Profile, 2011) and Alex Callincos' *Bonfire of Illusions* (Cambridge: Polity, 2010). The historian Eric Hobsbawn in *How to Change the World: Tales of Marx and Marxism* (London: Little & Brown, 2011) argued that the time was ripe to revisit Marxism: 'The globalized capitalist world that emerged in the 1990s was in crucial ways uncannily like the world anticipated by Marx in *The Communist Manifesto*.'

2 *Manifeste d'économistes atterrés* (Paris: Les Liens qui Libèrent, 2010).

3 Since March 2010, the French airline 'solidarity tax' has been supplemented by a new voluntary airline ticket levy ('Massive good' levy) paid by consumers when purchasing an airline ticket. This latest initiative was the brainchild of former French Minister for Foreign Affairs, Philippe Douste-Blazy, currently president of the Millennium Foundation. Nineteen countries have pledged to introduce a voluntary airline ticket levy. The international agency Unitaid which is hosted by the World Trade Organization provided 300 million dollars of funding in 2007 which was used to purchase medicines for developing countries. France is the leading contributor to Unitaid's budget and provides 60 per cent of its funding.

2

Globalization and French identity

A nation can have its being only at the price of being in search of itself, forever transforming itself in the direction of its logical development, always measuring itself against others and identifying itself with the best, the most essential part of its being.

Fernand Braudel, *The Identity of France*, vol. 1, 1988, 23

Recent studies attest to France's deep-seated difficulties in dealing with globalization, in adapting to structural and economic change and in negotiating its position in a changed international setting. Some believe the source of France's difficulties lies beyond its borders, in the process of globalization itself which has imposed a political and economic model that is sharply at odds with France's own structures, values and traditions (Todd, 1998, 2008; Rouart, 2003; Arthuis, 2007; Zemmour, 2010; Chevènement, 2011). For some, globalization is responsible for 'a moral and political crisis' and has plunged France into a spiral of political decline from which it is struggling to recover (Arthuis, 2007: 11–12). For others, France's problems lie closer to home and stem from its own domestic shortcomings and in particular, an outmoded economy, statist structures and a general unwillingness to reform. Pierre Dockès argues that 'hell is not other people' and the French need to look to themselves and to their own economic policies and political choices as the source of their difficulties (Dockès, 2007). Similarly, the Canadian economic historian, Timothy Smith believes that France has been gripped by a wave of 'globaphobia' characterized by an irrational fear of the outside world and a tendency to blame external markets for all of the country's domestic ills (Smith, 2004). Yet these recent accounts, written mainly by economists, trade policy specialists or economic historians, tend to treat France's relationship with globalization primarily as an economic problem, one that concerns the underlying structures and mechanisms of the French economy. One widely accepted view is that French opposition expresses a narrow corporatism that defends sectional interests at a time of modernizing transformation. This opposition, according to this viewpoint, does not reflect a general project for social transformation (a *projet de société*) or a broad ideological vision, but is simply a rearguard defence by specific groups seeking to protect their own social status and vested interests. If the French resisted globalization so strongly, this was because they wished to cling on to the generous privileges or 'acquis' afforded by the French welfare system and because they resisted change. In this chapter, I argue that France's relationship with globalization transcends the economic sphere and concerns more complex, deeply rooted and irreducible questions of identity, tradition and belonging. Because this relationship touches on the fundamental means by which the French define their identity, France's difficulties cannot be resolved by measures of economic adjustment or structural reform alone.

To understand why globalization has generated such tensions in France, we need to look more closely at aspects of national political culture and identity. What is French political identity and what has this notion come to signify in our contemporary globalized world? The question of French national identity has recently become the focus of intense political controversy, prompted by Nicolas Sarkozy's embrace of this theme during his 2007 election campaign. This recent controversy can be situated within a more long-standing debate about the meaning and substance of national identity that prevails within French scholarship on this theme. In this chapter, I will examine two opposing conceptions of French identity that characterize French Studies and that underpin many of the arguments made during recent political debates. On the one hand, there are those who see French identity as an essence, something primordial, hereditary and natural that is transmitted unchanged from one generation to the next. Classic historians such as Jules Michelet, Fernand Braudel and Pierre Nora, through panoramic historic self-portraits of France, produced an idealized and essentialist conception of identity that continues to influence the terms of political debates in the present day. On the other hand, there are those who see French identity as a mere construct, something that is constantly reinvented in response to changing contingencies and needs. Recently, some historians have sought to challenge a traditional conception of identity by examining the political and social conditions in which identity is produced and the instrumental ends to which it is put (Thiesse, 2001; Noiriel, 2007; Citron, 2008). This chapter draws on a constructivist approach that sees identity as something that is constructed in response to changing preoccupations and needs over time, but which nonetheless draws on enduring symbols and references that are specific to French political culture and tradition.

A key aim of the chapter is to consider how French identity has been renego-tiated at a time of globalization. National identity is not a constant, but something that becomes important at times of national crisis, when a community is expe-riencing profound transformation or is faced with an external threat. At such times, identity becomes a means to rebuild the cultural integrity of the commu-nity and to reaffirm threads of belonging, tradition and rootedness. The chapter focuses on a core dimension of French identity, that of the republican model which continues to define the contours of identity in the present day, condition-ing French perceptions of themselves and of the outside world. Republican identity is shaped by the past and by an historical legacy of state intervention-ism, republican values and a conception of universalism. Yet, republican identity today is also increasingly defined in response to the pressures of globalization itself. In particular, the Republic has become a symbolical and discursive means to confront the changes and uncertainties of a globalized world and to provide protection against them. On the one hand, the Republic is invoked as a bul-wark against change, conjuring up an idealized space in which traditions are preserved, identity is intact and social bonds are restored. It offers an antidote to all the perceived evils of a globalizing world, a place that is untouched by transformations in the present. On the other hand, the Republic provides a means to restore France's status in the world, projecting an imaginary vision of a France that is still at the centre of the world and a model for other nations to follow. Many French leaders believe that in a context of worldwide economic crisis, France's role is to lead the world out of its current impasse and to help lay the foundations for an alternative world order. French republican identity today is in many respects a product of globalization, in which an idealized past is reactivated as a means of dealing with unpalatable changes in the present. The chapter will begin by examining the different ways in which globalization challenges France and develop some of the points that were touched upon in the introductory chapter. I go on to review social sciences literature on France's relationship with globalization which has emphasized an economic interpre-tation of this process. The chapter then looks at work by major international scholars of globalization who have emphasized the link between globalization and identity. I then examine French scholarship on the theme of identity and conclude by looking at dimensions of republican identity in France.

How globalization challenges France

France is hardly the only country in the world where globalization has become a politically charged issue. In the period since the 2008 economic crisis in par-ticular, many countries have experienced a backlash against the neo-liberal economic model which is held responsible for an unprecedented collapse of the world economy, rising social inequalities, a massive reduction in state expenditure and declining public services. Political leaders in different countries across the world have denounced the failings of neo-liberalism and have made demands for radical reform, calling for tougher market regulation, a return to state interventionism and tighter financial controls. In France too, there has been intense criticism of neo-liberal globalization on the part of political leaders, trade unions, intellectuals and the general public. France was the first industrialized nation to witness a general strike in the wake of the economic crisis, when on 29 January 2009, hundreds and thousands of French workers took to the streets to protest against Nicolas Sarkozy's handling of the crisis. Meanwhile leftist intellectuals in a spate of books, newspaper articles and manifestos on the theme of the crisis, condemned the values and structures of the world economic order (Lordon, 2009; Ramonet, 2009; Juvin, 2010). At the same time, French political leaders, on the international stage, went further than their counterparts in any other European country in their demands for tough financial regulation and structural reform. Yet in France, this opposition was not a reaction to recent economic events, but instead reflected arguments and ideas that had been consistently and forcefully made over the preceding 20 years. During this period, France experienced an unparalleled backlash against economic globalization that gained the support of parties on the Left and Right and brought together groups as diverse as Parisian intellectuals, political activists, trade unionists and peasant farmers. If globalization generated greater conflict in France than elsewhere, this is because it was here that it came most sharply into conflict with the values and traditions that underpin political identity. In particular, it came into conflict with a republican model defined by a specific historical tradition, a distinct political order and a set of ideological beliefs. Globalization challenged the republican model and the foundations of French identity in a number of basic ways.

First, globalization was a threat to the nature and role of the French state which constitutes a core component of the republican model and of national identity. It has been linked to 'a fundamental shift in the constitution of world politics' and to the rise of a neo-liberal order that lays emphasis on an all-powerful market freed of all political and institutional control (McGrew cited by Bisley, 2007: 9).[1] Whereas France had been engaged in a process of European integration since the late 1950s and 1960s and this had brought its own challenges to a traditional conception of national sovereignty, globalization seemed to contest the role of the French state in new and fundamental ways. On the one hand, it accelerated the transfer of state powers from national to supranational level and more significantly, it extended these powers to new and more politically sensitive areas. Unlike earlier periods of European integration, questions of sovereignty were no longer limited to matters of customs tariffs, trade quotas or economic exchange, but involved an extension of negotiations to politically charged issues such as citizenship, workplace rights, public services and social spending (Gordon & Meunier, 2001). For instance, the Lisbon Treaty which provides the new framework for member-states within the European Union and which entered into effect on 1 December 2009, involved a considerable strengthening of the political powers of European institutions in relation to national governments. For some critics, this treaty marked a shift towards European dominance over national sovereignty with a change from unanimous to double majority voting, a removal of national vetoes in specific policy areas, new powers for the European Commission, European Parliament and Court of Justice and the introduction of a major new foreign policy role.[2] On the other hand, globalization increased the power and autonomy of multinational corporations whose power often supersedes that of national governments. For some critics, the rise of multinational corporations whose 'right to free trade' is enshrined within international institutions such as the World Trade Organization and who have the power to make governments rescind laws that are seen to interfere with free trade, is the defining feature of contemporary globalization. Hence, Amory Starr argues that globalization has created 'historically specific conditions' in which elected governments 'no longer have the right to enact the wills of their citizens into law as sovereign nations' (Starr, 2000: ix, viii). In the French context, where the state is regarded as the sovereign power and where there is a strict demarcation between the public and private sphere, globalization challenged the nature of the state and therefore the basic tenets of national identity.

Opposition to globalization in France is often articulated in terms of a defence of the French state against the external market forces that seek to undermine it or to diminish its authority. France was the first country to reject the terms of the Multilateral Agreement on Investment (MAI) negotiations that were championed by the United States and which sought to limit the authority of the state, where this interfered with the principle of free trade. In explaining the reasons for France's withdrawal from the MAI, Lionel Jospin explained in a speech to the French National Assembly that it endangered state sovereignty and therefore threatened the integrity of the French nation. He drew a distinction between European integration which was a process controlled by states and globalization which entailed 'an abandonment of sovereignty to private interests' (Jospin, 1998). The question of state sovereignty was also a key issue in the run-up to the 2005 referendum on the European Constitutional Treaty when the early 'no' campaign was dominated by arguments linked to a defence of French sovereignty and identity. For some, particularly on the Right, the new constitution threatened to create a 'super-state annexing nations' whose powers would surpass those of the French state (Garaud cited by Binet, 2008: 115). In their public pronouncements, French political leaders across the party spectrum, all vowed to defend the French state against globalization, presenting this as a question of defending the French nation itself. While Lionel Jospin, as Prime minister from 1997 to 2002, pursued a wholesale liberalization of the French economy, he also defended the principle of 'volontarisme' and the notion of an active state that would redistribute wealth and guarantee democratic rights. Similarly, Nicolas Sarkozy combined ultra-liberal reforms with an appeal to the image of a strong, independent and authoritative state that remained true to its own traditions and that provided a force for order and moral guidance in the world.

Secondly, globalization challenges the foundational values and principles on which the French Republic was built, values that continue to give substance to identity in the present day. In particular, it calls into question values of equality, justice and solidarity that are grounded in the national historical experience and which are seen as sacred and immutable. For Emmanuel Todd, conflict over globalization has little to do with material concerns, but involves an ideological struggle between two different systems, a French model rooted in equality and an 'Anglo-Saxon' model defined by freedom: 'What the French reject are the inequalities of a society entirely dominated by market forces, which demands continuous adaptation to improve the performances of the economic machine. That might be possible in the United States or the United Kingdom, but it is not in France. The French are searching for their own model, a model adapted to their specificities' (in Fougier, 2006: 87). Opposition to globalization in France has been articulated not only in a language of economic rationalism, but also with reference to abstract ideological principles that appeal to eternal and universal truths. In the 2005 campaign against the European Constitutional Treaty, some expressed their protest in terms of humanist principles that sought to place human interests above economic imperatives, as revealed by the Communist Revolutionary League slogan: 'Our lives are worth more than our profits' (cited by Startin, 2008: 94). Similarly, during the July 2010 protest against a raising of the legal retirement age from 60 to 62, trade unions legitimized their protest in terms of a defence of general social rights and this was 'the defence of a major conquest of the social state' (Aguiton et al., 2011: 11). Meanwhile, all French political leaders from Left to Right have explained their stance on globalization by invoking democratic and humanist principles. Jacques Chirac placed humanism at the heart of his campaign at international level during his second presidential term and called for an alternative world order that placed the human being at its centre. Meanwhile, Sarkozy affirmed that France's mission was to restore the values of French and European humanism to the core of the international economic system.

Thirdly, globalization is seen as an attack on France's social model which is intrinsic to the structures and principles of the Republic itself. Globalization is seen as the source of European and international directives that limit the state's capacity to intervene independently in society and to protect its citizens from the vagaries of the market. Many identify globalization as the cause of unpopular economic and financial austerity measures, reduced social spending, labour market reform and public sector redundancies. Social protest in France over the past 20 years has focused on a defence of the French social model in the face of external market forces that seem bent on destroying it. This was the case in 1995, during the public sector strikes against the Juppé reforms, during the 2003 demonstrations against pension reform, the 2005 demonstrations against the European Constitutional Treaty and the 2010 strikes against Sarkozy's pension reform. On 29 January 2009, French trade unions launched a mass-based demonstration against Nicolas Sarkozy whom they believed had betrayed France's social model by abandoning the interests of low-paid workers and the unemployed in favour of helping big businesses within a global economy. They argued that Sarkozy's raft of reforms including justice, hospital and school reforms were liquidating the legacy of the French social model. In the face of electoral pressures, French political leaders, compared with their counterparts in other European countries, have chosen to maintain core features of the French social model. Jonah Levy notes that in order to maintain electoral support and counteract some of the negative effects of economic globalization, French leaders increased social spending into the twenty-first century, giving France the biggest welfare state outside of Scandinavia (Levy, 2008). Successive political leaders have promised that they would defend France's social model in the face of globalization. While Nicolas Sarkozy made reform of the social model the explicit focus of his election campaign, his liberal economic policies were counterbalanced, particularly after 2008, by interventionist and protectionist measures. Hence during his presidency of the European Council, he called for a 'Europe that protects' its citizens and for a regulation of financial markets.

Fourthly, globalization is perceived as a threat to France's cultural identity and is equated with Americanization, the spread of a commercialized popular culture and a 'uniformisation of our cultures' (Chirac, 2008). For some observers, it is the cultural impact of globalization and its dangers for national language, culture and traditions which has become France's key dilemma in the twenty-first century (Warnier, 2004; Mattelart, 2007; Dauncey, 2010). While fears about Americanization and French cultural identity are not new and were prevalent during the *Trente glorieuses* of the 1950s and 1960s, they have reached a momentum in the contemporary period as trade flows, new technologies and accelerated consumerism made societies more susceptible than ever to foreign cultural influences.[3] Hence, Benjamin Barber referred to a McDonaldization of world culture and to the rise of a 'McWorld' that was stifling traditional national cultures with a bland, consumerist and inferior culture imported from the United States (Barber, 1995). Globalization was seen as a form of cultural imperialism or 'westernisation' that was redefining core facets of identity and culture (Latouche, 1996). France has been at the centre of international efforts to defend national cultures from what is seen as an onslaught of market liberalization. French leaders helped to define the principle of 'exception culturelle' at international level and the idea that cultural production should be exempt from free trade agreements and benefit from state protection and subsidies. They defended this principle during the Uruguay Round of multilateral negotiations within the framework of GATT and later at the World Trade Organization in Seattle. Whereas the United States sought to have trade in the cultural area treated under the same conditions as trade in other commercial goods, France argued that countries had the right to protect culture as a means of preserving national cultural heritage. For political leaders, the notion of cultural exception is regarded as sacrosanct and seen as a matter of national pride and self-affirmation. For instance, at the 2007 Cannes film festival, Sarkozy declared, via his Culture Minister: 'I am proud of our country which incarnates and defends the cultural exception, an exception that has given its vitality to contemporary creation' (*Le Point*, 20/5/07). In recent years, the notion of 'cultural exception' has given way to a campaign to defend 'cultural diversity' and France has seen itself as a spokesperson for all cultures and languages struggling to survive in a globalized world.[4] Under French and Canadian influence, the principle of cultural diversity was enshrined in the 2005 UNESCO Charter that was ratified by 150 countries against the sole opposition of the United States and Israel. More recently, France helped to launch UNESCO's 'international year of languages' in 2008. Opinion polls show that the idea of a protected national culture is strongly supported by public opinion and a LH2 poll for Radio RMC in March 2007 showed that 78 per cent of those questioned favoured an increase in the Culture Ministry's budget (Dauncey, 2010).

France's response to globalization tends to combine a sense of cultural elitism and pride in relation to a 'superior' European culture and also, a sense of victimhood in the face of an 'Anglo-Saxon tide' that has overwhelmed France and that threatens to stifle its national culture. Jacques Chirac, who during his presidency, championed the themes of cultural diversity and *francophonie*, manifested many of these contradictions between cultural elitism and victimhood. On the one hand, he saw France and the Francophone world as the repository of a rich traditional culture grounded in the values of the Enlightenment and a republican philosophy and which had a vocation for *rayonnement* in the world. Every French person, he argued, was 'heir to an old culture that manifested itself in the humanist effervescence of the European renaissance, was . . . enriched by the philosophers of the Enlightenment and Revolution and strengthened . . . by the social conquests of the 20th century' (Chirac, 2008). The Francophone world, he declared, had a mission to create a 'civilisation of the universal' that would combine cultural distinctiveness with humanist and republican ideals. On the other hand, he viewed French culture as a fragile and endangered entity, attacked on all sides by a rapacious market-driven culture which did not recognize its merits or respect its singularity. He equated globalization with the rise of 'a universe that is wholly rational and sanitized' which threatened France and other nations with 'cultural impoverishment' (ibid.).

Finally globalization represents a political challenge to French identity because it undermines France's status and self-image as a great power on the international stage. Intrinsic to French identity is a belief in France's exceptional position in world affairs and a consequent entitlement to influence beyond it borders. France's democratic model was a 'gift to the world' and it had a universalist duty to spread its Enlightenment values and political model to other nations (Boniface, 2007; Maclean & Szarka, 2008). As a major colonial power, the French establishment believed that it had a 'civilizing mission' to inculcate French values, French institutions and the French way of life. Under de Gaulle, France found new expression for this image of greatness in the notion of grandeur and independence. France's vocation was not just to defend its own borders but to project power beyond them. More than any other European country, national identity in France was built on a conception of a pre-eminent status in the world and a natural vocation for leadership and guidance. While the process of European integration challenged a conception of France as an independent nation, French political leaders succeeded in reconciling the national interest with a vision of an ongoing European project. They presented Europe as a means of transcending national limitations and of acquiring for France an amplified role on the world stage. Compared with its European counterparts, France exercised a profound influence on the institutions, ideology and organization of the European Union. Yet globalization challenged France's international status by creating a structure of international relationships based on American power which no longer seemed to recognize French status and pre-eminence in the world. For Hubert Védrine, former French Foreign Minister, the United States had become a 'hyperpower' in the face of which France could no longer aspire to exert influence and power. Since the 2008 economic crisis, the threat to France's international status is seen increasingly to come from China and India whose rising economic power seems to diminish European pretensions towards rank and influence in the world (Juvin, 2010; Chevènement, 2011).

An economic problem?

The question of France's difficult relationship with globalization has attracted considerable interest from scholars in the French- and English-speaking world. Some have focused on the impact of globalization on French culture and on the notion of French cultural exceptionalism (Farchy, 1999; Warnier, 2004; Mattelart, 2007; Dauncey, 2010). Others have examined this relationship from the perspective of international relations, exploring France's modified role and capabilities on the world stage (Cogan, 2003; Boniface, 2007; Maclean & Szarka, 2008). Others still have considered this question from the perspective of social relationships and have interpreted French opposition as a return of class-based conflict against a background of economic liberalism (Aguiton & Bensaïd, 1997; Wolfreys, 1999; Coupé, 2006; Kouvélakis, 2007; Dardot & Laval, 2011). However, it is economic interpretations which have prevailed in recent literature, within the social sciences at least, and which have shaped a broader understanding of France's relationship with globalization in the public sphere (Touraine, 1996, 2001; Gordon & Meunier, 2001; Kresl & Gallais, 2002; Bavarez, 2003, 2009; Smith, 2004; Dockès, 2007; Arthuis, 2007). According to these studies, France's difficulties with globalization stem from the under-lying structures and mechanisms of the French economy and are linked to problems of statism, corporatism, poor macroeconomic management and structural inefficiencies. They argue that the solution to France's difficulties resides in the economic domain in an 'adaptation' of France's economy, an adjustment of policy mechanisms and sweeping structural reform. It is a question of breaking down barriers, liberating economic potential, unleashing market competiveness and opening up the French economy to the full force of international markets. Each of these authors prescribes a different economic remedy to France's current ills, advocating a different 'economic strategy that should be followed in France' (Kresl & Gallais, 2002: 12). Such an economistic perspective, which has dominated public policy debates in France over the past 20 years, is shared by academics and government officials alike and led recently to a spate of government-sponsored reports that have sought to change public attitudes and promote a different 'economic culture', one that is better suited to the needs of the market (Lepeltier, 2004; Védrine, 2007; Bernardin, 2008; Cohen-Tanugi, 2008; Hamilton & Quinlan, 2008). Furthermore, this perspective helped to provide the moral and political context for widespread economic reform, laying the foundations for Nicolas Sarkozy's reformist drive and his appeal for a 'rupture' or break with the past as the only viable means to 'save' a France that was encumbered by archaic institutions, stuck in outmoded grooves and weighed down by ideology.

A widely held viewpoint is that French opposition represents a form of corporatism that seeks to protect sectional interests at a time of moderniz- ing change. For the leading sociologist, Alain Touraine who, during the 1995 public sector strikes, led the petition movement in support of Alain Juppé's social security reform, these strikes represented a 'great refusal' on the part of specific groups of workers who wished to defend their pensions and social security benefits: 'the strike was led from start to finish by protected workers' (Touraine, 1996: 49). Far from being a genuine social movement, this protest was defined by a complete absence of any project for society or any broad collective vision for the future of France. For him, French strikes were harmful to society and particularly to the most economically vulnerable, preventing a reform that might channel public resources to the most needy: 'For the past ten years, it is the growing anxiety and resistance of the protected sec- tor which has made protection of the marginalized sector difficult' (ibid., 44). Similarly, French political scientist, Jacques Capdevielle has pointed to the rise of a new phase of corporatism at a time of globalization that has mobi- lized groups of French workers in defence of 'specific, concrete, localized, sectional or corporatist interests' (Capdevielle, 2001: 171). This new corporat- ism has become the principal vector for social discontent among those who fear globalization, gathering widespread public support beyond French work- ers themselves. Similarly, Timothy Smith views French protest as a defensive reaction by the most comfortable sections of French society who are driven by 'selfish motives' and a desire to defend their generous social and economic benefits (Smith, 2004: 239). Drawing on the examples of the 1995 public sec- tor strikes and the 2003 demonstrations against pension reform, he argues that those who took to the streets were not marginalized or underprivileged groups but comfortable workers in secure employment: 'when *privileges* are won, they are, by definition, won by the most powerful (and/or potentially dis- ruptive) members of society: the people with the power to stop the trains and turn out the lights. The 4.5 million poor people of France have no privileges' (ibid., 22).[5]

According to this perspective, France is marked by a deeper opposition to globalization than elsewhere because corporatism is deeply embedded within French society and sustained by an extensive public sector and a generous welfare system. For Touraine, France's institutional model is characterized by bureaucracy, corporatism and inefficiency, a system that tends to suppress economic change and innovation:

in the economic realm, French society has taken refuge in its corporatism; at the ideological level, in its republicanism; and at the cultural level, in its past. By doing so, it transfers to the next generation the burden of artificial protections and the non-decisions, behind which it tries to hide from the world in which it lives. (Touraine, 1996: 66–7)

Similarly, for Smith, France's problems lie in a welfare system based on a post-war model that maintained a distribution of benefits to privileged sectors and that was completely out of touch with the changing composition of French society. This is a model suffocating under the weight of statist protection, an inflexible labour market and corporatist practices that excludes any possibility for reform. More importantly, he argues, this system exacerbates social inequalities and is responsible for France's endemic levels of unemployment. American political scientist Ezra Suleiman sees France's problems in terms of a complicity between the middle classes and political elites who have carved out for themselves a set of mutual privileges that they do not wish to lose: 'members of the French bourgeoisie fear losing their advantages through an opening up and democratization of French society' (Suleiman, 2007: 240). He points to a French state that cosseted its people during the post-war years, showering them with generous benefits that their counterparts in other nations simply did not receive. This overindulged and sheltered population, much like a spoilt child, now stubbornly refuses to face realities and to accept change. He suggests that those who protest against globalization today, invoke republican ideology not to express broad social ideals, but as a means to defend the status quo and prevent much-needed reforms.

Yet, these authors often accept implicitly a market-orientated perspective that sees globalization as progressive, rational and beneficial, a process to which France must inevitably conform and to which its economy and institutions must now adapt. The international economy is portrayed as a symbol of modernity that is driven by forces of dynamism, innovation and flexibility and which has become a yardstick against which French society should be measured and judged. While Touraine acknowledges the potential dangers of economic globalization for vulnerable social groups, he sees this as 'a great opportunity' that France must urgently seize (Touraine, 1996: 68). Those who invoke the spectre of a 'savage liberalism', Touraine suggests, are engaging in a kind of false consciousness that serves to impede change and prevent French society from facing the realities of the market. The French economy, he points out, is already internationalized and the rest of society must now follow suit. Similarly, Dockès sets out to dispel popular myths about globalization that see this as a source of inequality, social decline, unemployment and declining living standards. He argues that 'globalisation is fundamentally beneficial' and is a market system in which 'everyone wins' (Dockès, 2007: 21, 45,). In line with a neo-liberal perspective, he describes the market as a self-regulating mechanism which, if left to its own devices, will find a perfect equilibrium and soon bring universal benefits to all parties. While the costs in France of adapting to an international economy may initially be high, once the market finds its balance, France, like other nations will soon enjoy all the 'reciprocal gains' to be made in a globalized economy (ibid., 23). Recent government-backed reports reinforce this idealized vision of the market and set out to 'reconcile France with globalisation' by emphasizing out its considerable benefits for the French economy (Lepeltier, 2004). This is presented as a source of untapped wealth and opportunity that will bring France economic innovation, employment, raised living standards, cheap imports and new markets for its goods. Indeed, former Foreign Affairs Minister, Hubert Védrine in his report on France and globalization is puzzled as to why the prospect of massive cheap imports from China hasn't thus far been enough to convince the French of the merits of globalization and his ultimate goal is to 'shake up mentalities' (Védrine, 2007: 7).

While these studies ascribe centrality to the economic and structural dimensions of France's relationship with globalization, they also acknowledge the wider political and ideological sources of French opposition. Some signal the importance of a statist political model, of republican culture and of ideological values in preventing France from adapting to globalization. Yet, these wider factors are often considered only to the extent that they are seen as an obstacle to a compelling logic of market integration and economic adaptation. French opposition is often depicted as a misguided and illogical reaction that flies in the face of economic realities and that is costly for French society as a whole. For Touraine, those who railed against globalization were indulging in 'ideological scaremongering' that prevented French society from confronting economic realities (Touraine, 2001: 16). For Smith, ideological convictions have no place in a harsh and competitive global economy and the French need to peel back the layers of ideology and buckle down to the concrete business of reform.

As globalization is considered to be an economic and structural problem, the solution to this problem is also seen to lie in the economic domain. For Touraine, France needs to break completely with its statist tradition and evolve new forms of social control in relation to the challenges of the global economy that would shift emphasis from the state to collective action: 'Yes, we have to abandon the administered economy completely' (ibid., 6). He argues that France needs to adapt to globalization by a deep-seated reform of the state sector, a shift of investment from the public to the productive sector, technological innovation and a strengthening of trade unions and other forms of social representation. Smith shares the view that France's future lies in a 'thorough reform of French economic and social policy' and he posits a wide-ranging series of measures designed to reduce state spending, increase labour market flexibility, control wages and stimulate productivity. The French need to engage in broad macroeconomic reform, instead of short-term statist measures and the solution lies in a 'trimmed-down state which tolerates more flexible labor markets' (Smith, 2004: 219). Meanwhile, Bavarez, amidst an all-pervasive gloom about France's future, holds out hope for the French if they engage in 'a policy of radical reform' based on a principle of 'shock therapy' that would transform France's institutional model and shake society out of its endemic complacency and immobilism (Bavarez, 2003: 109). He proposes a deep-seated set of reforms to modernize the state sector, promote labour market flexibility and economic competitiveness.

These authors present economic reform as an urgent and inescapable remedy, as the only possible means for France to avert catastrophe and prevent a slide towards social stagnation, political immobilism and economic collapse. Such arguments, made by prominent public intellectuals, mainstream economists and experts, have profoundly influenced public debate about globalization over the past 20 years. They helped to reinforce what Ignacio Ramonet defined as a *pensée unique*, a single dominant and consensual system of thought that dominated the French establishment and that presented economic liberalization as the country's only viable course of action (Ramonet, 1995). Such arguments also helped to lay the moral and intellectual foundations for sweeping structural reform. In particular, they helped to legitimize Nicolas Sarkozy's ultra-liberal reforms and his promise to break with the past and to embrace a future of economic liberalization. Indeed, many of the French intellectuals who contributed to these debates supported the reformist aspirations expressed by presidential candidates during the 2007 election campaign. For instance, Nicolas Bavarez, the chief proponent of 'declinology', publicly supported Nicolas Sarkozy during the presidential elections and advised him on questions of economic policy and strategy. In one newspaper article, Baverez explained that he was voting for Sarkozy because he was 'the last chance for France to adapt to the new order of the 21st century'. Sarkozy alone, he believed, had the courage and vision to implement the 'indispensable reforms' needed to 'modernize France' (Bavarez, 2007). It is noteworthy that Sarkozy's economic programme was deeply influenced by the ideas set out in Bavarez's book, *La France qui tombe* (2003) and he incorporated many of the latter's key proposals on tax reductions, the abolition of the 35-hour working week, privatization, labour market reform and a European 'economic government'. Similarly, Alain Touraine who supported Ségolène Royal during the presidential elections and who endorsed the reformist aspects of her campaign, helped to emphasize the political need for urgent reform. In a book co-authored with Royal, he argued that France needed profound structural reform in order to overcome its 'administered economy' and 'corporatist management of society' (Royal & Touraine, 2008).

Globalization and identity

We have seen that France's relationship with globalization is often seen as an economic problem that is derived from structural causes and from the perceived costs and benefits of market integration. Yet, this perspective tends to overlook some of the deeper sources of French opposition. The question of what globalization is and how it transforms contemporary societies has spawned a rich and extensive body of literature across a diverse range of disciplines. Indeed, some of the most influential scholars in the world today have sought to analyse globalization, interpret its significance and examine its complex and multiple effects. These studies can provide a useful alternative to conventional economic interpretations and help to shed light on some of the more fundamental causes of French conflict. This section will focus on three dominant theoretical approaches by scholars whose work has helped to define the terms of contemporary debates on globalization, that of Michael Hardt and Antonio Negri's international best-seller, *Empire* (2000) and later *Multitude* (2005); American conservative political scientist Samuel Huntington's controversial work, *The Clash of Civilisations* (1997); and leading sociologist, Zygmunt Bauman's *Liquid Fear* (2006). While having very different disciplinary and political perspectives, these authors perceive globalization as a process that transcends economics alone and holds profound implications for the structures and functioning of modern democracies. They are all concerned with the relationship between economic transformations at international level and their implications for identity, collective values, social relationships and political belonging. For them, the meaning of globalization is not limited to market processes, but it concerns the emergence of an ascendant world order that is ineluctably imposing its power across the world and redefining the terms of human existence. Here the economy is merely an apparatus for furthering a logic of power that is characterized in terms of either 'empire', 'civilization' or 'liquid modernity'.

For neo-Marxist scholars, Hardt and Negri, globalization represents the coming of Empire with the rise of a new hegemonic system of power that has extended its influence across the world and created 'a single logic of rule' (Hardt & Negri, 2000: xii). Globalization, which freed the economy from all political control, has not diminished political sovereignty, but transformed its nature giving rise to a new decentred and deterritorialized system of power. Here the economy is subordinate to political power and economic exchanges and trade flows are a simple apparatus through which Empire has established itself:

> Along with the global market and global circuits of production has emerged a global order, a new logic and structure of rule – in short, a new form of sovereignty. Empire is the political subject that effectively regulates these global exchanges, the sovereign power that governs the world. (Ibid., xi)

Unlike older forms of imperialism, Empire is not limited to particular territories or institutions but stretches across the whole world and penetrates into every aspect of human life, aspiring towards a 'systemic totality' (ibid., 14). Globalization heralds the rise of absolute power that aims to control our social world and penetrate human consciousness itself. Hardt and Negri see globalization as a world of conflict and 'perpetual war' and when the nation state declines, they argue, 'conflicts begin to arise behind an infinity of emblems, ideologies, religious demands and identities' (ibid., 31). They believe that Empire produces its own inherent logic of resistance in the very sites of social life where it exerts its control. This resistance takes the form of the 'multitude' which like Empire itself, extends across the globe and into every facet of social and everyday life. It confronts its enemy by 'swarming' it, attacking it from all directions at once, like a swarm of insects or birds. In the face of a globalization that imposed 'organic unity', the multitude affirmed plural and multiple identities and the right to express differences freely:

> The multitude is composed of innumerable internal differences that can never be reduced to a unity or a single identity – different cultures, races, ethnicities, genders and sexual orientations; different forms of labor; different ways of living; different views of the world; and different desires. The multitude is a multiplicity of all these singular differences. (Ibid., 101: xiv)

The challenge facing the multitude is to find ways of acting and communicating in common in order to pursue a project for an alternative global society rooted in democracy.

For Hardt and Negri, conflict in contemporary societies, arises not from economic interests, but from deeper questions of identity, values and belonging. They believe that such conflict is not limited to sectional concerns, but embodies a broad project for social transformation, a distinctive ideological vision and a desire to build an alternative world order. The 'multitude' is driven by a democratic project that reaches beyond particular interests and identities and holds the promise of a new alternative society rooted in democratic and socialist ideals. Because resistance is not confined to sites of economic production alone, it has the potential to become a broad social, political and cultural force that transcends questions of material interest and becomes a new project for humanity as a whole:

> The project of the multitude not only expresses the desire for a world of equality and freedom, not only demands an open and inclusive democratic global society, but also provides the means of achieving it . . . these movements of resistance are driven at base not only by the struggle against misery and poverty but also by a profound desire for democracy – a real democracy of the rule of all by all based on relations of equality and freedom. (Hardt & Negri, 2005: xi, 67)

This is a utopian vision of a movement of resistance that will liberate the world from the chains of global capitalism and create a new and perfect society. It differs markedly from the orthodox economic viewpoint described above that sees opposition in terms of the 'selfish motives' and material interests of specific groups of French workers without any broader collective or ideological purpose.

Samuel Huntington points to a globalized world torn by conflict, war and antagonism between different civilizations, each locked into their own separate culture, institutional model and belief system. In the post–Cold War order, the bipolar division of the world had been replaced by the rise of multiple civilizations, each believing that they alone were at the centre of the universe and 'convinced that theirs is the final form of human society' (Huntington, 1997: 301). A civilization is defined not by economic relationships or even by shared institutions, but by deeper cultural affinities and this encompasses the political, ideological, historical and cultural means by which a culture defines itself: 'civilizations are comprehensive, that is, none of their constituent units can be fully understood without reference to the encompassing civilization' (ibid., 42). Huntington's central argument is that globalization tends to exacerbate rather than diminish conflict and antagonism between national cultures, as these seek to resist dominant forces of integration. The impact of increased trade, financial interdependence, technological innovation and cultural interaction does not, in his view, lead to greater homogeneity, integration and uniformity, but instead gives rise to a heightened state of conflict on an international scale. Faced with external pressures for change, cultures tend to reassert their own identities and 'civilizational consciousness' and to reaffirm their distinctive status in the world: 'The forces of integration in the world are real and are precisely what are generating counterforces of cultural assertion and civilizational consciousness' (Huntington, 1997: 36). The contemporary world is therefore marked by a reaffirmation of ideological and moral values, a revival of foundational myths and traditions and a defence of common institutions at the level of national cultures. He believed controversially that western civilization needed to assert its own distinctive cultural identity faced with civilizational threats coming from other cultures and from the Islamic world in particular.[6]

What distinguishes Huntington's approach is that he developed a broad civilizational paradigm arguing that conflict in a globalized world arises not from piecemeal economic or even political interests but from more fundamental questions pertaining to the civilization as a whole. People are concerned not with the terms of economic exchange or competition, but with the social and political relationships that bind them to their specific culture:

> Peoples and nations are attempting to answer the most basic questions humans can face: Who are we? And they are answering that question in the traditional way human beings have answered it, by reference to the things that mean most to them. People define themselves in terms of ancestry, religion, language, history, values, customs and institutions. (ibid., 21)

For Huntington, conflict in a globalized era is centered at the level of the civilization and this means that it is particularly intractable and intense. Whereas tradeable goods and merchandise may be open to negotiation and exchange, questions of identity, tradition and belief are part of a comprehensive and irreducible whole that is not open to compromise. To challenge any one of these aspects is to call into question the entire civilization itself, with its roots in history and defined by immutable values and beliefs.

Zygmunt Bauman examines the disastrous consequences of globalization for social and political relationships and for human existence itself. He conjures up a cataclysmic vision of a world hurtling towards its own self-destruction whose compulsive need for ceaseless market expansion will bring it inexorably towards its own end. His vision is of a wholly negative globalization in which the market possesses a transgressive power to break down all the human barriers and physical constraints that stand in its way. As political institutions can no longer control the market or curb its worst effects, individuals must face it alone and are assailed by a 'liquid fear' that seeps into every nook and cranny of modern existence. Bauman argues that the world through its own incapacity for self-limitation is doomed for a catastrophic end:

> The prospect of catastrophe is particularly difficult to avert since modern civilization owes its morbid (or rather suicidal) potential to the selfsame

qualities from which it draws it grandeur and glamour: to its inborn aversion to self-limitation, its inherent transgressiveness and its resentment of, and disrespect for, all and any borders and limits – especially the idea of final, ultimate limits. (Bauman, 2006: 75–6)

Bauman is concerned with the social and human consequences of globalization and he points to new forms of social polarization that divide a mobile elite who are free of the obligations and constraints linked to fixed places, from the immobile who are unable to escape their immediate conditions and who are confined to a situation of social deprivation and exclusion.

For Bauman, globalization intensifies struggles for identity as individuals seek to rebuild social relationships, political values and forms of cultural belonging in the face of a brutal market-driven world. Globalization is a process that destroys the fabric of social identity, loosening the anchors that bind the person to a community and casting him or her adrift in a hostile and meaningless world. Moreover, it strips territory of its identity-endowing capacity and disinvests locality of its social and cultural meaning, by reducing it to an abstract economic space. Unlike Hardt and Negri, Bauman sees little potential for resistance against globalization and he believes that its principal impact is to disempower society and diminish any capacity for human action, reducing the collectivity to a state of 'existential insecurity' (Bauman, 1998: 5). In today's world, the search for identity is therefore expressed in negative and destructive ways, through a desire to erect borders to keep the world at bay, to exclude others and to demarcate the lines that separate 'them' from 'us'. Identity struggles may take the form of religious fundamentalism in which simple incontrovertible truths are offered in response to the complexities of the contemporary world. They may also assume the guise of a perverse consumerism in which fear and uncertainty become a lucrative global market for security merchandise and 'fear-fighting products' (Bauman, 2006: 6). Bauman believes that globalization transforms the basic conditions of human existence and is experienced most acutely at a personal level through a generalized state of fear, insecurity and uncertainty. In a world in which the market destroys moral certainties, social relationships and political defences, we are all engaged in 'battles of identity and recognition' (ibid., 114). What is at stake is not merely a distribution of economic resources or material well-being, but fundamental truths about the nature of the human condition itself:

We are all strikingly alike in one respect: none of us, or almost none, believes (let alone declares) that they are pursuing their own interests – defending privileges already attained or claiming a share in the privileges thus far denied. All sides today seem to be fighting instead for eternal, universal and absolute values. (Ibid., 99)

Bauman sees no utopian outcome from this generalized state of human distress. Whereas modernity was linked to the notion of progress and to a collective vision of a better future society, in our 'liquid modern times', such collective ideals have been dissolved and each person must now confront individually the great dilemmas of our age. Yet, this is not a narrow individualism that turns inwards towards particular interests and concerns, but raises fundamental questions about the human condition and the future of the planet.

As we have seen, these theorists all view globalization as a comprehensive system that goes beyond economics and holds profound implications for identity. They tend to emphasize three important aspects of globalization and its relationship with identity: (i) globalization is a politically and ideologically determined process with deep-seated implications for democracy; (ii) globalization tends to exacerbate rather than reduce conflict in the world and this is a force for division, disorder and disintegration; (iii) conflict in a globalized world transcends the economic sphere and touches on more fundamental questions of identity, tradition and belief. Yet, we know that globalization is not a generic phenomenon, but affects societies differently according to the specific features of their national political culture and tradition. Indeed the impact of globalization in any one place is likely to depend on an interaction between international processes of economic transformation and nationally defined political values, institutions and traditions. Vivien Schmidt has shown how globalization affected European societies differently and in countries with a liberal political tradition, the shift to economic liberalization in the 1980s and 1990s was made compatible with the terms of national political culture and generated little opposition (Schmidt, 2002).[7] To understand why globalization was experienced as such a profound threat in France, we need to look more closely at dimensions of national political culture and identity. What is French national identity and why does globalization seem to pose a profound danger to this identity?

What is French national identity?

Contemporary France has been marked by an intense preoccupation with its own national identity, cohesion, historical origins and image. While French concerns with identity are hardly new and have surfaced periodically at moments of crisis throughout the twentieth century, some suggest that today these concerns have reached the proportions of a national obsession (Hayward, 2007; Noiriel, 2007; Schnapper, 2008; Thiesse, 2008; Martigny, 2009). Hence, Nicolas Sarkozy's embrace of national identity during his election campaign and the creation in 2007 of a Ministry of National Identity and Immigration sparked fierce controversy in France over the nature of French national identity and the relevance of this notion for society today. On the one hand, some prominent intellectual figures such as the conservative philosopher, Alain Finkielkraut and the historian, Max Gallo, welcomed a return to the themes of identity and the nation and they saw this as a means to strengthen and consolidate the fragile relationship that France had with its own past. In a jointly written newspaper article entitled 'How can we be French?' they criticized a culture of repentance over France's colonial legacy and saw this as a betrayal of French national history: 'It is our relationship with the dead that is today threatened and even broken by this repentance' (Finkielkraut & Gallo, 2007). On the other hand, many on the Left denounced what they saw as a dangerous populism that exalted the nation, stigmatized immigrants and pandered to the Far Right (Badiou, 2007; Noiriel, 2007). For them, national identity was a political instrument invoked in order to legitimize power and further the Right's nationalist agenda. This controversy can be situated within a more long-standing debate about the terms of French national identity and scholars in France have long been deeply divided about what this notion signifies and represents. This section explores two distinct approaches to French identity that oppose those who see identity as an essence, something primordial, fixed and organic and those who see it as a construct, something that is constantly reinvented in relation to changing contingencies over time. I will argue in favour of a constructivist approach that conceives identity as an artefact, but one that is shaped by an established repertoire of symbols and references that are specific to French national culture and tradition. Such a constructivist perspective can help us better understand France's dynamic relationship with globalization and the implications of that relationship for identity.

Of all European nations, France has traditionally been the most prolific in producing historical self-portraits that seek to capture the essence and contours of French identity. The very notion of French identity is deeply influenced by the work of major historians such as Jules Michelet (1798–1874), Fernand Braudel (1902–1985) and Pierre Nora (1931–) who each undertook extensive and multi-volumed projects in an effort to encapsulate French identity, to define its various dimensions and in particular, to preserve it for future generations. Their work gave rise to an essentialist notion of French identity, as something primordial, mysterious and elusive, a conception which continues to prevail in public debates in France today. Each of these historians was driven by a sense of patriotism and a self-proclaimed 'passion' for France which meant that they tended towards a romanticized account, shaped less by scientific objectivity than by nationalist sentiments and by a certain *amour propre*. Each saw their work in terms of a higher moral calling, an intellectual vocation and a nationalist duty to France. For Michelet, as a fervent republican, it was a question of celebrating the positive legacy of the French Revolution against the enemies of the Republic and of arousing widespread loyalty towards the republican regime. Similarly, Braudel was driven by a sense of 'filial piety' and a desire to devote to France the same historic scrutiny and attention that he had once devoted to his other subjects of study, from the Mediterranean to world capitalism (Kaplan, 1999: 294). Meanwhile, Pierre Nora's work was geared towards a specific nationalist purpose – to reconstitute the fabric of the nation in the face of processes of modernization and fragmentation that threatened to destroy or disperse precious repositories of collective memory. Each historian saw French identity as a 'mystery' that contained deep inner truths, yet that eluded easy capture (Detienne, 2010). All three believed that history and a common national past were the determining factors in shaping French identity. The French were French because they shared a common historical legacy and this determined who they were and conditioned their actions in the present.

In the preface to the first of his 17 volumes of *Histoire de France* (1833–1867), Jules Michelet describes how he was inspired to write his history in a moment of religious luminosity, when he suddenly perceived France in all its brilliance and completeness. His passion or 'flamme' for France, he goes on, gave him a unique vision that allowed him to perceive France in its essential wholeness, to reach beyond surface detail, to see past historical conflicts and glimpse 'the soul of the nation' itself (Michelet, 1881: 8). He defined history as a 'resurrection' and his aim was literally to bring France to life, to restore its integrity, to communicate its 'personality' and to set the scene for all its past glory and its future greatness: 'I saw it as a soul and as a person' (ibid., 1). Michelet's history is tinged with religious romanticism and he sees France as a divine entity that is indissociable from qualities of greatness, civilization and universalism:

> When France remembers that she was and must be the saviour of the human race, when she gathers her children about her and teaches them France as faith and religion, then will she discover her vitality. . . . Only France has the right to project herself as a model, because no people has merged its own interests and destiny with that of humanity more than she. (Michelet cited by Smith, 2004: 56)

Michelet saw the French Revolution as a unique historical moment, as God's 'second coming', which had revealed France to itself and confirmed its mission as the saviour of humanity and the harbinger of civilization. France's creed was not Christianity, but humanitarianism and through its republican ideals, it could transform the world and mould other nations in its own image: 'France, let it be known, will only ever have one inexpiable name, which is its true eternal name: the Revolution' (Michelet cited by Citron, 2008: 23). His history abounds with religious metaphors, invoking France in terms of 'resurrection', 'incarnation' and 'salvation' and just like any divinity, he believed that France required from its people, absolute devotion, sacrifice and even death. For Suzanne Citron, Michelet's national identity was shaped by two essential features: a religious devotion to his homeland and a cult of the Revolution which meant that he identified France with a singular destiny in the world and saw it as the fulfilment of history itself (ibid.).

While Fernand Braudel, a historian within the Annales School, sought to distinguish his approach from that of earlier historians and to evolve an innovative historical method, he too was driven by a profound sense of nationalism which coloured his perception of French identity. He undertook his three volumes of *The Identity of France*, published posthumously in 1986, partly to demonstrate his love for France and he opens the first volume with the following words: 'Let me begin by saying once and for all that I love France with the same demanding and complicated passion as did Jules Michelet' (Braudel, 1988: 15). His aim was to arrive at an understanding of the 'oneness of France' through a wide-ranging study of its diverse manifestations – historical, geographical, social and economic – over a long-term historical period (Braudel, 1990: 671).[8] Unlike Michelet who linked identity to a particular historical event (the Revolution), Braudel believed only long-term historical transformations could reveal the specific nature of French identity and France was shaped by an 'underlying history whose movement has drawn along and shaped all the various Frances of the past' (ibid., 678). Braudel's history was inspired by his childhood memories of rural France and of Lumeville, the village where he was born, a world in which daily routines were shaped by the dictates of soil and climate, where demographic and economic factors conditioned everyday life and where everyone knew what to expect from themselves and from others (McNeill, 2001). For Braudel, French identity literally sprang from the land, from a relationship between man and nature that endured over time and transcended political events and transformations. He believed that it is history that is the driving force behind national identity and this identity is something hereditary and predetermined that is created over time like the layers deposited by the sea-bed:

> What then, do we mean by the identity of France . . . if not the living result
> of what the interminable past has patiently deposited, layer by layer, just as

the imperceptible sedimentation of the seabed in the end created the firm foundations of the earth's crust. (Braudel, 1988: 23)

Braudel reveals a deterministic conception of a national identity that transcends time and space and that conditions who we are in the present, when he says: 'For men do not make history, rather it is history above all that makes men and thereby absolves them from blame' (Braudel, 1990: 679). For some, Braudel's identity is a 'depoliticized space' that exists outside human control and that relegates the state and political actors to minor characters on a stage in which time and space occupy the central roles (Dosse, 1994: 115). Others have suggested that his identity is influenced less by the rigours of empirical research than by 'fixed points of national ideology' (Anderson, 1999: 271) and this is a history driven by a 'civic duty' and a deeply rooted nationalism (Kaplan, 1999: 294). The result is a distinctly personal account of France that presents identity as a product of the historical specificities that distinguish France from other nations and which continue to persist over time.

In his seven volumes of *Les Lieux de mémoire* (1984–1993), Pierre Nora led a team of 120 historians in an extensive project which, over some 5,600 pages, laid out an inventory of 'realms of memory' in which French identity was seen to have crystallized. For Nora, identity is 'inscribed in the flesh of memory' and is reconstituted in the present through the act of remembrance (Nora, 2001: vii). His realms of memory cover an eclectic and at times, whimsical range of objects both material and immaterial, seen to symbolize either the nation, the Republic or Frenchness more generally and they include obvious national symbols such as the Tricolor, the Marseillaise, the Panthéon, Versailles, as well as more obscure examples of Frenchness, ranging from forests, the seaside, the art of conversation, coffee to the Tour de France bicycle race. Like Braudel, Nora was motivated by a sense of patriotic duty and a desire to defend France's past which was now, he believed, in danger of disappearing. Processes of modernization, fragmentation and international change had led to 'the rapid disappearance of our national memory' (Nora, 1984: vii) and had either destroyed or dispersed the key sites of memory. Nora's skills as a historian are therefore channelled towards a morally compelling task, that of reconstituting the fabric of the nation, of preserving the past and of restoring a 'France in the singular' (Nora, 2001: viii). He invites his readers to overlook the arbitrary and trivial nature of the whole exercise and to suspend their critical judgement in favour of embracing innocently the joys of journeying to France's past: 'And let us wish, for this handful of fresh and joyous essays – soon to be followed by armfuls more – a first innocent reading' (Nora cited by Anderson, 2009: 161). The selection of different realms of memory, he continues, was justified both by their historical importance and by 'the emotion that they arouse in each one of us' (Nora, 1984 xii). The result is a nostalgic and Gallocentric panorama of French identity conceived as a permanent and unchanging legacy, a relic of the past, that is free of all discord and division and that is represented as a unified whole. For Nora, identity is a 'pure form' (Nora, 1986: x) that is mysterious and fleeting, yet that defines who we are in the present and determines our future: 'it is as difficult to grasp as the air that we breathe and yet it gives us life' (Nora, 1984: x). He equates this essence with the nation, a powerful yet intangible force that can only be apprehended through a careful extrapolation of its various representations and symbolic forms. His *Lieux de mémoires* is a eulogy to France, to all its past glory, its diverse manifestations and its singularity. Nora defines identity as a conjuncture between history and collective experience that is produced through the act of remembrance. Whereas history reconstructs the past, memory is 'a link experienced in the eternal present' that is filtered through human emotions and is therefore 'affective and magical' (Nora, xix). Yet this memory is a more effective medium for accessing France's past and for reconstituting its wholeness because it is free of all the destructive and repressive processes of history itself: 'memory is an absolute and history knows only the relative' (ibid.). For Perry Anderson, Nora's identity is a nostalgic and consensual vision of the past, a kind of 'union sucrée' geared towards the political needs of the present and in particular the need to create a consensus in relation to the political establishment. Anderson notes that in Nora's project all discord and conflict has melted away and that France's entire imperial history is eliminated from his realms of memory and treated as a kind of 'non-lieu' (Anderson, 2009: 161, 162).

In contemporary France, many historians have challenged this traditional and essentialist conception of identity and argued in favour of a more dynamic, fluid and pluralist approach. They argue that the traditional notion of identity provides a unified and linear conception of history that distorts the past and creates a myth of national unity that fulfils the political imperatives of the present. Historians also criticize what they see as a narrow exclusionary concept of identity, one that is inextricably bound up with an ideal of the nation itself. Such a conception of identity is seen to exclude minority groups denying them their 'own' memory and a place in the 'official story' of France. Many historians have favoured a constructivist approach to identity that treats this as a construct or 'fiction' that is constantly redefined in relation to changing contingencies over time. Unlike the classic historians, they emphasize the invented, imagined, constructed and performed nature of identity and are interested in the political and instrumental uses to which it is put. For them, identity is not a natural or spontaneous phenomenon, but the outcome of purposeful fabrication on the part of political and intellectual elites and they set out to examine the political and social conditions in which it is produced.

In *La Création des identités nationales* (*The Creation of National Identities*, 2001), Anne-Marie Thiesse focuses on the historical context in which national identity was constructed and she locates this in the creation of nation states in eighteenth century Europe. She argues that the nation is not a spontaneous outcome of specific historical events such as the French Revolution, but the product of purposeful construction on the part of elites who sought to generate new forms of national mobilization and belonging. Challenging a nationalist perspective, she suggests that national identity is not the property of any one nation, but emerged as part of a broad European phenomenon that was deeply influenced by international processes of interaction and symbolic exchange: 'Nothing is more international than the construction of national identities' (Thiesse, 2001: 11). She describes eighteenth century Europe as an intense laboratory geared towards producing 'a symbolic and material heritage' that could provide the foundations for national identity (ibid., 12). Each nation constructed their national identity on the basis of a common set of elements or an identikit (identification of early ancestors, heroes fired by national ideals, a common language, folklore, cultural monuments, symbols of nationhood such as a flag, national anthem, national dress and gastronomy). These elements were mere constructs invested with symbolic meaning and designed to serve a clearly defined political purpose: 'To usher in the new world of nations, it wasn't enough to make an inventory of their heritage, rather, they had to invent it' (ibid., 13). The construction of identity involved reinterpreting the past and creating a common history that stretched back to the beginning of time and was seen to predetermine the emergence of the nation. This search for the past is always presented as a matter of great urgency, a task to be accomplished with great speed, lest the gateway to the past be closed forever. Thiesse shows how the nation provided a form of permanence, stability and continuity which allowed European nations to undergo profound social and economic changes without altering the basic structures of the political order: 'Everything can change, except the nation: it is the reassuring reference that affirms continuity despite all transformations' (ibid., 16). She argues that in a contemporary international context with a shifting of the boundaries and symbols of national identity, individuals have turned back towards their own national identities to provide the stability, belonging and community that they desire.

Suzanne Citron also views national identity as a construct, a 'national myth' and she is interested in the way this myth has been perpetuated by the French education system. She focuses on the relationship between French national identity and historiography and in particular, on the way primary school textbooks, with their origins in the Third Republic, served to inculcate an idealized, unitary and glorified vision of the past. This 'national story' can be found in the work of republican historians from Jules Michelet to Ernest Lavisse whose work provided the basis of the primary school curriculum (Citron, 2008: 10). History textbooks had a particular educational and nationalistic purpose and were intended to instil in school children, patriotic sentiments and a love of France, so that the purpose of history seemed inseparable from that of nationalism itself. This official history provides a mythologized vision of France which situates events in a 'natural chronological order' beginning with the Gauls, continued by the French kings and sublimated by the French Revolution which is seen to consolidate France's exceptional common destiny (ibid., 10). Yet this national history, she warns, has dangerous moral and ideological repercussions. It is a history that legitimizes or obscures abuses of power linked to events such as colonialism and the Vichy regime and that excludes those categorized as non-French from the national picture. Despite the rise of a new critical history, this version of national history, she suggests, and the 'staging of an imaginary past' has persisted and continues to provide a model for the teaching of history in French schools today (ibid., 9). Her purpose is to 'deconstruct the historical imaginary forged by the Third Republic and to reread the past' in order to help create 'a common and plural history' that reflects contemporary social realities (ibid., 16). She emphasizes the need to rewrite history for today's multicultural and plural France, so that all French people can lay claim to a collective past and memory.

Gérard Noiriel in *A Quoi sert l'identité nationale* (*The Uses of National Identity*, 2007), is interested in the contemporary political context and the way in which the theme of national identity has been re-appropriated by the Right as a means to justify their political goals. For Noiriel, national identity constitutes a political instrument that is bound up with the interests of nationalism and that serves to create a false division between 'them' (foreigners) and 'us' (French): 'my criticisms have always targeted the political uses of "national identity," because this expression has been used, most often, to stigmatize immigrants by creating an artificial divide between "them" and "us"' (Noiriel, 2007: 7). Focusing on Nicolas Sarkozy's 2007 presidential campaign, he examines the way in which the latter manipulated 'historical truths' in order to further a nationalist agenda that exalted the nation and excluded foreigners. Challenging Sarkozy's claim to have made a break with the past and to have lifted a 'taboo' on national identity, Noiriel situates Sarkozy's discourse within a classic right-wing tradition with its origins in the Third Republic and in particular, in the work of nineteenth-century writer and politician, Maurice Barrès. Writing in the aftermath of the Franco-Prussian war, Barrès appealed for a defence of national identity in the face of France's internal and external enemies and in particular in relation to Germany. Whereas from 1870 to the end of World War II, national identity was defined in relation to Germany, from the 1970s onwards, this identity was reconstituted by the Right and defined in opposition to immigrants. Noiriel seeks to expose the exclusionary logic in Sarkozy's rhetoric in which national identity is defined in terms of republican values that are portrayed not as products of history, but as eternal and hereditary attributes and which are therefore exclusively French. His aim is to reveal the instrumental and strategic uses of national identity and to encourage 'vigilance' in relation to the abuses of history made by politicians.[9]

In this book, I draw on the above studies to develop a constructivist approach that situates French identity in relation to globalization and to all the challenges, tensions and uncertainties that this process generates. If there has been a return of national identity in France today, this is because globalization is perceived as an external threat, one that encroaches on traditional forms of national belonging and tradition. National identity has been reaffirmed as a means to rebuild forms of cohesion and rootedness in a hostile and changing world. It acts as a kind of elixir, offering a cure for all France's ills and conjuring up a reified image of a nation in which traditions are preserved and in which a benevolent state continues to watch over its people. French identity often counterposes an idealized Republic against an Anglo-Saxon Other that is perceived as alien, dangerous and inferior. The Anglo-Saxon world serves as an oppositional myth, a means to reinstate a sense of common identity and to capture all the ill effects of a globalizing world. Yet French identity is not a pure construct or an 'empty vessel' that simply mirrors the concerns of the moment (Rogers, 2000). Rather, it involves a reactivation of the enduring symbols and references of French political culture and tradition. Identity may be based on an 'invention of history' but this act of invention draws on an established symbolic repertoire, a 'symbolic and material heritage' that shapes forms of belonging in the present day (Thiesse, 2001: 12). The following section will consider some of these critical and enduring aspects of French political culture and in particular the importance of the republican model in giving substance to representations of identity in the present day.

The republican model

National identity in France today is bound up with a republican model that is characterized by a particular institutional framework, a comprehensive ideology and a set of historical myths. While in the period after 1968, the symbol of the Republic seemed to have become obsolete and all but disappeared from mainstream political discourse, it has in the present day, become once again a critical reference for defining identity, one that mobilizes deep-seated support within French society and across the Left and Right. Different French observers have highlighted a resurgence of republicanism as a framework for representing national identity at a time of globalizing transformation (Spitz, 2005; Sieffert, 2006; Bernstein, 2007; Ferrand, 2007; Peillon, 2008; Rozès, 2009; Audier, 2010). Serge Bernstein refers to the rise of a republican political culture that revives the nationalist values and ideas of the Third Republic and that is characterized by a number of core elements: an attachment to the state, a defence of human rights both in France and in the world, an emphasis on the principle of solidarity and on a regulation of market forces (Bernstein, 2007). For Vincent Peillon, France has been marked by a 'return of the republican idea' and this provides a repository for meaning and identification, at a time when other forms of social and political identification seem to have been dissolved (Peillon, 2008: 36). Faced with the uncertainties of the market and fears of social breakdown, the French have found common ground in a republican discourse that exalts the nation and that bestows on France a universalist mission in the world. For Denis Sieffert, the rise of republican identity reflects a 'France in distress' that is fearful of globalization and of the spectre of national decline, a France in search of the terms of its own collective existence (Sieffert, 2006: 124). If France experienced a resurgence of republican identity, this was a reaction against a destabilization of the Republic itself. This section considers the nature of republican identity today and I argue that this is defined both by the past and by the challenges of globalization in the present.

In France today, republican identity has found a broad consensus across the Left and Right, overcoming previous ideological divisions and political differences. Indeed, the appeal of the republican model seemed to stem partly from its porous and malleable nature and its capacity to be harnessed towards entirely different political ends: 'who isn't a republican in 21st century France?' (ibid., 6). Hence the Republic could be used by the Right to justify the most hardline and discriminatory laws against immigrants, implemented in the name of strictly defined republican ideals and in particular, the principle of secularism. Nicolas Sarkozy's rhetoric of national identity was rooted in a conception of the Republic as a source of moral order, authority and leadership in a world that was chaotic, decadent and misguided. He saw the Republic as the pioneer of a new moral order that would overcome the excesses of Anglo-Saxon liberalism and restore authoritarian values in the world. Even Marine Le Pen, the Far-Right leader of the Front National, who has been in a leading position in the polls in the run-up to the 2012 presidential elections, conceives national identity in strictly republican terms and has distanced herself from the overtly racialist discourse of her father. Meanwhile, the Left in contemporary France has appealed for a 'social republicanism' based on the vision of a protectionist state guided by the principle of solidarity. For them, the Republic alone can provide a way out of France's current impasse and offer a pana-cea for its multiple social ills. Leftist debates often involve a re-examination of political traditions, the legacy of the Revolution and the significance of republican values in order to devise responses to today's social problems. In one recent volume, leftist thinkers agreed that only a 'revived Republic' could simultaneously resolve France's domestic problems and its external difficulties by countering 'a totalitarian extension of financial markets' coming from beyond its national borders (Ferrand, 2007: 12). Similarly, the project of *altermondialisme* that seeks to create an alternative model to neo-liberal glo-balization on the world stage, is articulated in terms of republican principles of equality, justice and solidarity.

French republican identity is characterized by the importance of history in determining the conditions of social and political belonging in the present. For Régis Debray, the French republican model was distinguished precisely by this weight of history and the fact that the French carried their past on their shoulders so that 'every child at birth is six thousand years old' (Debray, 1992: 35). The French tend to see themselves in a direct and linear rela-tionship with the past, based on a 'historical continuum of the nation' that stretches back to the French Revolution and continues seamlessly into the present (Slama, 1995: 52). The Republic was constructed though a unification of memory that overcame past divisions and conflicts in favour of a vision of national unity. Ernest Renan in his famous 1882 lecture 'What is the nation?' defined this as a 'daily plebiscite' and a 'common will' that was anchored in an awareness of a common past and an ancestral legacy transmitted from one generation to the next. For him, the nation was built not only on a common memory, but on the 'forgetting' (oubli) of the conflicts that divided the nation in the past. The continued importance of history in defining national identity in France today means that contemporary social and political problems often prompt a re-examination of France's past and of the principles of nationhood defined at the time of the French Revolution. According to Vincent Peillon, in his book *La Révolution française n'est pas terminée* (*The French Revolution is Not Over*, 2008), the French can only resolve their present social and political difficulties by rediscovering the meaning and significance of the Revolution. For him the Revolution was not merely an historical occurrence but a 'reli-gious event', an act of creation, and an 'absolute beginning' that forever trans-formed the terms of human existence. The solution to today's problems, from social exclusion to racism and globalization, resides in a re-examination of the Revolution and its profound significance for the present.

The French republican model is marked by a number of historically defined features which continue to provide a foundation for national identity in the present day. Bernstein and Rudelle observe that the republican model was not a simple variant of liberal democracy but a 'veritable political model' comparable to that of an absolute monarchy or socialist state and that it was grounded in philosophical ideas, historical references, ideological principles, an institutional model, a symbolic representation and political practice. This model was defined firstly by an attachment to a strong and centralized state, one that helped to construct the nation in the aftermath of the French Revolution and that gave substance to a conception of national identity. The state's mission was to create a 'one and indivisible Republic' by overcoming 'fragmented reality' and imposing a new sense of national cohesion (Hayward, 2007). Republican identity in France today is marked by a mistrust of the market which is often seen as a factor of social fragmentation and political disunity. French political culture is marked by 'the historical weakness of liberalism' which never acquired a clear and cohesive sense of political identity and conversely by an emphasis on a state-centred vision as the basis for organizing society (Hewlett, 2003: 119). Historically, the Republic gained legitimacy and mobilized widespread public consensus by claiming to protect 'les petits', embracing the interests of all ordinary French men and women and in particular the weak and marginalized (Bernstein & Rudelle, 1992). The state's role was therefore to limit individual freedoms where these were seen to interfere with the general interest of society, to protect its citizens and to guarantee social cohesion and equality. The resurgence of republican identity, particularly on the Left, is bound up with a conception of a state which takes precedence over the market and which incarnates the common good of society as a whole.

Secondly, republican identity is characterized by a set of ideological principles that have their origins in the 1789 Declaration of the Rights of Man and the Citizen that are seen as sacred and inviolable and that are deemed to be valid for all people and for all time. Régis Debray refers to the absolutist nature of France's ideological principles and sees this as the key feature that distinguishes the French Republic from other democratic systems. He suggests that the French are haunted by a 'totalitarian urge' seeing their own values as supreme, universal and incontrovertible and rejecting all other belief systems as inferior (Debray, 1992: 43). This republican legacy meant that the French held contempt for 'real men in favour of an idea of man' favouring abstract principles and ideals over social realities (ibid.). To transgress these foundational values was to violate the symbolic and historical origins of the Republic itself. In France today, national identity is increasingly defined in relation to republican values that are seen as a legacy of national history and an intrinsic component of Frenchness itself. On the Right, political discourse has been marked by a hardening of republican values which are increasingly interpreted in essentialist terms and which view French identity as a cultural predisposition to democracy (Noiriel, 2007; Emery, 2010).

Thirdly, national identity, as we have already seen, is closely linked with the French social model and with the principle of solidarity that underpins it. Defined by Léon Bourgeois in his book *Solidarité* (1896), this principle was based on the belief that all members of society were interdependent, sharing a 'natural bond' and that every individual had a duty towards society as a whole (Audier, 2010: 15). According to this ideal, the rich and fortunate were obligated to carry a greater social burden on behalf of the less fortunate in society. The principle of solidarity provided the main legitimizing principle for the creation of the Etat Providence in postwar France and national identity was increasingly linked with the image of a state that protects its citizens, guarantees equality and redistributes wealth. Smith notes that the French tend to define themselves in relation to their social model and contrast this negatively against an American model that is equated with social decline and moral decay (Smith, 2004). More than a provider of material benefits, of pensions, healthcare or welfare, France's social model is seen to embody enduring collective principles with their origins in the national historical experience. Recent surveys show that the French remain deeply attached to their social model and France has the second highest level of public satisfaction with its social model of all the countries in the European Union (after Luxembourg) and three quarters of French people believe that this provides a good basis for social protection (Damon, 2008).

Yet what distinguishes French national identity is not a disparate set of structures or beliefs but an attachment to the Republic as a comprehensive whole, a 'perfect and definitive system' that is viewed as all-encompassing and complete (Bernstein & Rudelle, 1992: 8). The French model is not one form of democracy among others, but an 'absolute Republic' that provides a lasting model for France and for humanity as a whole (Rudelle, 1982). The Republic is elevated to the status of a secular religion with its own forms of worship, its dogma, rituals and a strict moral code. In France today, many still distinguish the French republican model by its sacred and providential character: 'The religion of Humanity is not only a national religion. It is a religion for humanity as a whole' (Peillon, 2008: 159). As with all religions, republicanism tends to draw a strict line of demarcation between 'us' and 'them', between good and evil, between sacred and profane and between believers and nonbelievers. The Republic is not limited to day-to-day politics, but is seen to incarnate abstract ideological beliefs that transcend time. Here, history, ideology and institutions are all seen to be inextricably linked, forming part of an essential wholeness. This made France's relationship with globalization particularly difficult and intense. To touch any one aspect of this republican model is to call into question an entire political and social order, with its roots in the French Revolution and that continues to define national identity in the present day. Globalization is not only about economic reform, but it seems to invalidate French history itself and the dream of a society united around democratic principles and an interventionist state. Global market forces are not simply threatening social and economic rights, they are defiling the sacred burial ground of Robespierre and Danton.

If republican identity is defined by the past, it is also an explicit response to the challenges of globalization in the present. We know that identity becomes important in society during periods of profound transformation, when it provides a means to resolve tensions in society and to restore the cultural integrity of the community. Faced with deep-seated changes and uncertainties, republican identity has been invested with a new and compelling significance and this now offers 'an inexhaustible resource against the evils of neo-liberalism' (Berthet, 2007: 51). On the one hand, it provides a symbolic defence against changes in the present, conjuring up a perfect world, both timeless and pure, that is far removed from present contingencies. Increasingly, republican identity is defined in juxtaposition to globalization, so that it has become its very antithesis. It provides an image of an ordered and secure universe in which an authoritative and benevolent state watches over the people and this is counterposed against the chaotic, unpredictable 'casino economy' of contemporary globalization. The Republic is often presented as a rampart or a besieged fortress that is under attack from a globalization whose ultimate design is to 'dismantle the Republic' and to 'annihilate republican values' (Ferrand, 2007: 12). The Republic also provides a symbol of morality and this is a world guided by abstract universal principles that is contrasted with the dissolute market-driven value system of contemporary globalization. Finally, it provides a model of historical continuity that anchors the French to their past and provides a linear connection between past and present. It is counterposed against a globalization of ceaseless transformation that is identified by some with a 'dictatorship of the present' (Chevènement, 2011: 270).

On the other hand, as we will see in Chapter 3, republican identity is a symbolic means to restore French status and leadership in the world and therefore to reconstitute reality differently. On both Left and Right, writers invoked France's pre-given universalist vocation as a necessary platform for confronting the challenges of globalization and for restoring France to its rightful position in the world. For the leftist republican writer, Eric Ferrand, the solution to the dilemmas facing Europe is a renewed and strengthened French Republic that could once again provide leadership within a broader European civilization. The French, in his view, need to reaffirm their loyalty to the nation which alone holds the historical and moral legitimacy to provide leadership in the world: 'France which identified itself in the past with a vocation to offer values to the world must remain true to this image and provide an example of a revived Republic' (Ferrand, 2007: 14). Similarly Jean-Pierre Chevènement argues that in the wake of the 2008 economic crisis, the French need to reaffirm their identity, rediscover their historical roots and restore the Republic

> as a new concept, first in France, but also in Europe and the world. France, after all, was the first to provide a model of a 'republican nation' which then established itself in the rest of the world. We have nothing to be embarassed about. (Chevènement, 2011: 267)

He envisages a France at the helm of a new Europe, steering it towards a more steady and purposeful course, one that is guided by republican and Enlightenment traditions and that abandons its ill-fated trajectory as a Trojan horse for Anglo-Saxon neo-liberalism.

Conclusion

French opposition to globalization is often viewed as a regressive force that drags France backwards and that prevents modernizing change. Some situate it on a line of continuity with the corporatist, anti-modern movements of the 1950s and 1960s that had been mobilized to protect the social status of particular groups and to resist change. Many believe that contemporary protest is limited to narrow sectional interests and that it rarely looks beyond specific needs towards the general interest of society. This conception of protest is often counterposed against an image of the market as a force for modernity and universalism, one that transcends particular interests and brings benefits to all. This relationship between a modernizing market and an archaic resistance is central to neo-liberal doctrine and has been recently perpetuated in French public debates on globalization. Nicolas Bavarez, in his book *Après le deluge* (2009), written in the wake of the global economic crisis, defends globalization as a tremendous modernizing force ('globalisation constitutes a formidable economic, social and moral progress') and he equates this with an era of 'universal capitalism and the open society' which defines the twenty-first century (Bavarez, 2009: XXIX, 185). He urges the French to allow reason to prevail over fear and not to give in to the extremist and regressive elements that have emerged since the crisis: 'It is not the time for whining or hysteria, but for thought and action' (ibid., 188). He argues that France needs to accelerate the pace of reforms in order to integrate society more fully into the international economy. We have seen that Bavarez was a vocal supporter of Nicolas Sarkozy during his election campaign and his work helped pave the way towards the French government's ongoing neo-liberal reforms.

We will see in Chapter 3 that far from being regressive and particularist, French opposition has acted as a powerful force for political transformation that transcends the borders of France alone and increasingly intervenes on an international stage. Many activists and thinkers across the world see France as the nerve centre of movement that is helping to redefine the terms of globalization and to lay the foundations for an alternative world order (Pleyers, 2003; Fougier, 2008a). On the one hand, French activists helped to provide a new ideological framework for opposition, offering a countervailing set of political values, analytical tools, instruments of contestation and a vision of an alternative world order (*altermondialisme*). Yet beyond political ideals alone, France has helped to shape the process of globalization itself, influencing the substance of economic policies at European and international level, along progressive and democratic lines. Through their omnipresent role in international institutions, French political leaders helped to construct an alternative model to neo-liberalism based on a vision of *mondialisation maîtrisée* that emphasized market regulation, common international rules and social and democratic principles (Abdelal & Meunier, 2010).

Notes

1 According to Jack Hayward, 'France is a state-nation rather than a nation-state' and the state continues to give meaning and substance to identity today, providing a link with the past and incarnating sacred collective principles (Hayward, 1973: 17).

2 The French National Assembly (336 in favour and 52 against) and Senate (265 in favour, 42 against and 13 abstentions) voted strongly in favour of the Lisbon Treaty on 7 and 8 February 2008, a reworking of the European Constitutional Treaty that had been rejected by French voters in the 2005 referendum. As part of the Lisbon Treaty, a double majority voting system in the Council of Ministers will be phased in between 2014 and 2017 which means Germany's share of votes will double and small states such as Ireland will lose influence over decisions made in Brussels.

3 As Richard Kuisel points out, as early as 1949, when Coca-Cola began marketing its drinks in France, *Le Monde* alerted the French public to the dangers of Americanization which threatened the 'moral landscape of France' (Kuisel, 1995: 38). Similarly, Jean-Jacques Servan-Schreiber in his bestselling book *Le Défi Américain* (*The American Challenge*, 1967) warned that American companies were challenging American and European economic traditions.

4 In French and European public discourse, the term 'cultural diversity' has increasingly been supplanted by that of 'intercultural dialogue'. Hence, the European Parliament and member states of the European Union defined 2008 as the 'European Year of Intercultural Dialogue' and this concept emphasizes the importance of dialogue within diversity and between different cultures.

5 Smith draws on the example of the 1995 public sector strikes and the 2003 demonstrations against pension reform to argue that French protest mobilized privileged workers rather than the socially marginalized. Absent from his book is a discussion of the cycle of protest that began in the period after 1995 and that mobilized some of the most underprivileged sections of French society, often collectively referred to as the 'Sans' and including the unemployed (*sans-emploi*), undocumented immigrants (*sans-papiers*) and the homeless (*sans-abri*). Indeed, for many observers, these social movements are the critical social and political forces of this period, marking a return of social protest in contemporary France (Sommier, 2001; Waters, 2003).

6 Since publication, Huntington's book has come under virulent criticism from scholars who have contested his use of the word 'civilization' as a category for explaining patterns of conflict in a globalized world. For instance, Gilbert Achar, whose book, *The Clash of Barbarisms* was intended as a riposte to Huntington, has argued that the latter's approach is crude and reductionist and ignores the political motivations behind terrorism. Yet, Achar tends to reproduce his own form of binary categorization by replacing Huntington's 'civilization' with the notion of 'barbarism' seen to better reflect the 'darker' side of contemporary conflict (Achar, 2006). Similarly, Youssef Courbage and Emmanuel Todd, in their analysis of Muslim societies, argue that Huntington has exaggerated the potential for conflict in the world and they point instead to a convergence of cultures or kind of 'rendez-vous des civilisations' (Courbage & Todd, 2007). Some critics argue that Huntington's work fulfills a political agenda by conjuring up a new 'Other' for the United States in the form of Islam in order to replace the Soviet Union of the former Cold War order and runs the risk of creating a 'self-fulfilling prophecy' (Booth, 1997: 425). For instance, Robert Bonney in *False Prophets* argues that Huntington's thesis has had a profound influence on American political discourse and was used to legitimize an aggressive foreign policy against a perceived Islamic threat (Bonney, 2008).

7 Hence in Britain, globalization seemed to be attuned with a liberal tradition that emphasized market freedoms and a minimalist state. Yet in France, this same process generated an unparalleled scale of social protest, political opposition and popular malaise. Other studies have confirmed that globalization is perceived differently from one national setting to the next. One study comparing American and French perceptions of globalization showed that in the United States the role of the market is typically seen as central and there is a generalized mistrust of 'big government'. However, in France, it is the market that is generally looked upon with suspicion and the state that is seen as a 'natural' and central force within society (Fougier, 2001). These national

differences mean that globalization is perceived and experienced by different people in very different ways.

8 When he died in 1985, Fernard Braudel was one of the world's most influential academic historians. He made his reputation by a book published in 1949 entitled *La Méditerranée et le monde méditerranéen à l'époque de Philippe II* and later as editor of the influential journal *Annales: Economies, sociétés, civilisations*. The *Annales* journal was created in 1929 by Marc Bloch and Lucien Febvre and shaped a new historical approach that sought to embrace all aspects of human experience in what Febvre called 'total' history. When Febvre died in 1956, Braudel inherited his position as editor and over the next 12 years brought the Annales school to the peak of its influence. See François Dosse, *The New History* (1994).

9 His book also sought to justify his reasons for resigning from a national historical council in protest against the decision of Sarkozy's government to create a Ministry of Immigration and National Identity. Noiriel was one of eight members of the *conseil scientifique de la Cité nationale de l'histoire de l'Immigration* to declare his resignation from this post, on 18 May 2007, the same day that the government announced the creation of the new Ministry of Immigration and National Identity.

3

Political leaders: A new civilizing mission?

French political leaders seem to share a deeply contradictory, if not hypocritical relationship with globalization which consists of loving and loathing it, of embracing and rejecting it. On the one hand, politicians denounced the ravages of globalization and pointed to the shortcomings of an Anglo-Saxon neo-liberal model. They argued that France, in the face of globalization, would defend its own political traditions, assert its national identity and project its distinctive values on a world stage. On the other hand, political leaders were champions of globalization, opening up the French economy, privatizing state assets and initiating structural reform on a massive scale. Today's France, in economic terms at least, is one of the most globalized countries in the world, with a more open economy than either the United States or Japan (Meunier, 2004). For Sophie Meunier, French politicians have perfected the art of 'doubletalk' on globalization, loudly criticizing this from their podiums, while quietly adapting to the requirements of an international economy. They pursued a 'globalization by stealth' progressively integrating the French economy into a globalized market, but doing this far away from the public gaze (Meunier, 2003: 20). Jack Hayward, in a similar vein, suggests that the French political system operates according to a principle of 'organized hypocrisy' which consists of virulently defending the French social model, without creating the conditions for it to survive in a changing international environment (Hayward, 2007: 372). Meanwhile, for the French political scientist, Stéphane Rozès, political leaders display a 'schizophrenia' on globalization that reflects a deeper societal tendency to accept the economic and material aspects of globalization, while rejecting it as a political and cultural ideal. The French public, he suggests, were happy to flock to McDonalds restaurants and to watch American blockbuster films, while looking to their leaders to provide a 'national imaginary' based on an ideal of the Republic (Rozès, 2009: 46, 47). The ambivalent stance of French political leaders also perpetuates a more long-standing difficulty in negotiating France's role in Europe and in reconciling French national interests with European policy developments and constraints (Dyson, 1999; Cole & Drake, 2000; Howarth, 2002, 2008).

For many critics, France's contradictory relationship with globalization is the result of the competing pressures of pleasing the electorate, while responding to external market constraints. Politicians have been keen to rally the support of a public that is deeply fearful, pessimistic and anxious about globalization and that wishes to be protected from its worst effects. Yet, leaders also faced intense pressures from European and international institutions to open up the national economy, reform institutions, cut public spending and adapt to an international marketplace. The outcome of these competing pressures has been a kind of discursive high-wire act that holds in balance two diametrically opposed versions of reality. I argue in this chapter that the contradictory stance of French political leaders also reflects more deep-seated historical factors and in particular, the enduring impact of a legacy of republican universalism in the present day. France's universalist tradition is profoundly divisive and is marked by a conflict between two separate and opposing tendencies, on the one hand, a set of Enlightenment principles that advocated humanism and on the other, a relationship of power between France and the outside world, conditioned by the experience of colonialism. We will see that French leaders drew on the ideological resources of republicanism in order to challenge a dominant neo-liberal model, to question its fundamental assumptions and to further democratic and humanist ideals. French politicians have been at the forefront of opposition to globalization on an international stage and have gone further than their counterparts in any other European country in their demands for market regulation and structural reform. Yet, the response of French leaders has also been deeply influenced by a colonialist perspective that sees France at the centre of the universe with a mission to spread its values, exert political authority and enlighten others. For Dino Costantini, French political identity today is profoundly influenced by a legacy of colonialism which continues to shape representations of France's relationship with the outside world (Costantini, 2008). In this chapter, I argue that French leaders, at a time of globalization, revived a colonialist discourse as a means of confronting globalization and in particular, the consequences of national decline and waning international status. They conjured up a new 'civilizing mission' which reconfigured unpalatable external realities and restored France to a place of moral and political leadership in the world that seemed to be rightfully hers. In articulating France's relationship with other nations, political leaders transposed many of the metaphors once reserved for the colonial subject to the new Other of the globalized world: *le monde anglosaxon*. They increasingly defined national identity in opposition to an Anglo-Saxon Other portrayed as primitive, barbaric and inferior. We will see that many of the contradictions within French political discourse reflect the tensions inherent within republican universalism itself, between a desire to extend democratic and humanist values in the world and at the same time, to impose a relationship of power between France and other nations based on a belief in France's civilizing mission.

This chapter examines the response of three French political leaders to globalization: Lionel Jospin, Prime Minister of the Plural Left government (1997–2002), Jacques Chirac, right-wing president during two terms (1995–2002 and 2002–2007) and Nicolas Sarkozy who came to power as president in 2007. It will draw on political discourse from a variety of national and international settings including local and regional speeches, international summits and press conferences, as well as from books and newspaper articles written by these leaders. I argue that the response of French leaders to globalization has been both progressive – they challenged a hegemonic neo-liberal order and provided democratic and humanist alternatives – and regressive, in that they turned towards their colonial past and refused to see the outside world in anything but the narrowest and most self-referential of terms. In the face of globalization, French political leaders revived a conception of national identity rooted in all the metaphors and symbols of past colonial grandeur. Paradoxically, this appeal to a republican and colonialist identity by French political leaders was not intended to slow down or obstruct processes of economic liberalization, but rather to allow them to happen on a vast and unprecedented scale. The more France became integrated into an international economy, the more it became necessary to invoke the myth of a great universalist Republic. This was a discursive means to offset and cushion the effects of economic change, by anchoring it in a bedrock of stability, continuity and national pride. By conjuring up an idealized republican identity and images of colonial greatness, French leaders laid the discursive and ideological foundations for economic globalization to take place.

Facing decline

For Benedict Anderson, the nation was an 'imagined community' built not on objective structures or tangible realities, but on invented forms such as symbols, myths and rituals. He suggested that the nation, nationhood and national identity were ideas that 'rooted human lives firmly in the very nature of things, giving certain meaning to the everyday fatalities of existence (above all death, loss and servitude) and offering, in various ways, redemption from them' (Anderson, 1991: 36). French political leaders, in the face of globalization, have sought to reconstruct the nation symbolically and endow it with a power, prestige and influence that it did not otherwise have. They set out to create an imaginary community in which France was once again at the centre of the universe, a beacon of universalist values and a model for other nations to follow. During France's Third Republic, political elites drew on republican ideology and in particular, the notion of a 'civilizing mission' in order to articulate and justify France's relationship with its colonies. They sought to transform a colonial relationship based on power, domination and subjugation and to reconstitute it in terms that were consistent with French republican identity. Hence, they represented France's imperial expansion as a mission to civilize whereby a 'France généreuse' was spreading its values elsewhere and helping to elevate the lot of humanity as a whole. Just as during the Third Republic, political leaders today have invoked a discourse of republican universalism in order to redefine the terms of France's relationship with the outside world.[1] Yet here, it was not a case of reconfiguring a relationship based on imperial power and domination, but of dealing with a situation of powerlessness, national decline and loss of stature. If colonialism had placed France at the hub of the universe, globalization now reduced it to a shadow of its former self, confining its political influence to within its own national borders.

It has been well documented that globalization in France has been experienced as a process of steep and irreversible national decline. It is seen to have accelerated a loss of international power that began with the devastation of World War I, continued with the defeat of 1940 and was furthered by a loss of colonial empire. The impact of globalization in France has been one of increased national economic vulnerability, fading international prestige, accompanied by a loss of national identity. The belief that globalization has precipitated national decline is deeply rooted within French public opinion, among political elites and public intellectuals. This perception of French decline intensified after the 2008 financial crisis which discredited a belief that globalization was beneficial for France and put paid to the myth of a 'mondialisation heureuse'.[2] Hence, according to a 2010 IFOP poll, 71 per cent of people now consider France to be 'in decline' and only 46 per cent of those interviewed see France as a model for other nations. Nonetheless, the same poll revealed that 79 per cent of French people believe that France has considerable strengths and 70 per cent that France was capable of reform. There are signs that such pessimistic attitudes are becoming more entrenched within French public life. For instance, an earlier 2006 Barometer poll found that a more modest 52 per cent of people believed that France was in a state of national decline, while 8 per cent believed that France was experiencing progress in terms of its economic outlook, cultural influence and international status. Of these, 46 per cent of people attributed this decline to a loss of power on the international stage. A further 42 per cent attributed national decline to the lack of competitiveness of French firms within an international economy (Brouard & Tiberj, 2006).

Meanwhile, a debate about French decline has raged in France since the beginning of the decade and prompted a spate of books which all decry France's fading fortunes and seek to identify the key indicators of national decay.[3] Since the publication of Nicolas Bavarez's best-selling book, *La France qui tombe* (*France in Free-fall*, 2003) which helped to launch the national debate about French decline, this controversy has continued unabated and has been given expression in recent books by Eric Zemmour (*Mélancolie française*/ French Melancholy, 2010) and Jean-Pierre Chevènement (*La France, est-elle finie?*/Is France finished? 2011).[4] For some, the source of France's problems is of a domestic nature and stems from France's inability to adapt to a modified international context. Hence, Bavarez depicts a France that is paralysed by immobilism and that is incapable of reforming its own outmoded structures. He points the finger at political elites who have favoured grandiose rhetoric over concrete action and who have misled the public about the realities of France's declining geopolitical status and economic situation. For him, political leaders have helped create a self-deluded nation that 'maintains a discourse of power that is disconnected from its real means of influence and action' (Bavarez, 2003: 47). Similarly, the prominent historian, Jacques Julliard conjures up a catastrophic picture of a France that has sunk into a cesspit of despair, fear and melancholy, triggered by a collapse of France's international influence and a consequent loss of national self-belief (Julliard, 2005). Whereas Bavarez blames politicians, Julliard points to the French themselves whom he characterizes by an all-pervasive individualism that has destroyed the foundations of collective solidarity and idealism. Chevènement shares this apocalyptic vision, suggesting that France today has exited the stage of History, lost its natural vocation as a leader on the world stage and is 'a country without a future' (Chevènement, 2011: 7). He attributes France's woes to a fateful collusion between the French Socialists in government and an 'Anglo-Saxon capitalism' which sacrificed the French nation on the altar of economic 'liberalism' (ibid., 29). He traces the origins of the Socialists' liberal turn of 1983 to the legacy of defeat linked to two world wars during which France had 'lost its soul' and had become incapable of pursuing its own historic destiny (ibid., 192). For Chevènement, the way forward for French society lies in a reassertion of national identity and in particular in a revival of the concept of the Republic as a model for France and for the world. Bavarez, by contrast, believes that France's only option is to engage in deep-seated structural reform and he argues that the French need to show an increasing willingness to accept change and adapt to its constraints.

According to other critics, France's problems have their origins in the process of globalization itself which has imposed changes on France against its will and in contradiction with its own traditions, values and institutions. The novelist Jean-Marie Rouart in *Adieu à la France qui s'en va* (*Farewell to Departing France*, 2003) argues that the French nation is destined for decline under pressures of international change and is losing all the characteristics that once defined Frenchness. If France is facing decline, this is not because of its weaknesses but because other nations simply do not appreciate the greatness of France. His book is an attempt to rediscover the components of that greatness through an introspective journey to the author's own childhood, to rural France, to French literature and art and to France's colonial past. He suggests that France sits uneasily in today's Europe and finds it difficult to cooperate with other nations such as Britain and Germany which, in his view, are blinkered by a narrow patriotism and fail to understand France's universalist vocation:

> Will she be able to accept being reduced to the rank of one nation among others, she who has always believed, as the eldest daughter of the Church, the heir to Greco-Roman humanism, that she was made to instruct the world about its true civilising mission? She may suffer in this enterprise which can only be achieved through depersonalisation and uniformisation. (Rouart, 2003: 235)

He believes that the solution to France's decline lies elsewhere, in a Europe that needs to transform itself from a narrow economic entity into a broad cultural project, to reaffirm its own historical distinctiveness and its humanist tradition and thereby create a Europe that is truly worthy of French membership. Similarly, Eric Zemmour's book is a eulogy to France and to the illustrious march through history of a great French nation. He compares France's current decline to the fall of the Roman Empire and the collapse of a great civilization that had once enlightened and transformed the world. He locates the origins of French decline to seventeenth century Europe when England, through its domination of the seas, gained supremacy over France:

> We have never recovered from this history, this failure and this renunciation. A country that was destined for over a thousand years to bestow 'Roman peace' on Europe had to enter into rank. This wound is still open, even if we pretend not to see the blood flowing. (Zemmour, 2010: 35)

The real danger to France today, in his view, is mass immigration and the rise of an Islamic identity that is weakening the link between the present genera-tion and France's 'classic heritage' (ibid., 235). He observes that France, just like Rome is collapsing under the weight of an invasion by 'barbarians' that it is no longer able to assimilate or control. Like Rouart, Zemmour believes that France's salvation lies in a return to its roots, a recovery of its illustrious his-tory, a cultural renaissance and moral reconstruction which alone can reverse a path of ineluctable national decline.

For these authors, globalization has precipitated French decline in three important ways. Firstly, it is associated with the rise of American power which has usurped France's traditional status in the world and challenged France's universalist pretensions. Globalization is seen to have created a new geopolitical context, a post–Cold War world in which the United States exer-cises unprecedented political influence. Bavarez refers to a world shaped by the 'unrivalleled imperial power of the United States' and to a new 'uni-polar world' in the face of which, France can no longer project its power (Bavarez, 2003: 26). He argues that American political and military supremacy was intensified in the period after 11 September 2001, after which American neo-conservatives launched a project of 'global imperial domination based on force' (ibid., 126). For Julliard, globalization has reversed the historical rela-tionship between France and the United States. The latter now conceived its international role in terms of a singular, universalist and messianic mission to transform the world according to its own values. France, by contrast, had retreated to a defensive and pragmatic position which challenged American unilateralism and called for a more pluralist 'multipolar world', but which lacked a unifying vision with which to impose its own ideals. Chevènement notes that since the 2008 economic crisis, American supremacy has been rivalled by the economic power of Asian nations and in particular by 'the irresistible rise of China' and this is a source of new tensions in the world (Chevènement, 2011: 107). France and Europe, he observes, cannot hope to compete with a Chinese economy that draws on vast pools of cheap labour, rising internal demand and high rates of productivity and China's ascendancy has confirmed the Pacific region as the new centre of world power.

Secondly, globalization is linked to the rise of an ideological model based on neo-liberalism which has claimed hegemonic status and challenged France's own political model. Bavarez argues that globalization has exacerbated con-flict based on ideological values and principles and led to a 'frontal opposition' between the French and proponents of neo-liberalism (Bavarez, 2003: 42). In a world dominated by neo-liberal ideals, France has lost its claims towards universalism and is no longer capable of projecting power in the world. For Julliard, France no longer recognizes itself in a world dominated by an alien political, ideological and cultural model and has fallen into a state of despair, turning inwards with an increasingly melancholic and self-critical gaze: 'The world had become Anglo-Saxon' (Julliard, 2005: 10). For Chevènement, the French Socialists who ushered neo-liberalism into Europe had been corrupted by American capitalist ideology and their policies revealed the extent to which 'ideas coming from America had corrupted the French Left from within' (Chevènement, 2011: 33). France's salvation, he believes, lies in a return to the incontrovertible truths of the Republic which is the only viable model for France and for the world: 'France must recover its voice, that of the Republic which is indissociable from its own grandeur' (ibid., 12).

Thirdly, globalization is linked with a loss of state sovereignty as a result of a transfer of competences to international institutions which has diminished the autonomy of the French state. For Pierre Dockès, French decline is inextricably bound up with the process of European integration which has weakened the state's capacity to intervene in the economy, without producing an effective common policy at European level. Similarly, for Bavarez, European integration has created a 'democratic deficit' which political leaders have been unable to fill, resulting in growing voter apathy, political disillusionment and the rise of the Far Right (Bavarez, 2003: 65). Chevènement links French decline to a progressive transfer of sovereignty from national to European level through successive treaties including the Single European Act (negotiated under 'the diktats of Margaret Thatcher'), the Maastricht Treaty and the Lisbon Treaty which had led to the 'domination of financial markets' over democratically elected governments (Chevènement, 2011: 41).

In the face of this state of apparent decline, political leaders have sought to reconfigure the nature of France's relationship with the outside world in a way that is more congruent with the terms of French national identity. Just as in the past, they have invoked republican ideology and colonial myths in order to provide the symbolic and rhetorical resources necessary to build a new 'imagined community'. This discourse allowed political leaders to fulfil two urgent political needs. Firstly, it was a means to reaffirm national identity in the face of apparent decline and help to restore a sense of greatness, historic mission and collective purpose in the world. For instance, Lionel Jospin who embraced economic liberalization during his term as Prime Minister and who privatized more state assets than any previous right-wing government, appealed in his discourse to France's universalist vocation in a globalized world: 'France has a universalist vocation. National identity, European capacity, universalist vocation are the three axes which give France its specific weight' (Jospin, 2002b: 195). Just as in the past, France's duty was to project its values and offer leadership to others: 'We can shape the world according to its values' (Jospin, 1999: 10). He argued that France shared with Europe a distinctive civilization, one in which humanity had reached its greatest accomplishments and which could provide a model for the rest of the world, and he reminds the French public that this is 'the land where respect for the human person had reached its pinnacle' (Jospin, 2002a: 16). This meant that France had a special mission to fulfil in helping 'to find a better way of organizing the world' and in seeking a 'redefinition of the world order' (ibid., 5).

Similarly, Jacques Chirac who always sought to place France in a position where it most benefited from economic globalization, argued that France had a universalist vocation to affirm the values of the French and European tradition in order to help reconstruct the world order: 'France still pursues the same dream: to bring alive at international level the ambitious slogan that it chose for itself: liberté, egalité, fraternité' (Chirac, 2000a: 3). He argued that such values had universal significance and were applicable to 'all people, all nations, all religions' (UNESCO, 2001: 2). It was not a case, he suggested, of seeking to impose a western model elsewhere, but of 'searching in every civilization for a common ideal' (ibid.). Nicolas Sarkozy expressed a conception of national identity rooted in a universalism that was seen to spring from the depths of time and which conferred on France a singular destiny in the world: 'France is a dream of greatness and of universality' (Sarkozy, 2007a: 3). To be French was to share a set of universal ideals and to possess an aspiration to elevate humanity towards greater heights. This universalism was a product of the past, but also a vocation yet to be fulfilled and France had a 'collective destiny' to project values and provide leadership to others (Sarkozy, 2007b: 5). At a time of globalization, Sarkozy called on the French people to recover the republican values that were intrinsically theirs, to reaffirm their own identity and to help show other nations the way.

Secondly, this was a means for political leaders to galvanize public support and to build confidence in their leadership. Faced with public anxieties about national decline and a 'disappearing France', political leaders repeatedly promised the electorate that they would defend French national identity, preserve French traditions and protect France's distinctive political model. By appealing to a republican identity, political leaders have been able to assume for themselves a singular political mission, one that corresponded with the higher interests of the nation itself. Politicians presented themselves as brave and fearless leaders, steering an unwavering course through a 'sea of globalization' and remaining true to their convictions, faithful to French traditions and resolute in their political ambitions (Jospin, 2002a: 15). Hence, Lionel Jospin sought to demonstrate that despite external pressures, he would vigorously defend the core values and traditions of the Republic. While emphasizing the need for economic reform, he advocated a political model that was 'both faithful to its values and modern' (Jospin,

1999: 6). He argued that France must preserve its republican values within a wider Europe that 'keeps alive the consciousness of being a civilization and the desire to remain one' (Jospin, 2005: 56). At the international level, Jospin presented himself as an authoritative and visionary leader, resolute in his principles, faithful to French traditions and assuming 'the collective mastery of our destiny' (Jospin, 1999: 7). He saw himself as the architect of an alternative French-led model that would help transform globalization in the interests of France and the whole of humanity.

Similarly, Chirac promoted a conception of France as a leader on the world stage engaging with the key challenges of a globalized era and helping to lead the world towards a more humane and 'civilized model'. In his final presidential speech of 15 May 2007, he evoked a vision of a 'generous nation' with an exceptional role to play in the world, providing guidance for others on questions such as peace, international development and the environment: 'we are heirs to a great nation, an admired and respected nation which counts in Europe and the world'. For Third World countries, France's role was to extend the hand of friendship, helping them along a path towards progress and democracy (Chirac, 2007). Finally, Sarkozy styled himself as a guardian of French national identity, defending French values and traditions in the face of the external forces that conspired against them: 'I want to be the one through whom France will defend its universal values. Values that cannot be transgressed because they are the foundation of our policies both internally and externally' (Sarkozy, 2007b: 12). He made national identity the leitmotif of his election campaign, presenting himself as a 'man of the people' who would champion the French nation against all the odds. France's republican model, he suggested, could provide an alternative model for the world, by restoring a system rooted in the values of European civilization.

Challenging the market

A critical impact of France's legacy of republican universalism was that it provided an ideological framework rooted in democratic and humanist ideals that could be used to challenge contemporary political developments, to affirm the primacy of democratic and human rights and to legitimize demands for progressive reform. Over the past 20 years, French political leaders have been at the forefront of a movement of opposition to neo-liberal globalization that has mobilized across an international stage. At a time when the neo-liberal model enjoyed hegemonic influence and when policies of economic liberalization were accepted by most European nations, France was one of the few countries to contest this model. French political leaders have gone further than their counterparts in any other European country in their demands for market regulation and a reform of the international economic system. In international settings including the European Union, the G20, the United Nations and the World Economic Forum, they have denounced an economic model that places precedence on profit alone and demanded that democratic and humanist rights be placed at the centre of the international system. They have opposed an extension of economic liberalization to new spheres of human activity and called for a reassertion of state power over private interests. Challenging a dominant laissez-faire doctrine, they have put in place innovative measures to regulate the market and promote wealth redistribution and international solidarity. Since the financial collapse of 2008, it is again French leaders who have made the strongest demands for a reform of the global economic system, arguing for a tougher regulation of the market, for a redistribution of wealth and for a globalization that places people before profits. Some commentators have suggested that in the wake of this crisis, which served to discredit an American-led neo-liberalism, a French-inspired alternative model could gain increasing influence and legitimacy in the world (Abdelal & Meunier, 2010; Jacoby & Meunier, 2010).

If French political leaders have become a voice of opposition to globalization, this was because they were deeply influenced by a republican legacy that laid out a set of ideological principles and provided a countervailing political model to that of neo-liberalism. Theorists of radical democracy, such as Chantal Mouffe have shown how the 'founding narratives' of western democracies and the values of European humanism can have an important ideological and mythological force in the present day (Mouffe, 1994). She defines radical democracy as a project to instigate political change within the existing structures of contemporary democratic societies, by modifying and extending the values at their core. The aim is to challenge the system, not according to an alternative doctrine or political order, but according to its own inherent principles, demanding that it remains true to the democratic inspiration on which it is based. The foundational values of democracy, Mouffe suggested, can provide a blueprint for a genuinely democratic society in which equality is guaranteed and rights are deepened and extended to an ever-increasing range of groups in society. French political leaders in their relationship with globalization can be seen to have furthered the goals of radical democracy by challenging the neo-liberal system according to its own principles and by drawing on the ideological resources of the democratic tradition to legitimize demands for progressive reform.

French republicanism provided political leaders with a framework of opposition to neo-liberal globalization in two important ways. In the first place, it provided an ideological framework with its roots in Enlightenment values that affirmed the natural and inalienable rights of all human beings, principles that were later enshrined in the 1789 Declaration of the Rights of Man and the Citizen. It is in relation to these principles that French leaders from Left to Right articulated their response to globalization and measured its effects on society. Hence, Lionel Jospin's speeches were marked by a constant appeal to values and he identified his political outlook in terms of a 'social republicanism' that drew on French democratic tradition to justify demands for a deepening and extension of social rights (Jospin, 2005: 42). He believed that 'the republic gives a framework to democracy' and if its values were transposed to a European and international level, then it could provide a model for an alternative world order (ibid.). Yet Jospin's arguments were not simply empty rhetoric and they helped to inform his distinctive approach to globalization. Jospin's government was at the centre of international efforts to regulate the market economy and curtail its worst effects. For instance, France, under Jospin's government, was the first to reject the terms of the MAI negotiations led by the United States, which sought to extend the reach of market competition to new realms and to limit state autonomy where this was seen to interfere with market freedoms. Similarly, Jospin and his ministers aligned themselves with a rising movement of international opposition to neo-liberalism (*alter-mondialisme*) and formed links with groupings within this movement and in particular, with the French grouping, Association for the taxation of financial transactions for the aid of citizens (Attac). As further evidence of this support, Jospin's government sent six ministers to the first World Social Forum[5] held in Porto Alegre Brazil in 2001, while only three ministers attended its official counterpart, the World Economic Forum in Davos, Switzerland. After some prevarication, Jospin also threw his weight behind the principle of a taxation of international financial exchanges: in November 2001, the French National Assembly, in an unprecedented move, voted in favour of the principle of introducing a new tax on international financial transactions (Tobin tax) to be used to alleviate global poverty.[6]

Similarly, Jacques Chirac defined the French Republic in terms of a humanist tradition that gives primacy to the natural and inalienable rights of all human beings and which, in his view, helped to define the modern world: 'Our history is that of a nation of old Europe which gave the modern world its essential values and which never gave up when they were threatened, making them the heritage of each one of us' (Chirac, 2009: 453). France's role on the international stage, in Chirac's view, was to act as a beacon of democratic and humanist values seeking to assert these in the face of destructive market forces and to extend them to a wider group of nations. Chirac made global poverty the centrepiece of his international campaign, drawing on principles of equality, justice and solidarity to emphasize the obligations of richer countries towards the world's poor. For instance, in his address to the international conference on development in Mexico on 22 March 2002, he attacked an economic model that brought unprecedented wealth to the few while pushing other countries into a situation of grinding poverty: 'How can we put an end to a situation that is morally unacceptable, politically dangerous and economically absurd, that of a world in which the growing accumulation of wealth is not enough to allow the poor to pull themselves out of poverty' (Chirac, 2000a: 2).

Yet Chirac did not simply pay lip service to grand ideals and he also put in place concrete measures to promote a redistribution of wealth, to protect the environment and to restrict further market liberalization. Following the United Nations' agreement to increase development aid as part of the Millennium Development Goals agreed by all 191 member countries in 2000, Chirac criticized those nations that had failed to meet their financial commitments and highlighted the gap in development aid under the agreed projections. As part of his commitment to promote aid, Chirac also increased France's aid budget from 2001 onwards and pledged at the Johannesburg Earth summit in 2002 that France would raise aid levels to the United Nations target of 0.7 per cent of gross national product by 2012. Alongside his appeal for increased aid, Chirac echoed the demand of many non-governmental organizations for an abolition of Third World debt and implemented new mechanisms to promote a redistribution of wealth to poorer countries. Hence, he set up a working group of French and international specialists to examine the possibilities of new forms of taxation in favour of the poor, which resulted in the 2004 Landau report. In his address to the World Economic Forum at Davos in 2005, he set out to convince other world leaders that these mechanisms were not only economically rational but also, technically feasible. His proposals presented at Davos included a 'solidarity' tax on financial transactions, a tax on countries using tax havens, a carbon tax to be levied on the transport industry and a new airline ticket tax. Under Chirac's initiative, France was the first country to introduce an airline ticket tax on 1 July 2006 for all flights departing from French territory and intended initially to fund the provision of anti-HIV medicines for Third World countries. Similarly, Chirac was the driving force behind the creation of a new international aid agency Unitaid, established jointly by France and Brazil in September 2006.[7]

Chirac also campaigned for a sustainable model of development and signalled to other world leaders the profound dangers of accelerated globalization for climate change, deforestation and a depletion of primary resources. Ironically, Chirac's discourse went further than that of any of the ministers within the Plural Left government in his demands for urgent environmental reform. Hence, a Greenpeace representative noted that Chirac's speech at Mont Saint-Michel in March 2002, 'was ten times stronger than that of Jospin' (Guiral & Losson, 2002). Chirac called on other nations to meet environmental targets and fiercely criticized the United States for failing to ratify the Kyoto agreement. At Chirac's initiative, a Charter for the Environment was approved by the French Parliament on 28 February 2005 and incorporated into the Preamble of the Constitution. Chirac gained an international reputation as an environmental campaigner following his impassioned address to the Johannesburg Earth Summit in 2002, where he warned other leaders in prophetic terms: 'The earth and humanity are in peril and we are all responsible.' He also called on other nations to reach an agreement on 'a world alliance for sustainable development' (Chirac, 2002b: 182). Finally, in the face of American opposition, he led the campaign to defend cultural products from economic liberalization and helped to define the principles of the Convention for Cultural Diversity which was adopted by UNESCO in October 2005 and ratified by 148 member states.

Like Chirac, Nicolas Sarkozy defined the Republic in terms of democratic and humanist ideals, yet for him, these were attributes specific to France, rather than belonging to a wider European tradition. For him, Frenchness was defined by a set of inviolable principles that were specific to French national tradition and he describes the Republic as 'an ideal tirelessly pursued by a great people who has believed since the beginning of time in the strength of ideas and in their capacity to transform the world and bring happiness to humanity' (Sarkozy, 2007b: 11). The French Republic, in his view, transcended ideological divisions and united all citizens around collective democratic principles. He saw himself as a champion of these nationally defined principles advancing them on an international stage in response to the challenges of a globalizing world. Sarkozy defined his approach to globalization in terms of a campaign to 'moralise capitalism' in order to reinscribe core values at the centre of the workings of the international economic order (Sarkozy, 2008b: 2). For him, the problems of globalization did not stem from the structural weaknesses of the capitalist model itself, but from a 'moral crisis' and a dilution of the values and principles that defined French and European civilization. He argued that the nations of the world had lost sight of the virtues of honest labour, hard work and competition and had been seduced by the 'cult of the money king, short-term profit, speculation' (Sarkozy, 2007b: 8). In the wake of the 2008 economic crisis, Sarkozy cultivated a virulent moralistic rhetoric that denounced the 'excesses' of a financial capitalism which had led the world astray. The solution to this crisis, in his view, lay not in structural reform but in a recovery of the moral values that were the foundation of western civilization: 'it is our vision of the world that we need to correct' (Sarkozy, 2010: 1).

He called on other leaders to agree on the terms of a 'common morality' which alone could provide a path out of the crisis (ibid., 2).

In keeping with his conception of a republicanism that transcended the Left/Right divide, Sarkozy pursued a political campaign at international level that appealed to leftist concerns to regulate financial markets, to promote social rights and protect citizens from globalization. Having played a leading role in the negotiations that led to the adoption of the Lisbon Treaty, Sarkozy during his tenure as president of the European Council (30 June 2007 to January 2008), insisted on a regulation of market forces and a 'Europe that protects' its citizens (cited by Dimitrakopoulos et al., 2009: 455). He succeeded, symbolically at least, in challenging the neo-liberal bias of the European Union by insisting that the reference to free and undistorted competition be removed from the list of EU objectives. In the wake of the economic crisis, Sarkozy supported the announcement by the European Commission of a 'major Recovery Plan for growth and jobs'. Similarly, he has been credited with the successful conclusion of the negotiations on the EU 'climate-energy' package to reduce European greenhouse-gas emissions (ibid.). Sarkozy also promoted a vision of globalization that defended and advanced social rights. Following his speech to the International Labour Organization on 15 June 2009, he launched a project to promote the social dimension of globalization and develop proposals to further 'social justice', so that France became a leader in the 'definition of a new social regulation of globalisation that reconciles economic development with social development' (Elysée, 2009). In the run-up to the G20 conference that took place in France in November 2011, Sarkozy declared that his central ambition was to 'reinforce the social dimension of globalization'.

In the second place, French republicanism provided a countervailing political model, one in which the state took precedence over market forces and was responsible for defending the general interest of all members of society. What united political leaders from Left to Right was their emphasis on regulation as a core principle for the international economy. Lionel Jospin's political vision was orientated by a fundamental belief that 'the political should take precedence over the economic' (Jospin, 1999: 1) and that market forces needed to be 'tamed', 'harnessed and 'mastered' by an authoritative state. Without state regulation, he argued, the international market system was a disorderly, unpredictable and potentially dangerous force that threatened the general interest of European nations. He called for a strong Europe, empowered international institutions and common 'ground rules' which would together constitute a new system of 'global governance' (Jospin, 2005: 65). Only a regulated market system, controlled by an 'active state' could ensure social progress, order and stability: 'rules are indispensable to the proper functioning of the market economy' (Jospin, 2002a: 6).

Similarly, Chirac, in a rhetoric that was remarkably similar to that of Jospin, advocated market regulation as a means to further democratic and humanist goals. Hence, he confided to his aides that 'the regulation of globalization has become a central element of diplomacy' (Guiral & Losson, 2002). Likewise, Nicolas Sarkozy particularly in the period after the economic crisis, went further than any other European leader in his demands for tighter regulation of the global economy. In the run-up to the G20 negotiations in London in April 2009, in a joint letter written with the German Chancellor, Angela Merkel to the President of the European Union, he called for a global financial regulator, a proposal that went further than either the United States or United Kingdom would have liked. Similarly, in Davos in January 2010, Sarkozy made forthright demands for a regulation of markets according to common rules.

The appeal by French leaders for greater state control and market regulation was certainly used as a rhetorical device designed to please uncertain voters. In Sarkozy's case, it allowed him to assume the guise of an authoritative and moralistic leader, without the need to actually implement any concrete reforms that might constrain market freedoms. Yet, beyond its rhetorical dimension, the French approach to globalization also helped to shape processes of international decision-making, influencing the substance of European and international policy on trade and finance. Rawi Abdelal and Sophie Meunier have shown that the international economy over the past 20 years has been dominated by two contending visions of globalization: a neo-liberal model promoted by the United States and a French-inspired *mondialisation maîtrisée* that emphasized regulation and state control and which was enshrined by the European Union. They show that French leaders, through their dominant presence in international institutions including the European Union, International Monetary Fund, World Economic Forum and Organization for Economic Cooperation and Development (OECD) helped construct a distinctive political model at international level that challenged a hegemonic neo-liberalism. First conceived by French left-wing policy-makers, the notion of 'managed globalisation' was integrated into European discourse by the French socialist Pascal Lamy when he was European Trade Commissioner (1999–2004) and has since become the official doctrine of the European Union. It has been the key driver of European policy-making over the past 20 years, laying emphasis on economic regulation, on a 'social' Europe, common 'ground rules', multilateral negotiations and strong international institutions. In the wake of the economic crisis of 2008, French leaders were once again at the helm of the international organizations responsible for steering the world economy out of crisis (Jean-Claude Trichet at the European Central Bank, Hervé Hannoun at the Bank of International Settlements, Christine Lagarde at the International Monetary Fund and Pascal Lamy as head of the World Trade Organization).

For Abdelal and Meunier, the financial crisis has been perceived as a failure of regulation and has given fresh impetus to a French-inspired model of mastered globalization (Abdelal & Meunier, 2010). France's influence in promoting an alternative counter-model was reinforced during France's presidency of the G20 in 2011.

Political doubletalk

Vivien Schmidt has shown that it is in France that political leaders have had the greatest difficulty in making globalization consistent with the terms of national political identity. Whereas in Britain, processes of economic liberalization, pursued over the past two decades, have been easily reconciled with an established liberal tradition and a conception of a minimal State, in France, these processes seemed to come into conflict with the foundational values and structures of the French Republic. Instead of constructing a 'legitimizing discourse' that situated globalization in relation to the French Republic, political leaders preferred to maintain a polarized discourse that conjured up two opposing realities and two very different narratives of France and of its place in the world (Schmidt, 2002: 271). The one presented a France that was unchanged, resolute in its principles, true to its own traditions, that refused to bow down before external pressures and that was providing a model for other nations to follow. The other, was of a France that accepted globalization and the need for reform and that was steadily reforming its structures in response to external constraints. Political leaders tended to pursue a delicate balancing act that separated the political realm (seen as a repository for identity, tradition and collective values), from the economic realm, seen as purely material and contingent and therefore without deeper implications for national identity. This allowed French leaders to pursue economic liberalization without appearing to encroach on the fragile boundaries of national identity.

Indeed, republican discourse was a powerful discursive tool that seemed to facilitate economic liberalization, making this possible on a vast and unprecedented scale. The more France became integrated into an international economy, the more it became necessary to appeal to a grandiose Republic. This discourse served to further the goals of economic liberalization in two important ways. Firstly, it was a means to assuage French public opinion at a time of profound societal transformation and uncertainty. By invoking the Republic and by appealing to French traditions and values, political leaders were able to anchor economic transformations within a bedrock of stability, permanence and continuity. They offset policies of economic liberalization against an image of the Republic as stable and unchanged, faithful to its own traditions and extending its political influence elsewhere in the world. Secondly, this was a means to rally electoral support and to build public confidence and trust in their leadership. French leaders sought to demonstrate that, despite external pressures, they were not 'selling out' to globalization and remained true to the values of the Republic. Paradoxically, such public trust was essential to mobilize the public support needed to implement policies of economic liberalization. French political leaders, these 'craftsmen of discourse' found themselves hovering between the devil and the deep blue sea and became adept at walking a tightrope between two seemingly irreconcilable worlds (Dyson, 1999: 181).

As Philip Gordon and Sophie Meunier have shown, the real story of France over the past 20 years is that of progressive economic adaptation, as France has become gradually integrated into the global economy (Gordon & Meunier, 2001). Successive governments of Left and Right have pursued deep-seated structural reform, to liberalize the economy, to privatize state assets and to reform the labour market. As a result, France today, in economic terms at least, is one of the most globalized country in the world, with an economy twice as open as that of Japan or the United States and reaping many of the benefits of economic globalization (Meunier, 2003). For instance, while France holds 1 per cent of the world's population, it is the fifth economic power, the fourth biggest exporter of goods and services and the second largest producer of agricultural exports. French companies are among the most successful in the world and France has a higher number of firms that appear in the international ranking of top businesses than either the United Kingdom or Germany (Védrine, 2007). Meunier shows that French firms are world leaders in sectors such as car manufacturing (PSA, Renault), aeronautics (Airbus), building and construction (Bouyges), advertizing (Publicis) and cosmetics (L'Oréal) (Meunier, 2004). Similarly, the supermarket chain Carrefour comes second only to Walmart in size as a market retailer. France has become more open to overseas investment and is ranked second in the European Union for the number of foreign-owned companies on its soil. This has had positive effects on French employment and according to one economic survey, one in seven French workers is today employed by a foreign company (Hamilton & Quinlan, 2008). At the same time, French businesses are increasingly engaged with the international economy and France is ranked fourth in the world in terms of its investment in foreign-owned companies outside of France.

Yet, as we have seen, this economic liberalization was grounded in a political discourse that asserted French identity, that appealed to the past and that affirmed French authority in the face of outside change. Lionel Jospin was a master of the 'art of verbal and linguistic acrobatics' that seemed to characterize French politicians on the question of globalization (Hazareesingh,

1994: 255). On the one hand, he asserted a conception of identity rooted in the republican state that would fulfill a collective destiny and allow France to adapt to globalization, without losing any of the specific features of national culture. France, he suggested, was not afraid to open up to globalization, but would only do so on its own terms: 'she intends to do so in her own way, a controlled way, which takes account of her economic situation, social balance, political traditions and cultural background' (Jospin, 2002a: 5). On the other hand, Jospin argued that: 'globalization is a reality full of promise that we must succeed in shaping so that it benefits the whole of humanity' (ibid., 11). He presented this as a kind of modernist dream through which France would be able to fulfil the foundational goals of its own civilization: 'globalisation can become a milestone in the progress of civilisation' (ibid., 9). Jospin's core message was that France could reap the economic and political benefits of globalization without compromising its traditions, values and institutional model.

While Lionel Jospin denounced an uncontrolled globalization, he pursued a liberalization of the French economy on an extensive scale. Hence, he privatized some 36 billion euros worth of state enterprises, more than the previous six governments combined. Faced with the pressures of European and international directives, he cut France's historically high rate of taxation, made France home to the world's second-highest volume of executive stock options and increased labour market flexibility (Meunier, 2003). Reneging on his campaign promises to end budgetary cuts, Jospin continued with the cuts in state expenditure of the previous right-wing government, particularly in defence. To increase labour market flexibility, Jospin introduced the 35-hour working week which, despite protest from unions, gave companies the possibility to freeze wages. In keeping with this market-driven agenda, Jospin refused to intervene during the highly politicized factory closures of the Renault plant in Vilvorde in Belgium in 1997 and the massive lay-offs in Michelin in 1999. He attracted fierce criticism for his remarks on television following Michelin's decision to lay off 7,500 workers despite an increase in turnover of 17.3 per cent when he commented: 'the state can't do everything' (cited by Desbos, 2006).

Many of the contradictions in Jospin's stance were evident in his discourse on Europe. While Jospin championed France's integration into Europe, favouring greater openness and a transfer of competences, he envisaged a European Union moulded in France's image, that incorporated key features of the French political and social model (Cole & Drake, 2000; Howarth, 2002, 2008). He therefore called for a Europe 'fired by social democratic ideals' that was attuned to French conceptions of public service, social regulation and state economic interventionism (Jospin, 1999: 9). Europe was a means to fulfil France's own political goals and to assert French power on an inter-national stage and thereby transcend its own national borders: 'it is through Europe that France can best fulfil its universalist mission' (Jospin, 2005: 50). He called for a strong political Europe that could regulate globalization, pro-tect its citizens and act as a counterweight to American power. Hence the European Union played a central role in his vision of a multipolar world in which the United States' 'hegemonic tendencies' would be curtailed: 'In order to build a multipolar world the democratic principles which operate at national level must be projected onto an international stage. There should not be a single superpower imposing its own vision on the world' (Jospin, 1999: 3). Jospin's ambivalence towards globalization seemed to accentuate many of the features of his stance on Europe in which he sought to reconcile the often con-flicting imperatives of European integration and the French national interest.

Jospin's doubletalk seemed to give his government a measure of success in its early years when he maintained strong levels of support in public opinion. However, cracks soon began to appear in this façade, as the contradictions of his stance became increasingly apparent. It was when Jospin could no longer reconcile an image of a strong republican state with processes of economic liberalization that he faced mounting political opposition, especially on the Left and Far Left and this would culminate in his defeat in the 2002 elections. For many, even former members of his own party, globalization was the decisive issue in Jospin's defeat in 2002 and more generally in the splintering of the French Left that followed this defeat (Meunier, 2003). For them, Jospin's gov-ernment had failed to provide a coherent stance on globalization that either rejected neo-liberalism and aligned itself firmly with the Left or that openly and honestly accepted the market economy. Hence, for Arnaud Montebourg who formed the Nouveau Parti Socialiste in 2002, following Jospin's defeat in the presidential elections, the Socialist Party 'completely misunderstood the nature of this issue' (Cited by Desbos, 2006: 219).

Jacques Chirac typified the contradictions of French politicians for whom globalization seemed to blur the traditional ideological divisions between Left and Right. To some extent, his stance was consistent with a broader Gaullist legacy and the ideological ambiguities of a political movement that combined both classic right-wing elements (order, authority, national independence) with typically left-wing tendencies (statism, *dirigisme*, anti-americanism). Beginning his political career as a right-wing conserva-tive faithful to the teachings of the Chicago School, he ended it as a self-proclaimed champion of leftist opposition to neo-liberal globalization. His politics have been described as deeply contradictory, if not schizophrenic, leading one commentator to remark: 'He has no convictions. He believes in nothing' (Guichard, 2002: 33). Even his wife Bernadette Chirac confirmed this political ambivalence when she declared in 2009: 'You know my husband has always been on the Left' (LeParisien, 2009). As President of the Republic, Chirac, the 'cameleon' forged a discourse that would pass for gauchiste or tiermondiste, championing the causes of equality, international solidarity and global justice (Agence Presse France, 16 May 2007). His leftist inclinations were already apparent during his first presidential campaign in 1995 when he promised to heal the 'social fracture' of the nation. Yet, it was in the international domain that these were brought to greatest effect, as he presented himself as a champion of egalitarian and humanist values. During the Johannesburg summit of September 2002, Chirac, in his new guise as 'planetary Robin Hood', defended environmental goals, denounced Third World debt and spoke out in favour of taxing wealthier nations in favour of the world's poor. As was the case with Nicolas Sarkozy who succeeded him, the international stage provided a perfect arena in which to cultivate an idealistic and moralizing discourse that appealed directly to the French electorate, but that didn't necessarily require any concrete political action. Free of the obligations of domestic politics, Chirac favoured a political style based on grand rhetoric, emotive language and moralistic claims.

When he was Prime Minister (1986–1988), Chirac pursued a rigid right-wing agenda, implementing ultraliberal economic policies based on privatization, labour market reform and tax reductions. Similarly, during his first presidential term, he supported the economic policies of his Prime Minister, Alain Juppé (1995–1997) who pursued privatizations and proposed a sweeping reform of the social security and pensions system to meet the convergence criteria of the Maastricht Treaty. It was Juppé's proposed reform that sparked the massive public sector demonstrations of the winter of 1995. However, shaken by the scale of this protest, Chirac increasingly avoided a reformist agenda and focused during this second presidency on non-contentious domestic campaigns, such as cancer prevention and road safety. Chirac was criticized by his opponents during this period for being timorous and incapable of initiating reform. Hence, his Prime Minister, Dominique Villepin's proposals for a new youth employment contract designed to combat unemployment and which was endorsed by Chirac in a televised address to the nation on 31 March 2006, were like Juppé's 1995 reforms, withdrawn following widespread student and trade union protest. Meanwhile, the 2005 riots in French suburbs proved to some that Chirac had failed in his ambition to overcome France's 'fracture sociale'. Others have seen the rejection of the European Constitutional Treaty as a personal failure for Chirac who had made the decision to put the treaty to the people by referendum in November 2005. Following his withdrawal from politics in 2007, one newspaper observed 'Domestically the Chirac years will go down as 12 years of wasted time' (Lichfield, 2006).

Yet, Chirac always sought to place France in a position where it would draw the most economic benefits from globalization. Hence he fiercely defended the protection of French agriculture and opposed a reform of the Common Agricultural Policy, even when this seemed to interfere with his campaign for solidarity with the Third World. Hence, in one international meeting in 2002, where he shared 'vigorous exchanges' with Tony Blair, he was criticized by the latter for defending the cause of international solidarity, while locking poorer countries out of European markets by insisting on a policy of agricultural protectionism. Chirac reacted with great consternation by cancelling the Anglo-French summit that was due to take place in December of that year (Wintour & Black, 2002).

It is on the question of France's relationship with Africa that Chirac's doubletalk was most blatant. Chirac styled himself in the international arena as an advocate of poorer African countries, articulating their demands in international settings and affirming democratic and humanist interests. Yet these values often came into conflict with a national interest that was intent on maintaining France's privileged relationship with specific African leaders and continuing a traditional family relationship (Françafrique) with former colonies which had prevailed since political independence (Chafer, 2005; Hugeux, 2007; Majumdar & Chafer, 2010). He continued to cultivate these relationships in the annual Franco-African summit which brought together French and African leaders in a celebration of their special relationship. This 'family relationship', for some critics, often took precedence over a concern with democratic principles and human rights. Hence, Chirac was criticized for maintaining close ties with authoritarian regimes with poor human rights records. Chirac was responsible in 1997 for the decision to support Zaire's dictatorial leader, President Mobutu, resulting in French diplomatic isolation. In the same year, he was accused of backing the return to power of his friend and ally, the former Congolese dictator, Denis Sassou-Nguesso who was more sympathetic to French economic interests than the incumbent political leader (Chafer, 2005). This led The Washington Post, when Chirac stepped down as President in May 2007, to welcome the departure of 'a leader with a deep scorn for fostering democracy' (Applebaum, 2007). Chirac's doubletalk on globalization, like that of other leaders, seemed to stem from the difficulties in reconciling the French national interest with a changing economic and political conjuncture at international level.

It was Nicolas Sarkozy who brought this doubletalk to dizzying heights, veering erratically between a conservative right-wing discourse on economic policy and a leftist idealism on the international stage. Some critics have explained these contradictions by situating Sarkozy within a right-wing populist tradition that sought to transcend the Left/Right divide and to appeal to the nation as a whole. For instance, Alain Badiou, describes Sarkozy's politics as a 'transcendental' populism typical of the French Right that endangered democracy and that had its roots in the rise to power of Marshall Pétain following France's defeat in World War Two (Badiou, 2007: 114). Sarkozy, just like Pétain, had come to power during a period of national crisis, shock and 'organised disorientation' and promised, like him, to save France and deliver a programme of 'national regeneration' (ibid., 22, 106). Other critics, explain Sarkozy's contradictory stance in terms of a crude opportunism and a desire to rally all sides of the electorate at once. Far from being a danger to the Republic or a totalitarian threat, Thomas Legrand argues, Sarkozy was a mediocre politician, an uncommitted liberal and a weak leader driven by the vagaries of public opinion and he was a 'waste of time' for a France in urgent need of reform (Legrand, 2010). On the one hand, Sarkozy called for a 'return of national identity' and sought to affirm French traditions, ideals and its collective purpose in the world. On the other, he made economic reform the explicit focus of his election campaign, calling for a clean break with the past and with all forms of 'conservatism and archaism' which dampened economic growth and stifled France's entrepreneurial spirit (cited by Marlière, 2009: 376). From the outset of his time in office, Sarkozy urged the French people to 'play the game of globalization' and to accept the need for modernization, liberalization and reform (Bennhold, 2007). His ambition was to reconcile the French people to the joys of the market and to a vision of France grounded in hard work, enterprise and honest competition: 'I want to reconcile my country with capital, success and ambition' (Acutalité, 2006: 2). A champion of free markets, 'Sarko, l'américain' presented the United States as a model to which the beleaguered French should aspire. For instance, following a visit to the United States in 2006, two years before the collapse of Lehman Brothers bank, Sarkozy proposed a wholesale reform of the French banking sector to create a model based more closely on the American subprime and derivatives model.

Barely two months in office, Sarkozy pushed through a hardline neo-liberal programme, starting with a handsome 'cadeau pour les riches' that reduced income tax for the wealthiest earners (up to a maximum of 50 per cent of personal income) and he also scrapped inheritance tax. In a bid to get France to 'work more and earn more', the Tepa law, voted in August 2007 also reduced taxes on overtime pay which led to a voluntary circumvention of the 35-hour working week. This was followed by the 2008 financial law which reduced taxation for shareholders whose investment shares were henceforth exempt from income tax. Sarkozy also set about reforming French public services with the aim of initiating sweeping cuts in public expenditure. His public policy reform launched in July 2007 (Révison générale des politiques publiques) made a commitment to replace only half of all public sector employees departing for retirement. Between 2007 and 2010, this reform led to a loss of 56,000 jobs in the education sector alone. Other measures introduced during his first year in government included a reform of special pensions on the railways, a lowering of taxation in the restaurant sector and ongoing liberalization of energy suppliers and railway services.

While Sarkozy, along with other European leaders, was forced to take emergency interventionist measures to stabilize the banking sector and wider economy, following the 2008 economic crisis, he also saw this crisis as an 'opportunity' for deepened economic reform. In his speech in Toulon on 25 September 2008, Sarkozy insisted on the need to accelerate the pace of reform, to embrace change and overcome fears which served only to dampen economic growth and entrepreneurship: 'fear is the main threat which today hangs over the economy' (Sarkozy, 2008b). He declared that interventionism was but a short-term palliative response to crisis and that his government was committed to even greater economic reforms: 'the crisis will push us to go further and faster in our reforms' (ibid.). Alongside interventionist measures, Sarkozy therefore introduced reforms to tighten access to employment benefit and provide stringent incentives to return to work in order to help those 'trapped by welfare'. Meanwhile, he pushed ahead with a massive reduction in state spending and the finance bill presented to government on 29 September 2009 projected a reduction of public funding of 10 billion euros between 2011 and 2013 (Le Monde, 28 September 2010). New legislation was also passed to liberalize further gas and electricity and the railway sector and his pension reform of July 2010 raised the legal age of retirement from 60 to 62.

It was in the international arena that Sarkozy's doubletalk on globalization was most apparent and where his rhetorical claims were directly contradicted by the substance of his own policies. Hence, he cultivated a strongly denunciatory stance on the international stage that combined moral reprobation, idealistic rhetoric and high-profile posturing. He tended to treat the international arena as a great echo chamber for resounding French principles and ideals without the usual obligations to fulfill any promises made. Hence, prior to the G20 meeting in London in 2009, he threatened to walk out of the negotiations unless his demands for greater regulation were met: 'If things don't advance in London, there will be an empty chair. I'll get up and leave' (Chrisafis et al., 2009). While making a show of denunciation and playing to the gallery, behind the scenes, as some journalists noted, Sarkozy privately agreed to all the G20 plans. Similarly at the international meeting of political and business leaders in Davos in January 2010, Sarkozy delivered a blistering attack against a 'morally unacceptable' capitalism and chastised other nations for succumbing to the profanities of the market. Yet, his rhetorical claims were directly contradicted by the substance of his own policies. While in Davos, Sarkozy called for a taxation on excess banking profits, yet the UMP majority in parliament, under government pressure, had voted against a proposal to introduce such a taxation at national level. In Davos, he fulminated against a culture of excessive pay and yet refused to reconsider his own tax reduction for the wealthy (*bouclier fiscal*) introduced in 2007. While vowing to 'save the human race' with a new tax on carbon, this proposal was later abandoned by his government, as it threatened, in the words of his Prime Minister François Fillon to 'sink the competitiveness of French businesses' (Davies, 2010).[8] While emphasizing the need to strengthen international aid in Davos insisting that 'we must help poor countries', France along with Italy was one of the two G8 countries which reneged on its aid commitments to Africa in 2008.

The response of French political leaders to globalization has been characterized by a disjuncture between two separate discourses, two languages and two opposing visions which seem on the surface to be completely irreconcilable. Yet France's doubletalk on globalization operated according to its own reciprocal and self-fulfilling logic that helped to lay the foundations for large-scale economic liberalization. Instead of producing a 'legitimizing discourse' that emphasized the potential benefits of globalization, French leaders chose, in their speeches, to reject it completely and to extol the virtues of France's own republican identity. The more they liberalized the French economy, the more they appealed to an idealized republican discourse. Paradoxically, this was a means to legitimize policies of economic liberalization by offsetting them against a discourse of stability, continuity and tradition. As we will see in the following section, this republican discourse also drew on the myths and symbols of colonial ideology, which for over two hundred years, had conditioned France's relationship with the outside world.

The Anglo-Saxon Other

During the Third Republic's imperialist expansion, political elites perceived the colonized peoples as an 'Other' who were defined in binary opposition to the French and ascribed with specific cultural traits. Whereas the French were seen to inhabit a realm of civilization, the colonized peoples were categorized as inferior, barbaric and unenlightened. This conception of a colonial Other was a means to reaffirm French national identity at a time of imperialist conquest so that this project was better attuned with the democratic ideals of the Third Republic.[9] Edward Said, whose book *Orientalism* helped define the concept of the Other in the context of European imperialism, noted that 'European culture gained in strength and identity by setting itself off against the Orient as a sort of surrogate or even underground self' (Said, 1991: 3). The Other was also a means to emphasize the primacy and naturalness of French colonial policy. The French, according to this view, were called upon to intervene in the colonies and indeed, had a moral duty to do so, in the interests of civilizing barbaric peoples, liberating them from the forces of nature and bestowing on them the fruits of western culture. Said emphasized that colonialist ideology was not confined to the period of empire, but tended to be reproduced from one generation to the next, through the enduring influence of national language, cultural production and public discourse. At a time of globalization, political leaders on the Left and Right have perpetuated the key metaphors of the colonial period in order to conceptualize France's relationship with the outside world. Globalization is rarely portrayed as a neutral economic reform or as a disembedded market process, but is seen instead as a culturally and politically defined entity, an Other possessing its own irreducible characteristics. What is striking about contemporary political discourse is that many of the categories once reserved for the colonized peoples have been transposed to an Anglo-Saxon Other that is perceived as inferior, uncivilized and backward. Just as in the past, this new Other served to strengthen national identity and reinforce the bonds of community and belonging at a time of profound transformation and upheaval. It was also a means to reconstitute political reality very differently and to legitimize France's claims towards renewed power and influence on the international stage.

For the American critic, Michael Veseth, in his controversial book *Globaloney*, France's colonial past is critical to understanding its relationship with the outside world in the present day. In addressing the question 'why do the French hate globalization so?', he suggests that the French have experienced this as a kind of reverse colonization and consider it as the cultural antithesis of the values and ambitions that inspired France's own colonial model: '*This* globalization is simply crazy – the culture of the *idiots* is being imposed on the island of civilization' (Veseth, 2005: 215). Whereas French colonialism is often viewed as an extension of civilizing influences in a dark barbaric world, globalization is the revenge of the savages, whereby the United States is imposing its primitive and backward culture on the island of civilization. French leaders tend to view globalization as a far-reaching and all-encompassing external threat which is identified with the 'Anglo-Saxon world', the face of a new anti-France and an order that seems fundamentally at odds with the values of the French Republic. Lionel Jospin saw in globalization an ascendant political order of American origin that was imposing its influence in the world, sapping democratic rights and endangering collective values. Hence, he equated globalization with an extension of American hegemony and a political system driven by a belief in its own 'crushing superiority' (Jospin, 2005: 81).

He described an American model of neo-liberalism, rooted in 'Anglo-Saxon culture' and characterized by 'ideological narrowness, political interventionism and economic inefficiency' (ibid., 17, 60). For Chirac, the threat of the Anglo-Saxon world was political, ideological and cultural. What was at stake in accepting the Anglo-Saxon model was the loss of a civilizational model in which humanism had reached its highest pinnacle. Globalization, in his view, represented a 'cultural impoverishment' as a uniform and homogenizing cultural model extended its influence in the world and threatened the survival of national cultures (Chirac, 2008). Similarly, Nicolas Sarkozy attributed responsibility for the financial collapse of 2008 to the 'excesses of the Anglo-Saxon model' that had spiralled out of control and plunged the world into crisis (Sarkozy, 2009b: 8). In the face of this crisis, France's role was once again to act as a beacon of civilization, restoring order, values and direction in a lost and misguided world.

Political leaders draw on essentialist and irreducible categories to describe the underlying nature and dimensions of Anglo-Saxon globalization. Firstly, the Anglo-Saxon world is seen as 'primitive', a place that exists outside the boundaries of civilization itself. It is a savage and disorderly world in which base physical instincts and desires prevail and where natural laws or the 'survival of the fittest' determine human relationships (Jospin, 2005: 65). Lionel Jospin evokes metaphors of primitivism referring to a 'jungle capitalism' that has broken free of the civilizing influence of the state. For Jacques Chirac, the Anglo-Saxon world was the antithesis of a French and European model and he defined this as 'inhumane', a system that endangered the fundamental rights of all human beings. France's duty was to help constrain savage market impulses and to help 'master the power and appetites of man' (Chirac, 2002b: 2). Similarly, Nicolas Sarkozy in the wake of the economic crisis evoked a financial capitalism driven by 'the law of the jungle' in which the greed, excesses and 'indecent behaviour' of the powerful, held the whole of society to ransom (Sarkozy, 2008b, 2).

Secondly, Anglo-Saxon globalization is seen as 'regressive', a system that turns the world backwards, plunging societies into a dark and premodern place. Hence for Lionel Jospin, neo-liberalism represents an 'historic regression' and is a model that 'sends us backwards' (Jospin, 2005: 223). This is counterposed against a French and European model defined by 'an ideal of progress' and by shared democratic rights and social gains or *acquis* acquired through 'a long history of political and union struggles, of social conquests' (ibid., 108). Jacques Chirac argued that France and Europe's role was once again to become a force for progress in the world, to overcome the regressive impact of the market and help to create a new 'universal civilization' (Chirac, 2002a). Similarly, Nicolas Sarkozy saw the Anglo-Saxon model as a 'perversion' of a true model of European capitalism and this was a system that 'pulls everyone downwards' (Sarkozy, 2010: 6). He calls for a return to a European model grounded in a 'human ideal' and a notion of progress, a model 'which permitted the extraordinary blossoming of western civilization for over seven centuries' (Sarkozy, 2008b).

Thirdly, Anglo-Saxon globalization is 'uncivilized' because it operates outside the realm of collective values and ideals that are seen to define Europe. It is perceived as a form of moral and social decay in which the foundations of the social order have been destroyed by a rampant individualism, leaving a world without ideological principles or moral direction. For Jospin, globalization was driven by a dissolute ideology that exalted the individual and undermined the moral foundations of modern society. Driven by the law of the market, globalization had burst free of all democratic constraints and threatened the world with 'precarious disorder' (Jospin, 2005: 17). For Chirac, globalization was an affront to 'humanist civilization' because it discarded democratic principles and exacerbated inequality in the world (Chirac, 2005: 2). Characterized by 'egoism and blindness', the neo-liberal order was 'morally unacceptable' and needed to be 'humanized' in the interests of all the nations of the world (ibid., 3). Sarkozy saw globalization as a tide of moral decay that had engulfed France and Europe, sweeping away social norms, common values and collective bearings and plunging society into a quagmire of permissiveness, moral decay and stagnation. This was 'a capitalism without scruples or ethics' which had plunged the world into crisis (Sarkozy, 2007b). The revival of the notion of the Other in a globalized context was for political leaders an essential means to reconstitute and sustain the boundaries of national identity. At a time of contingency and instability, this was also a means to legitimize France's claim to assume a new civilizing mission in the world.

Lionel Jospin: Taming the jungle

According to the Third Republic's colonial ideology, France's vocation was to 'master' the colonies by achieving control over the forces of nature and by overcoming the tyranny of the elements over man: 'French imperial ideology consistently identified civilization with one principle more than any other: mastery' (Conklin, 1997: 5). Jospin's discourse on globalization reproduced the key references of colonial ideology and in particular, the conception of a French mastery of untamed external forces. He portrayed globalization as a 'jungle capitalism' that operated outside the rule of law and therefore beyond the realm of civilization itself. This was a primitive system, governed by 'natural' economic laws and by the brutish force of the market in which mankind had returned to a primitive state. France's duty was to 'tame', 'domesticate' and 'master' globalization in the interests of France and a wider civilization. He believed that France had a 'historic vocation' to construct an alternative model for the world economy, a *mondialisation maîtrisée* in which market forces would be subject to the higher authority of the state and in which other nations would be welcomed into France's civilizing embrace (Jospin, 2002b: 234). A mastery of globalization would allow France to extend the benefits of its civilization elsewhere, helping to lift others onto a path towards modernity and progress. Jospin's model of 'mastered globalization' rested on three key elements: (i) a regulation of world capitalism; (ii) a reassertion of state authority; and (iii) agreement on 'worldwide rules'.

Jospin's key demand was for a regulation of global capitalism in order to create a more ordered, rational and controlled economic system: 'France must be an advocate of world regulation' (Jospin, 2002b: 228). He believed that neo-liberal globalization was an irrational process in which the economy 'invades all spheres of life' (Jospin, 2005: 60). Moreover, this system was dangerous and unpredictable threatening to unleash chaos and disorder on civilized societies: 'The world remains dangerous, unjust and often irrational' (ibid., 312). Jospin's key aim was to extend the rule of law to the global economy and help curtail the worst effects of this barbaric system:

> Wherever there is a risk that the only effective law will be that of the jungle, where private interests challenge the public interest, where the quest for short-term profit undermines social justice and harms the environment, states must define the 'ground rules'. (Jospin, 2002a: 5)

Jospin believed that the state alone could provide order, authority and collective purpose in an unenlightened globalized world. He criticized the Anglo-Saxon model as fundamentally flawed as it seemed to reverse the proper balance between the state and market, one that had defined the French Republic for over two centuries. He argued that market forces, if left to their own devices, were devoid of meaning, value or direction: 'capitalism is a force that moves, but it does not know where it is going' (Jospin, 1999: 8). Whereas the state was seen as an instrument of civilization that embodied democratic and humanist ideals, guaranteed social order and equilibrium and extended its benevolent hand over the whole nation, the market was the domain of the savage, irrational and dangerous. For Jospin, the republican state had a vocation to help construct a different world order grounded in state authority and which would provide an alternative to deregulated capitalism. He saw Europe as an essential vehicle for exerting French influence in the world and for projecting an alternative economic model: 'Europe offers a model, a model open to the world' (Jospin, 2002: 20). France shared with Europe a specific 'political architecture', an institutional model, common traditions and in particular, a distinctive civilization (ibid., 15). He argued that Europe 'must keep alive the consciousness of being a civilisation and the desire to remain one' (Jospin, 2005: 56). In his international engagements, Jospin called for a strong political Europe 'a Europe that speaks with a single voice' and a strengthening of international institutions (International Monetary Fund, World Trade Organization, World Bank) which together could provide a 'new world governance' that would assert political authority over a deregulated economy (Jospin, 1999: 3; 2005: 65).

For Jospin, the means to 'bring globalization under control' was through regulation and the introduction of 'worldwide rules' (Jospin, 2002a: 35). He sought to overcome the arbitrary, 'erratic' and unpredictable nature of the market by submitting it to regulatory control (Jospin, 2005: 62). Jospin's government played a key role in introducing new regulations at international level, designed to control and harness a global economy. Common rules were also the means to define an alternative vision for the world economy in the interests of humanity as a whole. He emphasized the need to define a new common project for the world, particularly for those nations who looked to France and Europe and who were unable to do this for themselves: 'But the whole world needs a common project and some countries are too poor or have been too overwhelmed by history not to benefit fully from international solidarity' (ibid., 68). In the contemporary context, it was necessary to 'offer humanity a universalist vision with common values' (ibid., 69). At a meeting of the United Nations General Assembly in September 1999, Jospin argued that 'the more the world globalizes, the more it needs rules'. World regulation could be established only by institutions that emanated from the international community, operating according to rules under which all states were equal before the law (Jospin, 1999: 3).

Jacques Chirac: Humanizing globalization

During the Third Republic, political elites legitimized the forcible acquisition of empire by evoking France's universalist vocation to spread values and to civilize others. On the basis of a belief that the French 'were the foremost people in the universe' with a vocation to extend the universal principles of 1789, colonialism was articulated as a project for 'regenerating humanity' (Conklin, 1997: 8, 17). Jacques Chirac's discourse was suffused with references to colonial ideology, as he defined France's role as to 'humanize' globalization, to export values and to help elevate humanity as a whole. He incorporated the core principles of the Third Republic's official ideology, those of universalism, humanism and civilization in order to articulate and justify France's role in a changed globalized context. He argued that France, by virtue of its unique history had a vocation to intervene in the world and was, destined, just like in the past 'to open up and clear the paths of the world' (*Le Monde*, 3 January 2000). France had a duty to help build a 'new international order' and its leaders were entrusted with the task of 'civilizing globalisation' in the interests of all peoples. (UNESCO, 2001). Whereas Jospin believed France's role lay in 'mastering' globalization through state intervention, Chirac believed that France could transform the world through the force of its values alone. His ambition was to lay the foundations for a new universalism 'founded on a clear and universally recognised ethic' that would define human relationships in a globalized era and awaken in other cultures a common humanist ideal: 'to find in each civilization the expression of a common ideal' (UNESCO, 2001, 2003). It was not a question, he asserted, of imposing a westernized model elsewhere in the world but of rediscovering a humanism that was 'of all people, of all nations, of all religions'. For Chirac, France was also a beacon of culture that could provide meaning, values and direction for the nations of the world. This culture, rooted in Enlightenment values, could provide a response to the world's problems by becoming 'a weapon of intelligence against brute force' (RFI, 2004).

If Chirac sought to assert humanist ideals in a globalized context, he also perpetuated a clichéd colonialist outlook that counterposed French and European civilization against an 'inhuman' globalizing world. Globalization was represented in binary opposition to France as a system that was feral and depraved, that lacked civilized values and was 'neglectful of humanist culture' (UNESCO, 2001). Chirac argued that globalization in its present guise attacked 'human dignity' by exacerbating inequality, global poverty and injustice. Driven by crude market imperatives, this system reduced human beings to mere merchandise to be bought and sold and stripped them of basic rights and dignity. He highlighted the illicit practices of child trafficking, forced adoption and commercial surrogacy as evidence of a model of globalization that was fundamentally unjust. In its place, he projected a utopian vision of a new 'universal civilization' and a humanity united around collective ideals and grounded in a model of progress, where prosperity, well-being and common values were available to all. It was in the name of this alternative globalization that France, he believed, was now called upon to play a leading role on the world stage.

While Chirac defended the cause of international solidarity, he also perpetuated a paternalistic stance in relation to poorer African countries, seeing himself as a benevolent father figure, speaking out in international settings for an Africa that could not speak for itself. In his address to the Davos summit in 2005, he presented himself as a champion of the poor, vulnerable and oppressed who by their own efforts were unable to help themselves: 'Because the poor do not have the means to protect themselves physically, even less financially from the dangers of existence' (Chirac, 2005). During his 12 years as president, he visited 39 African countries, 11 in the context of international summits (Hugeux, 2007). In these diplomatic visits, he constructed an image of himself as the leader of a *France généreuse* that was helping to show the way and to lead other nations on a path towards progress and development.

Nicolas Sarkozy's civilizing project

During his election campaign, Nicolas Sarkozy told the French people that they needed to think differently about their colonial past and overcome a sense of national shame and repentance linked to the legacy of French imperialism. Colonialism was part of a unified national history of which the French should be proud and while this had had negative effects, it also had a positive impact as a vehicle for extending the fruits of civilization in the world: 'the truth is that there have been few colonial powers in the world who worked so much for civilization and development' (Sarkozy, 2007a). Sarkozy's discourse on globalization, unsurprisingly, comes closest to reproducing the colonialist language of the Third Republic. He defined France's relationship with globalization in terms of a 'civilizing project' that aimed to export values, enlighten others and help elevate humanity. In his press conference at the Elysée Palace in January 2008, where he set out the terms of this 'projet de civilisation', Sarkozy argued that France's mission was to construct a new 'human ideal' that would redefine the relationship between man and society and set the terms for human progress over the coming century. He compared this great mission to that which was accomplished during other major periods of historical transformation, such as the renaissance, the Enlightenment, the industrial revolution and the post-war recovery, when it was also necessary to construct a new project to guide humanity. At a time of globalization, he saw France at the centre of a world stage, acting as 'the soul of the new renaissance that the world needs' whose duty was to 'radiate the universal values that are ours'. By projecting its values outwards, France could help transform the world in order to 're-humanise society' and 'moralise capitalism' (Sarkozy, 2008a).

Sarkozy's civilizing project was predicated on a conception of the Republic as the heir to a great civilization, steeped in history, defined by abstract ideals and endowed with a universalist vocation. He shared with Chirac a belief that France and Europe, by virtue of their unique and superior civilization, had a

duty to intervene in the world and to guide others. Yet where Chirac emphasized a shared humanist tradition, Sarkozy pandered to a purely nationalistic
and self-referential view of France's role in the world. He constructed an image
of the French nation as pure myth, an eternal and universal ideal that transcended history and reached beyond the borders of France to touch all mankind. Humanist values were seen as an exclusive preserve of France by virtue
of its distinctive national history and a predefined national character. Instead
of seeing France as one nation sharing a wider European tradition, he defined
Frenchness as humanism itself: 'France is everywhere that values are alive
in the hearts and minds of men' (Sarkozy, 2007a: 3). France had a vocation to
look outwards towards other nations and help include others in its civilizing
embrace. Yet, France was also an 'old nation' with an exceptional history that
could help provide an example for others. Sarkozy defined French history as a
trajectory of human accomplishment that stretched back to the beginning of
time and continued seamlessly into the present. France was identified with
the Republic, which had its origins, not in 1789 but in the depths of time, in the
imagination of the Gauls and the ambitions of feudal kings and the Republic
fulfilled 'the old dreams of unity of the French kings' (ibid.). The French nation
was also identified with the people who were seen to keep alive, in their
hearts, the flame of the Republic. He saw France as a spiritual essence that
was intrinsic to all French people and this was a 'mysterious fabric of individual
and collective memories' (ibid.). Each French person was therefore cast as a
leading actor in the great drama of the nation and in a future of unfulfilled greatness on the international stage. If France had a great role to play in the world,
this was because its people embodied a distinctive history and a set of ideals
and therefore had an exceptional destiny to fulfil in the world.

Sarkozy's discourse reproduced a binary opposition between France as
the locus of civilization and a globalized world that was uncivilized because it
lacked foundational values and ideals. For Sarkozy, the problems of contemporary globalization stemmed less from the structures of capitalism itself, but
from a kind of moral transgression that had derailed the economy, corrupted
the values of European civilization and led the world astray. The outside world
had lost sight of the values and ideals of European civilization and sunk into
a morass of permissiveness, individualism and moral decay. The brand of
financial capitalism that characterized the world economic system was driven
by the 'excesses' of human nature, by base physical needs and desires that
were unconstrained by collectively defined principles. For Sarkozy, the crisis
of 2008 represented the collapse of a morally bankrupt economic system
which had spiralled out of control and plunged the world into decline: 'the
crisis we are experiencing is not a crisis of capitalism. It is a crisis of a perversion of capitalism' (Sarkozy, 2010: 3). He counterposed this against a 'good'

European capitalism that was rooted in the values of hard work, honest competition and entrepreneurship.

France's vocation in a globalizing world, just like during the colonial period was to exert moral influence and thereby help civilize others. Sarkozy revived the colonialist idea of a 'conquête morale' defined in 1889 as 'the moralizing role of France among these peoples so far from civilization' (Conklin, 1997: 14). Like Chirac, Sarkozy identified France's role with that of moral influence, without a need for state intervention or to modify significantly the structures of the international economy. His new moral project would cleanse the economic system of its worst excesses and restore the certainties of the past. In the face of the crisis, France's role was to construct 'a new model of growth' that would help lift the world out of crisis (ibid., 2009b). He pointed to a France at the helm of an economic and moral recovery on the world stage, providing leadership through its presidency of the European Union and its role in the G20 negotiations.

Conclusion

Of all European nations, it is in France that political leaders have had the greatest difficulty in reconciling globalization with the terms of national identity and in making this process consistent with dominant perceptions of national culture. Whereas in countries with a more liberal tradition, globalization was reconciled with the key references of national identity, in France, this process seemed to challenge the Republic and the foundations of Frenchness itself. Globalization was seen to threaten the integrity of the French state, to undermine republican values and to challenge France's universalist vocation on the world stage. Vivien Schmidt noted that political leaders in France failed to construct a legitimizing discourse that justified globalization in the eyes of the public and made this acceptable in political life. Rather than accommodating globalization within the parameters of French political culture, politicians preferred instead to denounce it and to reassert a traditional conception of national identity rooted in republican universalism and images of a colonial past. In the face of external changes, they projected a myth of a great Republic with an exceptional 'collective destiny' to fulfil in the world, one that remained unchanged in the present. They therefore tended to keep the realities of France's economic liberalization hidden from the public eye, pursuing globalization quietly and steadily. While successive governments liberalized the economy, reduced state spending and reformed the labour market, they did this discretely, far away from the public gaze. The result was a deeply ambivalent political response, a doubletalk that consisted of loudly denouncing globalization while quietly adapting to it (Gordon & Meunier, 2001; Meunier, 2003).

I argued in this chapter that political leaders' contradictory stance on globalization had its roots in deep-seated historical factors and in particular, the impact of an enduring legacy of republican universalism suffused with colonial symbols and myths. At a time of profound transformation and upheaval, this republican discourse became the means to fulfil two urgent political imperatives. First, it was a means to reaffirm national identity and to restore a sense of national greatness, collective purpose and historic mission. For an anxious and uncertain electorate, the Republic offered a symbol of stability, tradition and continuity, one that anchored them to the past and that protected them from changes in the present. Second, this was a means to mobilize the public support needed to implement policies of economic liberalization. The more France became integrated into the international economy, the more it became necessary to appeal to a mythical Republic. Paradoxically, a republican discourse that loudly rejected globalization became the principal means to usher this in on an unprecedented scale.

French political leaders' contradictory stance on globalization reflected many of the contradictions of republican universalism itself. On the one hand, it provided an ideological framework that could be used to affirm fundamental rights, to promote humanism and to challenge a market-driven neo-liberalism. On the other hand, it defined a relationship of power between France and the outside world that was conditioned by the historical experience of colonialism. As Costantini notes, the ideological dimension of republicanism is in fact inseparable from its political application by the French state, especially during the Third Republic's imperial expansion, when this ideology reached its apogee (Costantini, 2008). The response of French leaders to globalization has been deeply influenced by a colonialist perspective that sees France at the centre of the universe with a mission to spread its values, exert political influence and help enlighten others. Instead of confronting the reality of France's diminished political status in the world, political leaders have taken refuge in delusions of grandeur within a France that 'sees itself as the center of the world and writes its history as the central drama of human history' (Huntington, 1996: 54–5). Eschewing objective economic and political realities, they have preferred to reduce other nations to crude essentialist categories, reflecting France's own desperate need for self-image and status in a changing international order. Political leaders have refused to see themselves as equal partners on an international stage shared with others and continue to see the outside world in the most binary and chauvinistic of terms. If French leaders helped to transform globalization in many constructive and progressive ways, this was often driven by a nationalistic self-belief that masqueraded as abstract universalism.

Notes

1 Different writers have shown how colonial ideology continues to influence political discourse today, independently of the fact of empire, and how this ideology is reproduced over time within political culture, official discourse and national traditions (Chatterjee, 1986; Said, 1991; Costantini, 2008). For instance, Alice Conklin in her book, *A Mission to Civilize*, observed 'what is striking is how little French discourse has changed despite the disappearance of empire' (Conklin, 1997: 247).

2 The term was coined by the French investment banker, economist and political advisor, Alain Minc whose book *La Mondialisation heureuse* championed the virtues of market integration and state reform and was seen as a key reference for the *pensée unique* which was seen to dominate French political thinking during the 1990s (Paris: Plon, 1997). Minc was a founding member of the liberal think tank, Fondation Saint Simon and is close to Nicolas Sarkozy.

3 The debate about declinology has not been confined to France and reflects a wider preoccupation within western industrialized societies, prompting what Madeleine Bunting has described as 'a publishing boom in doom across Europe and the United States' (Bunting, 2011). Recent titles which point to a decline of the West, include economist Dambisa Moya's *How the West was Lost: Fifty Years of Economic Folly and the Stark Choices that Lie Ahead* (New York: Farrar, Straus & Giroux, 2011); Stephen King, chief economist at HSBC's *Losing Control. The Emerging Threats to Western Prosperity* (New Haven & London: Yale University Press, 2010); Walter Laqueur's *The Last Days of Europe: Epitaph for an Old Continent* (New York: Thomas Dunne Books, 2007); and Bruce Thornton's *Decline and Fall. Europe's Slow Motion Suicide* (USA: Encounter Books, 2007).

4 Nicolas Bavarez is a right-wing liberal and an economic historian. He is a member of the French employer's association, MEDEF and an executive member of the right-wing think tank, Institut Montaigne. He supported Nicolas Sarkozy during the 2007 election campaign and his work influenced the economic policies of the new president. Jean-Pierre Chevènement is on the nationalist Left and describes himself as republican and a Europsceptic. He was Minister of Defence from 1988 to 1991 and Minister of the Interior from 1997 to 2000. He was a presidential candidate in the 2002 elections and since 2008 has been a member of Senate. Eric Zemmour is a French political journalist and author who is situated on the anti-liberal populist Right. He is a columnist for *Le Figaro* and presents a daily editorial on RTL, France's most popular national radio station. He has attracted controversy for his conservative views and is routinely accused of racism, sexism and homophobia. On 30 March 2010, SOS-Racisme summoned him to appear before a criminal court on charges of racial defamation following his comments on a Canal + television programme when he was speaking about his book, *Mélancolie française*. He commented that blacks and Arabs were targeted by the French police 'because the majority of trafficers are black and Arab; that's how it is, it's a fact'. He was convicted on 18 February 2011 and ordered to pay a fine of 2000 euros.

5   The first World Social Forum was held in Porto Alegre, Brazil on 25–30 January 2001 and was organized by groups including Attac and sponsored by the Porto Alegre government led by the Brazilian Workers' Party.

6   Until the 2008 financial crisis, the notion of a global tax on financial transactions was dismissed by most European leaders as hopelessly naïve. Since then it has gained increased momentum and support within civil society and among political leaders. G20 leaders in Pittsburgh asked the International Monetary Fund to consider introducing a Tobin tax of 0.005 per cent on currency trading based on the model first introduced in France. Gordon Brown became the first G20 leader to back the plan publicly, renamed the 'Robin Hood tax'. In 2010, Gordon Brown, Angela Merkel and Nicolas Sarkozy all declared their support for the introduction of such a tax. In March 2010, the European Parliament voted overwhelmingly in favour of it (536 votes for and 80 against). In Britain, it is backed by some 100 organizations from Oxfam to the Salvation Army.

7   Since retiring from politics, Chirac has devoted himself more fully to the cause of international development and through the charity, that he set up in June 2008 (Fondation Chirac), has launched projects in several African countries to promote access to water, medicine and education.

8   The French carbon tax was a culmination of the Sarkozy government's conversion to ecology that began in autumn 2007 with the launch of the *Grenelle de l'Environnement*, a new development strategy based on ecological sustainability. Following a heated public debate, the Constitutional Council censored the government's proposal on 29 December 2009, only 48 hours prior to its implementation. Three months later, the Prime Minister François Fillon announced a definitive postponement of the carbon tax. See Laurent (2010).

9   The notion of the Other was first philosophically conceived by Georg Wilhelm Friedrich Hegel and was later made popular by Edward Said in his well-known book *Orientalism* (1991). For Said, the creation of the Other was done by highlighting their weaknesses as a way of justifying the moral responsibility of the stronger Self to educate, convert or civilize them. The Other was bound up with a project of political power and was a means to legitimize the domination of individuals or groups in the periphery. More recently, Jack Hayward referred to the persistence of an Anglo-Saxon Other or counter-identity within French political life, based on a long history of 'enduring rivalry' between France and Britain and later the United States (Hayward, 2007). Similarly, Gérard Noiriel traces the construction of the Other to its origins in the 'nationalist' universalism of the French Revolution and from the late nineteenth century onwards, to the work of French writers such as Maurice Barrès who, in the wake of the Franco-Prussian War of 1870, defined national identity in opposition to Germany which was seen as the embodiment of barbarism and backwardness. He shows that while the notion of national identity was widely discredited after World War II, it was revived in France from the 1980s onwards when 'immigrants' were increasingly designated as the new Other (Noiriel, 2007).

4

French intellectuals: A war of worlds

Over the past 20 years, leftist intellectuals in France have engaged in a new phase of political activism in opposition to what they saw as a rising tide of economic globalization. Against a background of neo-liberal hegemony or *pensée unique* within mainstream politics, conditions of enduring socioeconomic crisis and a rising militancy on the Far Left, French thinkers engaged in renewed activism, taking to the streets, writing books and newspaper articles, launching petition movements and forming an array of new intellectual clubs and think tanks. This mobilization seemed to mark a break with the 'silence of intellectuals' that characterized the period from the 1980s onwards, signalling a return of intellectual engagement after a prolonged phase of apparent inactivity and quiescence (Lemieux, 2003; Sommier, 2003; Noiriel, 2005). Leading leftist thinkers, including Pierre Bourdieu, Cornelius Castoriadis, Ignacio Ramonet, Viviane Forrester, Susan George and Alain Badiou became the figureheads of a new anti-liberal critique that denounced globalization and called for a radical alternative. On the one hand, they set out to provide a new framework for leftist opposition and to create the conditions for popular mobilization on a national and international stage. For a nascent movement of opposition to globalization, they helped to provide 'intellectual and cultural weapons', analytical tools and theoretical categories that could be used to challenge neo-liberalism in all its forms (Bourdieu, 1998: 60). On the other, they actively participated in protest activities during this period, throwing their weight behind social movements and endorsing demands for social and political change. The public sector strikes of 1995 are widely seen as a turning-point in this new phase of intellectual engagement, giving rise to a synergy between leftist thought and militancy that would define the political context in the years that followed. Recent studies of contemporary France often overlook the significance of this leftist, anti-liberal current and empha-size instead, the rise of a 'new liberalism' as the dominant feature of French intellectual life during this period. They point to the pervasive influence of lib-eral intellectuals who seemed to have established a hegemony in the political and cultural spheres. Yet this trend towards liberalism often obscures a dif-ferent and countervailing reality, that of the rise of a leftist intellectual current that challenged the political establishment, rejected neo-liberalism and called for radical political and social change.

This chapter examines leftist intellectual debates on globalization focus-ing on a number of major polemical books published over the past 15 years. Written by well-known intellectual figures (Pierre Bourdieu, Viviane Forrester, Ignacio Ramonet and Emmanuel Todd), these books found considerable reso-nance within public opinion and often reached best-seller status. At a time of profound social and political upheaval, they helped to give shape and rep-resentation to a process that seemed otherwise distant, abstract and com-plex and to 'give visible and recognisable form' to invisible external forces (Bourdieu, 2001: 40). These texts can be seen both to shape and reflect wider public opinion and they give us a critical insight into attitudes and percep-tions that are found in more diffuse form elsewhere within French society. Furthermore, many of the metaphors of globalization that are invoked by French political leaders in the present day, have their origins within these texts. I argue that French intellectuals saw neo-liberal globalization not as a piecemeal economic reform or a market transformation, but as a broad civili-zational threat. At stake for them were not matters of economics or trade, but the defence of an entire 'civilization' with its roots in the French Revolution, defined by social gains or 'acquis' and by immutable collective principles. In evoking globalization, intellectuals tended to displace economic terms in favour of more urgent and prophetic metaphors of 'invasion', 'tyranny', 'barba-rism' and 'dictatorship'. They seemed to experience globalization as a kind of war of worlds between two separate universes whose differences seemed basic and irreconcilable.

If French intellectuals shared a civilizational perspective of globalization, this had contradictory effects on the nature of their opposition. On the one hand, French intellectuals helped to produce a radical critique that contested a dom-inant neo-liberal doctrine and helped to provide a countervailing interpretation of the market transformations taking place. In particular, they challenged a conception of the market as a 'natural', logical and disembedded process that was free of political and ideological implications. For the American sociologist and activist Amory Starr, political opposition is only possible where the nature of the enemy is understood and where a structure of power is made clear. French intellectuals contributed to what Starr has called 'naming the enemy' by revealing globalization as a comprehensive order, a coherent ideology and a structure of power, one with direct causal links to the social conditions that determined everyday life (Starr, 2000). In doing so, they helped to politicize globalization and create the conditions for a new current of leftist opposition. On the other hand, French intellectuals, in seeking to inscribe the market within a specific political and ideological context at national level, tended to invoke an essentialist vision of globalization that linked it to predetermined cultural factors. They often ascribed globalization not to economic causes, but to a *monde anglosaxon* defined by a dominant set of cultural characteristics and traits. While challenging what they saw as the narrow economistic perspective of neo-liberal theory, they often tended to replace this with their own form of cultural reductionism that saw globalization as the expression of a cultural essence.

The chapter goes on to explore French intellectual debates in the wake of the 2008 economic crisis. Recent books by French thinkers have sought to demonstrate that the crisis is not a spontaneous or natural occurrence, but has been prepared in advance through the conscious actions and decisions of political leaders, under the sway of a dominant neo-liberal ideology. The purpose of their writing is to attribute the causes of the crisis to an overarching neo-liberal order and therefore to emphasize the need to construct an alternative world order in its place. Leftist thinkers provide a radical critique that challenges the myth of a 'self-regulating market' and argues for radical political and social transformation. Yet recent books also perpetuate the notion of a conflict between France and Europe on the one hand, and the Anglo-Saxon world on the other, which was already evident in earlier literature on globalization. In the context of the economic crisis, this conflict is recast in terms of binary couplings based on good versus evil, innocence versus guilt and perpetrator against victim. Whereas the United States is portrayed as an evil perpetrator driven by clear ideological designs and political ambitions, the French and Europeans are portrayed as its innocent victims, beguiled by promises of untold prosperity and ensnared in an economic apparatus over which they had no control. As some critics have argued, this viewpoint tends to obscure the specific role of French leaders in creating the conditions for economic crisis in Europe (Lordon, 2009).

Networks of radicalism

Different observers of contemporary France point to the rise of a new stratum of liberal intellectuals since the 1980s, who became increasingly dominant on the political and intellectual scene and who helped create a new consensus in relation to the political establishment (Drake, 2002; Lindenberg, 2002, 2009; Hewlett, 2003; Anderson, 2009). Daniel Lindenberg signalled the rise of a class of 'new reactionaries', intellectual elites who challenged French democracy in the name of order, authority and nation. In his view, these intellectuals were responsible for reversing an Enlightenment tradition based on values of progress and equality and turning France backwards in a kind of 'conservative revolution' (Lindenberg, 2002, 2009). Whereas post-war France had been marked by a widespread *engagement* or commitment of leftist thinkers, who participated massively in the political causes of the period, the key feature of present-day intellectual life was a shift towards political liberalism. Influenced by the anti-Marxism of the New Philosophers of the 1970s, contemporary intellectuals rejected revolutionary politics, embraced the political establishment and made peace with the market. They were identified with the rise of an ideological hegemony of liberal ideas that found its expression in mainstream politics in the form of *pensée unique*, a single dominant doctrine that saw economic liberalism as the only path open to France. Leading historians such as François Furet and Pierre Nora were seen as figureheads of this new liberalism, whose histories of France sought to reinterpret the past, to remove sources of conflict and division and to help build a new consensus in the present (Anderson, 2009). Nicolas Sarkozy's rise to power can be seen as a crowning moment for this new liberalism, as some of its chief luminaries threw their support behind his presidential campaign and even joined his new government (in the case of Bernard Kouchner, nominated as Minister for Foreign Affairs).[1] Yet this account of intellectual life, with its emphasis on a pervasive liberalism, often obscures a countervailing reality, that of the rise of a new leftist intellectual current that challenged the establishment, rejected neo-liberalism and called for a radical political alternative. Many recent studies either ignore the role of leftist intellectuals during this period or treat them as a marginal and insignificant force in relation to a hegemonic liberalism.

The period from 1995 to 2005 in France was characterized by a widespread and intense mobilization by left-wing intellectuals. Challenging what they saw as a profoundly dangerous and unjust system, they wrote books and newspaper articles, took to the streets, formed petition movements and created new intellectual clubs and think tanks. In fact, some of those who had bemoaned the 'silence of the intellectuals' during the 1980s, now complained about 'the deafening noise of their quarrels' (Touraine, 2001: 111). Some observers situated this intellectual current in relation to the political context of the time and in particular, the impact of the Socialist Party in government (1997–2002) which, for many on the Left, was seen to have abandoned socialist values in favour of a conservative neo-liberal line. For Didier Eribon, this mobilization represented a backlash against the mainstream Left and represented an attempt to recover 'true' socialist values and ideals and to redefine the very terms of leftist opposition (Eribon, 2007). Similarly, Jérôme Vidal points to the rise of 'a new radical and democratic tendency' in French intellectual life that was opposed to the liberalism of the mainstream Left (Vidal, 2008: 34). For others, this current has deeper historical roots and reaffirms a tradition of intellectual engagement with its origins in the Dreyfus Affair of the nineteenth century and that was perpetuated by the *engagement* of intellectuals during the post-war years. For Raymond Boudon, intellectuals have reactivated, in the contemporary context of globalization, a long-standing hostility of French thinkers towards liberalism that has its origins in the Enlightenment period (Boudon, 2004).

This new phase of intellectual engagement was made evident in two important ways. Firstly, by an increased political activism on the part of leftist thinkers. The public sector strikes of 1995 which mobilized several hundred intellectuals within petition movements, either in support or opposition to the strikes, are generally recognized as the turning point for this new interventionist phase. These strikes seemed to give rise to a new political and ideological framework for the Left ('politics against markets frame') that was critical in shaping subsequent patterns of mobilization (Ancelovici, 2002). Following his dramatic speech at the gare de Lyon in Paris in December 1995, Pierre Bourdieu ('the most influential intellectual in France'), became the figurehead of a new leftist current, the 'gauche de la gauche' which threw its support behind the main protest movements of this period (mobilized by groups including the unemployed, undocumented immigrants and the homeless) and challenged the politics of the Plural Left government (P. Girard cited by Drake, 2002: 201). Bourdieu's ambition was partly to reactivate the role of the intellectual within French society based on a conception of the 'collective intellectual' someone who would place his/her expertise at the disposal of the social movement as a whole, rather than at the service of specific struggles. In this way, the intellectual grouping, Raisons d'agir that Bourdieu helped to create in 1996, was intended to give rise to 'an autonomous collective intellectual capable of intervening in the political field' who would draw on his/her specific competences and moral authority in order to support social causes (cited by Crettiez & Sommier, 2002: 403). After 1995, intellectuals went on to support the key demonstrations of this period including the 2003 demonstrations against pension reform and the 2005 campaign against the European Constitutional Treaty that mobilized scores of leftist economists.[2] At international level, French intellectuals were an influential force within the World Social Forum that was held annually in different countries across the world and intended as a forum for critical opposition to neo-liberalism. The meetings of the World Social Forum were marked by a close interaction between political activists and intellectuals who together sought to construct alternatives to neo-liberalism. As was the case during the European Social Forum that took place in Paris in 2003, the prominent role of intellectuals and the strong emphasis placed on critical debate, analysis and discourse within these events, led to accusations by some, of an excessive intellectualism and elitism (Agrikoliansky & Sommier, 2005).

This period was also marked by the creation of an array of new intellectual clubs and think tanks that mobilized leftist thinkers in opposition to neo-liberalism: 'a proliferation that largely surpassed the period from the 1960s to 1970s' (Poulet, 1999: 54). For instance, clubs such as Attac, Raisons d'agir, Pénombre, Fondation Copernic, Acrimed and Fondation Voltaire were meant to act as a site for critical reflection and for the production of ideas, aiming to 'diffuse the knowledge that is essential to reflection and political action in a democracy' (Crettiez & Sommier, 2002: 405). Fondation Copernic set up in 1998 by intellectuals close to the journal *Politis*, epitomized this close relationship between intellectual and political circles. Created as a forum for 'critical reflection', Copernic's purpose was to draw on the expertise of researchers and activists in order to challenge a dominant neo-liberal orthodoxy and in particular, to contest the legitimacy of the right-wing think tank, Fondation Saint Simon seen as an 'auxiliary to liberalism' (Sommier, 2003: 157). Its founding manifesto signals the dangers of a free market ideology that is seen to have taken hold of the political establishment and to have led France on a path towards 'social disaster'. Signed by 319 researchers and activists, this founding manifesto includes key names from Left and Far-Left circles including Christophe Aguiton, Daniel Bensaïd, Robert Castel, Didier Daeninckx, Christine Delphy, Gisèle Halimi, Pierre Khalfa, Jacques Kergoat and Stéphane Rozès. Through its different working groups, Copernic reacted to key debates in the public sphere (on questions such as pension reform, immigration, taxation and social rights) by producing a countervailing set of arguments and ideas to that of the official government line. Yet, its role was not limited to critical debate alone and Copernic also participated actively in the political causes of this period. It played a leading role in the 'no' campaign in the run-up to the 2005 campaign on the European Constitutional Treaty and supported the nomination of a unitary anti-liberal candidate in the 2007 presidential elections. In April 2010, it campaigned against the government's pension reform and launched a petition movement with Attac that called for an alternative system of pension funding. While some of these intellectual clubs have a broad aim of challenging neo-liberalism, others have a more specific target. For instance, Pénombre created in 1993 mobilizes statisticians, economists and sociologists in order to challenge what they see as a misuse of statistics in the public domain as a means to justify neo-liberal policies.

Similarly, Acrimed created in 1995 focuses on a critique of the media, while Réseau Voltaire created in 1994 campaigns against censorship and in support of free expression and of secularism.[3]

Secondly, this period was marked by a proliferation of new publications on neo-liberalism in the form of books, newspaper articles, reports, tracts, pamphlets: 'Without doubt, not since the pre-1968 period and the era of Editions Maspero has one seen so many newspapers and books flourish, feeding protest against the system' (Poulet, 1999: 53). Many intellectuals believed that critical analysis, discourse and theory were essential tools in the struggle against neo-liberalism and they shared a belief in the intrinsic value of knowledge in the public sphere. For them, the power of neo-liberalism was derived partly from its claims to represent an expertise and therefore to assume a guise of economic rationalism and scientific objectivity. It was necessary to challenge this discourse with a 'counter-expertise' that mobilized the intellectual resources of left-wing 'experts' for the purposes of opposition. On the one hand, the leftist intellectual press experienced exponential success with newspapers such as *Le Monde diplomatique, Politis, Economies alternatives, Charlie Hebdo* expanding their readership within French public opinion. For instance, *Le Monde diplomatique*, which became a critical site for anti-neo-liberal discourse, doubled its sales during this period (Sommier, 2003). At the same time, critical leftist journals such as *Mouvements, Multitudes, Contre-temps, Lignes, Chimères* and *Vacarme* increasingly acted as a 'political avant garde' constructing new analytical categories and a framework for leftist opposition (Agrikoliansky & Sommier, 2005). *Multitudes*, founded in 2000 by Yann Moulier-Boutang, defined itself as a political and cultural journal committed to social and political transformation that supported emerging social movements and that explored the possibilities for resistance against a profoundly modified capitalist system. On the other hand, there was an outpouring of new books that set out a radical critique of neo-liberal globalization. Written by well-known intellectual figures, these books were intended not for narrow academic circles, but for as wide a public audience as possible. Produced in an accessible style and sold in cheap pocket-sized versions, they found widespread resonance within public opinion, often reaching best-seller status. They helped shape broad public perceptions of globalization and contributed to a deep-seated opposition of market transformations within French society. At the same time, many of the key metaphors and symbols by which globalization was represented and conceptualized within mainstream political discourse have their origins in these texts. Pierre Bourdieu, whose political intervention dominated this period, laid out a set of 'counter-arguments' against neo-liberalism in his two volumes of *Contre-feux* (*Counter-fire*, 1998, 2001). This work became the 'intellectual reference' for movements opposed to neo-liberalism in France and elsewhere (Johnson, 2002). Viviane Forrester, a reputable novelist and literary critic for *Le Monde* launched a virulent attack on neo-liberalism in her two books *L'Horreur économique* (*The Economic Horror,* 1996) and *Une étrange dictature* (*A Strange Dictatorship,* 2000), the former selling 350,000 copies in France alone and awarded the prestigious Prix Medici (Forrester, 1996, 2000). Ignacio Ramonet, former chief editor of the newspaper *Le Monde diplomatique* wrote two books, *Nouveaux pouvoirs, nouveaux maîtres du monde* (*New Masters of the World,* 2001) and *Géopolitique du chaos* (*Geopolitics of Chaos,* 1999) and sought to analyse the political and ideological determinants of the current neo-liberal phase. Meanwhile in his controversial best-selling book *L'Illusion économique* (*The Economic Illusion,* 1998), the prominent historian and anthropologist Emmanuel Todd alerted his readers to the dangers of the 'Anglo-Saxon world' that was gradually encroaching across Europe.[4]

In this chapter, I focus on the books outlined above, as these encapsulate the key arguments made by leftist intellectuals during this period. How was globalization represented and conceptualized in these texts? What were the dangers that globalization was seen to represent? What is striking is that each of these books is imbued with a sense of urgency and foreboding in relation to the perceived dangers facing France. If these intellectuals decided to write these books, this is because they believed that France, just as during other periods of crisis from history, was again facing a profound external threat. Globalization is portrayed as a horror, an impending disaster or cataclysm that threatens the world with deep-seated and irreversible change. For instance, Pierre Bourdieu explains in the prologue of the first volume of *Counter-fire* that he felt impelled to write by 'a legitimate fury, often close to a feeling of duty' and by an awareness that the 'dangers' facing France were of a deep-seated and lasting nature. He warned the reader of a 'neo-liberal invasion' with profound repercussions for the future of democracy (Bourdieu, 1998: 7). Similarly, Viviane Forrester presents a world characterized by 'economic horror', as human beings reduced to mere cogs in a vast profit-making machine and are eliminated from society once they cease to be productive. She warns her readers that: 'For the first time in history, the human species is no longer materially necessary' (Forrester, 1996: 165). Her purpose is to alert the French public to the dangers that lay beneath the benign democratic face of globalization, by evoking images of an ascendant totalitarian order. Ignacio Ramonet sought to delineate the contours of an emergent hegemony and reveal 'the new masters of the world' that were ineluctably taking control of people's lives (Ramonet, 2001). Meanwhile for Emmanuel Todd, globalization represents the imposition of a degenerate American model on European societies and on the rest of the world (Todd, 1998).

At stake for these authors is not mere economics, but the defence of a civilization, defined by democratic traditions, by immutable collective values, by social rights and by unique institutions. When Pierre Bourdieu addressed striking rail workers at the Gare de Lyon in 1995, he declared that they were engaged in a pivotal struggle that transcended narrow sectional interests or economic concerns and implicated a whole 'civilisation'. In his speech, reproduced in the first volume of *Counter-fire*, Pierre Bourdieu declared: 'I am here to express support for those who struggle . . . against the destruction of a *civilisation* linked to the public service'. It was not a question of resisting economic reform but of defending 'an entire society and even a group of societies' (Bourdieu, 1998: 30, 58). Similarly, Viviane Forrester implores her readers not to be fooled by politicians into thinking that globalization was a simple economic process. This was a civilizational transformation with repercussions not only for the present, but for future generations as well: 'When will we realize that there isn't a crisis or crises, but a mutation? Not that of a society but . . . of a civilization' (Forrester, 1996: 10). Meanwhile, Emmanuel Todd argued that the economic dimensions of globalization were a mere smokescreen for a deeper 'civilizational crisis' which had allowed the United States to impose its own regressive and nihilistic social model across the world.

If globalization was a civilizational threat, then the only recourse available to the French people was one of resistance. In 2004, a group of prominent public intellectuals, all former members of the resistance during World War II issued 'an appeal to the younger generation'. Just as they themselves had mobilized against the Nazi occupying forces, so they called on young people to engage in a new phase of resistance against the 'dictatorship of the markets' (Appel des résistants aux jeunes générations, 2004). The theme of resistance has become increasingly popular as a metaphor for expressing the unforeseen and dreadful consequences of globalization and for emphasizing the urgency of popular protest against it. Hence, associations such as Citoyens Résistants d'Hier et d'Aujourd'hui (Citizens of the Resistance of Yesterday and Today) created in 2008, seek to connect the legacy of the Resistance with political challenges in France today and call for its spirit to be revived in a context of neo-liberalism. Similarly, Stéphane Hessel, a former resistance hero, published a 30-page call to arms, *Indignez-Vous* (*A Time for Outrage*, 2010) which sold nearly a million copies in France in just ten weeks. Hessel urged young people to revive the spirit of the French Resistance and to get angry again with the state of French society and with injustices in the world. At the root of today's problems lay 'the international dictatorship of financial markets' which had created an unprecedented gap between rich and poor: 'the power of money, that was fought against by the Resistance, has never been so great, insolent, selfish, with its own servants that are found in the highest echelons of the state' (Hessel, 2010: 3).[5] He called on his readers to embrace the ideas of the Resistance, those of solidarity, equality and cooperation as a means to challenge the destructive effects of global capitalism.

Each of the authors examined here invokes the theme of resistance as a means to galvanize popular protest aiming to 'trigger a mobilization' (Bourdieu, 1998: 8). For instance, Viviane Forrester calls on her readers to take action immediately and argues that neo-liberalism has been allowed to flourish in a climate of indifference, resignation and tacit complicity: 'to resist is primarily to refuse. The urgency today lies in this refusal which contains nothing negative, which is an indispensable, vital act' (Forrester, 2000: 213). For her, resistance should take precedence over a search for concrete solutions or alternative models to global capitalism. Evoking memories of World War II, she argues that a refusal to act by some, during this dark period of French history, resulted in genocide and the horrors of the Holocaust. To avoid a similar fate, urgent action was now essential: 'To allow a nail, a hair of whomsoever to be touched is already to consent to genocide' (ibid., 218). Similarly, Pierre Bourdieu aimed to launch a resistance through intellectual arguments and the purpose of his writing was to 'serve the resistance' to neo-liberalism, by providing 'useful weapons' to challenge the economic order (Bourdieu, 1998: 7). Finally, Ignacio Ramonet believed that intellectuals were at the forefront of a struggle against financial power, by contesting the established order and rejecting its forms of indoctrination: 'they resist, challenge and rebel. They propose other arguments, other theses to escape from the mind control and help to transform the world. They help us to better understand the meaning of our times' (Ramonet, 2001: 28).

This new phase of intellectual activism prompted very different reactions from French observers. Some saw it as a significant ideological force, an 'avant-garde' that was challenging the establishment and opening up possibilities for social and political transformation (Aguiton & Bensaïd, 1997; Duval et al., 1998; Poulet, 1999; Aguiton et al., 2011). It was heralded as 'the return of radical intelligence' that was redefining the terms of leftist opposition at a time of neo-liberal globalization (Weill, 2010). Many situated it within a broader trajectory of left-wing renewal that had its origins in the 1995 public sector strikes ('this decisive moment in intellectual history') and which had continued unabated to the present day, reasserting itself in the 2010 demonstrations against pension reform (Duval et al., 1998: 9; Aguiton et al., 2011). Leftist thinkers were reviving the role of the classic French intellectual, by defending the oppressed, articulating social and political causes and elucidating the nature of changes taking place within society. For others, this intellectual current was marginal, reactionary and self-defeating and reflected the broader powerlessness of the French Left in the face of a rising tide of neo-liberalism. For instance, Alain Touraine criticized what he described as republican intellectuals or 'left-wing social conservatives' whose role was limited to a 'denunciation of the modern economy' and who sought a return to a France of the past (Touraine, 2001: 17, 19). In his view, contemporary intellectuals were impeding social transformation by speaking on behalf of emergent social movements and by failing to recognize their capacity for autonomous political action. Similarly, Jérôme Vidal criticizes leftist intellectuals who, he believes, are incapable of grasping the new historical situation and the changing nature of power in a post-Fordist context. Instead of constructing a genuine political alternative, one that reaches beyond narrow scholastic circles, intellectuals had taken refuge in sterile and outdated concepts linked to the post-war social compromise and which had lost their relevance in France today. For him, it is futile to seek a return to the past and to the post-war social model and leftist intellectuals need to construct a 'politics of radical emancipation' attuned to the sociopolitical realities of the present day (Vidal, 2008: 35).

A leftist critique

French intellectuals seem to share a civilizational perspective of globalization, seeing this as a comprehensive political order driven by a distinctive ideology, a set of power interests and specific cultural values. This is not about economic processes, but the rise of a malevolent political order that seems to be imposing its power across the world and destroying the fabric of democratic societies. Because they perceive globalization in broad civilizational terms, French intellectuals have been able to produce a radical critique that challenges neo-liberalism and provides an alternative interpretation of the market transformations taking place. For a burgeoning movement of opposition to globalization, they provided a new leftist critique, an analytical framework, and 'new forms of struggle' that could be used to challenge neo-liberalism in all its forms (Bourdieu, 2001: 53). French thinkers believe that opposition to globalization is only possible where this is revealed as a politically and ideologically determined force, one driven by powerful hegemonic interests and ambitions. They set out to expose behind piecemeal economic changes, the workings of a comprehensive order, an all-encompassing system or 'totality'. Their aim is to give visible form to otherwise abstract economic processes, to provide a clear target for political opposition and thereby to create the conditions for leftist mobilization.

For French thinkers, the strength and influence of economic globalization stems from its underlying ideological apparatus. Neo-liberalism, in their view, has become a dominant ideology, a hegemonic discourse or a *pensée unique* that has taken root within western societies, that has achieved consensus on the Left and Right and which has invalidated all opposing systems of thought. First defined by Ignacio Ramonet in an article in *Le Monde diplomatique*, 'la pensée unique' is a 'doctrine that imperceptibly engulfs all rebellious reasoning, inhibits it, disrupts it, paralyses it and ends by stifling it'. The core tenet of the pensée unique is that 'economics takes precedence over politics' and it advocates market freedom, competition, free trade, financial globalization, deregulation, economic liberalization and privatization. It treats the social domain as a cumbersome obstacle to be overcome in the interests of economic growth and sees this as a 'source of regression and crisis' (Ramonet, 1995). By drawing on economic theory, proponents of neo-liberalism are seen to have a scientific framework at their disposal and can present globalization as a force for social progress, rationalism and modernity: 'we are dealing with an enemy that equips itself with theories and it is a question, it seems to me, of opposing it with intellectual and cultural weapons' (Bourdieu, 1998: 60). Only an equally persuasive discourse, a countervailing theoretical viewpoint or radical critique could challenge globalization effectively and reveal its shortcomings as an economic model. French intellectuals believe that it is on the terrain of political ideas, theory and analysis that the battle against global capitalism will be won.

For French thinkers, neo-liberalism has imposed an economistic interpretation of the market which means that globalization has been rarely questioned. This doctrine reduces the market to an abstract economic mechanism that is detached from its links to national territory and that is determined by economic processes alone: 'a separate domain governed by natural and universal laws' (Bourdieu, 2001: 26). This is 'a pure and perfect order' that operates independently of power structures and political interests and is guided by the invisible hand of the market (Bourdieu, 1998: 108). Furthermore, the market is portrayed as a neutral and universal force, free of ideological values or any one belief system: 'an autonomous sphere independent of ideology or morality' (Boltanski & Chiapello, 1999: 48). The prevalence of this neo-liberal conception means that globalization is generally viewed as natural, benign, progressive and inevitable and it is seen as a pure economic process without wider implications for politics, society or ideology. In the face of what they see as a 'modern dogmatism' French intellectuals have set out to challenge this prevailing doctrine by reinscribing the market within a specific national territory, a set of power relationships and a specific ideological context (Ramonet, 1995). Their purpose is to reconfigure globalization as a broad civilizational process that holds profound implications for the future of France and Europe as a whole.

French intellectuals have challenged a neo-liberal conception of the market in a number of fundamental ways. Firstly, they situate globalization within a specific national territory arguing that it has its origins within a distinctive social and cultural model defined at national level. Their aim is to contest a notion of the market as a disembedded force that glides above the nation and that is free of connections to national territory. All of the authors see globalization as the product of an American cultural tradition, reflecting its particular social model and more deep-seated cultural values. For Pierre Bourdieu, globalization embodied 'the historical characteristics of a particular social tradition, that of the United States of America' (Bourdieu, 2001: 27). He saw the origins of globalization within a specific ideological juncture in the United States, with the rise of neo-conservative economic thought within the Chicago School and subsequently within the American government. In his view, globalization was impregnated with all the values of American individualism, a vision of society that exalted individual action and distrusted all modes of collective representation. Far from expressing the universal, globalization for Bourdieu, simply 'universalizes the particular case of the American economy' extending throughout the world a social model based on a minimalist state, social precariousness and cultural uniformity (ibid., 26). Similarly, Ignacio Ramonet seeks to challenge the economic abstraction of neo-liberal theory by identifying the precise historical context in which it has arisen and he situates this within a confluence of factors linked to the recent American past. He refers to a 'new geopolitical context' at the international level marked by events such as the collapse of the Soviet Union, American military intervention in the Gulf War and the rise of Bill Clinton to power, which together allowed the United States to gain unprecedented influence on the world stage (Ramonet, 1999: 23). For Emmanuel Todd, globalization has its origins in a civilizational crisis within an American society of the 1980s ravaged by social decline, cultural stagnation, intellectual regression and political impotence. Faced with its own implosion, the United States sought to assert itself by aggressively imposing its power elsewhere. For each of the authors, globalization is an extension of an American social and cultural model whose intrinsic inequalities and shortcomings have come into conflict with a more equitable French and European model. The market was not a pure, neutral or universal force, but a product of the American way of life, embodying all its intrinsic cultural values and traits.

Secondly, French intellectuals have sought to politicize globalization by grounding this within a set of power relationships at international level. They challenge a vision of the market as a neutral mechanism driven by economic rationalism alone or by 'pure reason' and argue instead that this is the product of powerful political interests and ambitions (Bourdieu, 1998: 59). All of the authors see globalization in terms of a power struggle in which the interests of dominant elites are being imposed on other nations across the world and this is variously described as 'empire' (Todd), 'colonization'

(Bourdieu), 'neo-hegemony' (Ramonet) or 'dictatorship' (Forrester). Forrester seeks to dispel a myth of globalization as pure economics and urges her readers to see this as a coherent political project: 'Are we able to perceive this as a political regime and understand the kind of politics we are dealing with? (Forrester, 2000: 20–1). She points to the rise of a new and terrifying world order characterized by the 'brutal imposition' of a free market system across the world with devastating consequences for the whole of humanity (ibid., 24). Similarly, for Bourdieu, globalization reflects a 'relationship of domination' whereby powerful nations were imposing their interests on others ('the dominated') by means of political coercion, institutional control and symbolic violence. This new political order was bent on 'limitless exploitation' and a 'submission of governments and citizens' to the implacable laws of the marketplace (Bourdieu, 1998: 108; 2001: 57). Faced with this new political regime, Bourdieu argued that we need to 'restore politics' by reaffirming the power of the state, by safeguarding social gains and by constructing new forms of collective mobilization (ibid.). Finally, Ramonet's core argument is that globalization is a vehicle of American neo-hegemony, a new period of imperialism comparable in its political ambitions to the European colonial empires of the nineteenth century: 'There are periods in the history of the world where the hegemony of a State, as a result of the defeat or deconstruction of its main rivals, exerts itself suddenly and without equivalent across the whole planet' (Ramonet, 1999: 62–3). For him, globalization therefore constitutes a 'new world order', one that has been conceived in Washington in order to advance America's strategic ambitions, historic objectives and political interests (ibid., 56). In this current imperialist phase, the United States wields power not through territorial domination, but through a control of economic exchanges, trade, financial transactions and technological innovation.

Thirdly, French intellectuals have argued that globalization constitutes an ideological project, one that envisages a comprehensive transformation of the structures and values of European democracies. Contesting a vision of globalization as a neutral, random or spontaneous force, they argue that economic processes are underpinned by an overarching ideology or belief system. Each of the authors seeks to reconfigure globalization as an ideological project and this is a 'dominant ideology', a 'powerful discourse' or a 'justifying myth' (Ramonet, 2001; Bourdieu, 1998: 39, 43). They argue that the force of globalization is derived precisely from this ideological apparatus rooted in neo-liberalism. As intellectuals, they see it as their duty to expose and examine the mechanisms by which this ideology is produced, propagated and imposed. For Pierre Bourdieu, it is impossible to understand the nature of economic globalization without reference to its underlying ideological structure: 'I evoked globalisation: it is a myth in the strongest sense of the term, a powerful discourse, an *idée force*, an idea that has social power, which commands belief' (Bourdieu, 1998: 39). He argued that globalization is the product of 'prolonged and constant intellectual endeavour' on the part of think-tanks, pressure groups, private corporations and lobby groups (Ramonet, 2001: 35). This neo-conservative ideology invokes a discourse of modernity and progress in order to justify a return to the most archaic and regressive aspects of liberalism. Propagated by political and economic elites and by the mainstream media, in a kind of 'symbolic drip-feed', the validity of this ideology is often left unquestioned (Bourdieu, 1998: 35). For Bourdieu, this was a highly destructive system of thought, that substitutes the values and traditions of the Welfare State with 'a radical capitalism without any other law besides that of maximum profit' (ibid., 40). Similarly, Ramonet sees neo-liberalism as a 'crushing ideological consensus' that has been propagated by the media on behalf of powerful economic elites (Ramonet, 2001: 27). He argues that this ideology now exerts a form of mind control, presenting itself as the only possible model for society and suppressing all alternative ways of thinking. Emmanuel Todd locates globalization within a nihilistic and destructive system of thought that has Anglo-Saxon origins. This ideology posits inequality as a 'social absolute' and an economic necessity with devastating consequences for society and for the nation state. In the face of this *pensée zéro*, Todd calls for a reassertion of collective values and beliefs and in particular those linked to the ideal of the nation state. Forrester goes further still, seeing behind the workings of the market, a 'totalitarian ideology' which uses propaganda, coercion and violence to further its ends (Forrester, 2000: 60). This 'dictatorial discourse' serves the interests of an ascendant power structure in which profit is seen as the ultimate goal of all human endeavour: 'An ideology of profit has been imposed, one which has no goal other than that of limitless financial power' (ibid., 21, 52). This ideology of profit is, in her view, used to justify and legitimize the worst attacks against human rights and social interests.

Le monde anglosaxon

Because French intellectuals share a civilizational perspective of globalization, they have been able to produce a radical critique of neo-liberalism and what they see as its narrow economistic paradigm. They set out to politicize globalization by reinscribing the market within a comprehensive political and ideological order. Yet this civilizational perspective has also had negative and reductionist effects on the nature of their critique.

In seeking to identify globalization with a coherent political and ideological system, a clearly defined order or civilization, French intellectuals often equate this with a *monde anglosaxon* that seems to be imposing its model on France and on the rest of the world. The Anglo-Saxon world is treated less as an objective analytical category, than as a set of dominant cultural traits and characteristics. It serves as a kind of oppositional myth, a means to capture all the perceived ill effects of globalization and at the same time, to reinforce a sense of political identity at a time of profound transformation and upheaval. Some critics have noted a tendency of French leaders to externalize the causes of globalization and attribute it to the workings of an Anglo-Saxon world beyond French control. For Timothy Smith, Anglo-Saxon globalization has become a means to assign blame for unpopular socioeconomic transformations on external economic forces outside of France (Smith, 2004). Intellectuals tend to share a Manichean tendency that situates the Anglo-Saxon world in juxtaposition to the French Republic so that it became its irreducible opposite. Where the Republic is seen as a symbol of civilization, the Anglo-Saxon world becomes an embodiment of barbarism. Where the Republic is seen as quintessentially democratic, the Anglo-Saxon world is cast as a totalitarian order. Where the Republic is seen as a stable, ordered and regulated universe, the Anglo-Saxon world becomes its opposite, a place of chaos, disorder and anarchy.

Barbarism

Anglo-Saxon globalization is characterized in these texts as a form of barbarism that is counterposed against France's own 'civilization'. Each of the authors portrays globalization as a form of regression, backwardness or social decline and this is a 'barbarism', a 'neo-darwinism', a 'jungle', a 'savage capitalism' (Bourdieu, 1998: 41, 48; Ramonet, 1999: 258; Forrester, 2000: 81). This is a backward social model that destroys collective values and rights and which ultimately poses a threat to the project of modernity itself. What is at stake in accepting globalization is that France will be plunged back into a dark and primitive place, a kind of social Stone Age where no laws exist, where human rights are trampled upon and where each man turns on his neighbour. Frequent references are made to France's own past and in particular to the pre-revolutionary regime as a way of denoting the regressive effects of globalization and this will lead to 'a return to the conditions of the Old regime' and represents 'a modernity consisting of a regression to the 19th century' (Ramonet, 1999: 260; Forrester, 2000: 53).

Pierre Bourdieu compares the rise of neo-liberalism to a 'conservative revolution' that threatens to drag France backwards and undo centuries of civilizing progress (Bourdieu, 1998: 40). It is contrasted with the French Revolution that has propelled France forward to ever greater social progress and enlighten-ment. Bourdieu argues that globalization has assumed a discourse of moder-nity and progress to disguise what is in effect a model of social regression and decline: 'neo-liberalism brings back under the guise of a very chic and very modern message, the oldest ideas of the oldest employers' class' (ibid.). Behind much of this rhetoric lies a fear that France will leave itself open to an Americanization of its social model that will endanger the principle of equality seen to define the French way of life. For instance, Forrester summons up a cataclysmic image of American society as a future that France must avoid at all costs. This is a ghetto society driven by endemic poverty, weak social pro-tection, poor working conditions, deplorable healthcare and minimalist public services and she observes that 'the major world economic power is also amongst the industrialised nations, the first in terms of the levels of poverty of its population' (Forrester, 2000: 73). American society is the image of a future nightmare society that will destroy the foundations of the French social model and propel it into a spiral of ceaseless decline: 'because we are now at the frontiers of barbarism' (ibid., 81).

This vision of an impending barbarism is most vividly expressed by Emmanuel Todd in *The Economic Illusion*. For him, the economic dimension of globalization is illusory, a mere smokescreen for the deeper cultural and anthropological forces at work. He describes globalization in terms of an ascen-dant American model marked by stagnation, cultural decline and 'intellectual and ideological reversion' (Todd, 1998: 294). Yet, he believes that the causes of this transformation have little to do with economic processes, but instead reflect all the inherent characteristics of a pre-defined cultural type identified with the Anglo-Saxon world. Indeed, his purpose is to analyse the origins of this cultural model, to uncover its cultural and anthropological 'subconscious' and thereby to better understand changes that are taking place in the present day. He traces the origins of this model to its English and Calvinist roots and characterizes this as a convergence of influences including the nuclear fam-ily structure, Protestantism and individualism. In the contemporary context, Anglo-Saxon globalization has given rise to a rampant individualism that is now threatening the 'destruction of civilized worlds' (ibid., 14). He views glo-balization in terms of a conflict between opposing cultural models and in par-ticular, 'an anthropological opposition between France and the Anglo-Saxon world' (ibid., 340). Whereas the Anglo-Saxon model is rooted in individualism, the French model is 'driven by cultural progress' is socially egalitarian, intel-lectually advanced and defined by its 'foundational values' (ibid., 337). In his more recent book, *Après la démocratie* (*After Democracy*, 2008), Todd con-tinues to interpret France's current social and political situation in terms of an opposition between 'the French and the Anglo-Saxons' (Todd, 2008: 112). He argues that Nicolas Sarkozy's rise to power reflects a profound cultural, ideological and educational crisis in France, whereby it has become increasingly distanced from its own inherent anthropological and cultural roots. Sarkozy, in Todd's view, is a champion of 'American-style inequality' and has attempted to impose on France an Anglo-Saxon model characterized by 'primitive democracy' that is completely at odds with France's cultural predisposition towards equality. For him, globalization is not about economics, but about a clash between two opposing cultures whose differences are fundamental and irreconcilable.

Dictatorship

Because the Republic is perceived by leftist intellectuals as the quintessential site of democracy, the Anglo-Saxon world is reconfigured in these texts as a model of totalitarianism. Each of the authors sees behind market transformations the rise of a new authoritarian regime, an ascendant world order that is assuming ever greater powers and crushing the foundations of democracy. This is a 'tyranny of profit', a 'financial terrorism', an 'infernal machine' or a 'market dictatorship' that is taking control of the entire planet and which is sapping democratic rights and freedoms (Bourdieu, 1998; Ramonet, 1999: 97; Forrester, 2000: 33, 52). Through its dogmatic neo-liberal creed, globalization has unleashed the power of capital onto the world to the extent that it now dictates to society, supersedes elected governments, imposes a single ideology and quashes all opposition. This 'authoritarian regime' imposes the will of a dominant financial elite across the entire planet and brings untold suffering to the many (Forrester, 2000: 26). Moreover, by concentrating power in unelected supranational institutions, it violates the sacred bond between citizen and state and a precious legacy of the democratic tradition.

For Ignacio Ramonet, the market has become a vehicle for American tyranny and the 'new masters of the world' have established a ruthless and oligarchic power structure that aspires towards absolute power: 'they recognise neither borders, not states, nor cultures and they deride national sovereignties' (Ramonet, 2001: 13). Just as during other periods of totalitarian rule, this new order establishes itself as a 'modern divinity' that requires absolute submission, that exerts forms of coercion and imposes its own ideology. By placing emphasis on profit above every other consideration, globalization threatens to destroy the sociopolitical edifice of western democracies and in particular, the notion of progress enshrined by the French Republic. Ramonet seeks to delineate the contours of this new order in which power is increasingly displaced from the political to the technological sphere and the media becomes a key instrument of manipulation and control.

It is Viviane Forrester who expresses most forcefully this conception of globalization as a form of totalitarianism. In her *Une Etrange dictature* (*A Strange Dictatorship,* 2000), she argues that through propaganda, ruthless exploitation and an obsessive profit-making doctrine, Anglo-Saxon globalization has become as destructive in its effects as any other period of totalitarianism. This is a system that discards whole swathes of humanity, treats them as superfluous and consigns them, through mass unemployment, to a sort of living hell. Like other forms of dictatorship, globalization attacks the very fabric of society, its traditions, structures and values and is also characterized by a systematic destruction of human life. Thus, she evokes historical precedents that are both terrifying and extreme, those of European colonialism, apartheid in South Africa, racial segregation in the United States and the Holocaust of World War II to describe the true nature of this regime. Yet, globalization is a 'strange' dictatorship which is all the more dangerous because it extends its power in hidden and surreptitious ways and assumes the benign face of democracy: 'a dictatorship without a dictator has established itself without attacking any specific nation' (Forrester, 2000: 52). She suggests that this regime could however easily dispense with the apparatus of democracy and make the transition to a full dictatorship. Forrester's representation of globalization as an ascendant totalitarianism has attracted criticism for its alarmist and conspiratorial nature and some have denounced it as an 'apocalyptic vision' and others as an 'alarmist diatribe' (A. Supiot cited by Gollain, 1999: 485; Smith, 2004: 59).

Chaos

Anglo-Saxon globalization is portrayed in terms of chaos and this is a disorderly, unstable and unpredictable process, a 'casino economy' that is spiraling out of control and unleashing havoc across the planet (Ramonet, 1999: 38). Without rules, political direction or ideological purpose, globalization hurtles along driven by the brute force of a market and respects neither social norms nor cultural differences. It has created a world of ceaseless change, dislocation and flux, a place where all rules have been swept away, where common values have been dissolved and where states are left powerless. This chaotic system is presented as a binary opposite to the ordered and stable universe of the French Republic, a world regulated by the benevolent hand of the State, guided by an overarching political framework and having a clear sense of ideological purpose. Whereas the Republic raises society upwards towards greater social order and progress, the Anglo-Saxon world drags society downwards into a quagmire of chaos and dissoluteness.

In *Geopolitics of Chaos,* Ramonet points to a contradiction between a 'new world order' driven by American imperialist ambition and a triumphant liberalism and a world system that has been plunged into chaos, instability and lawlessness. He describes a 'civilization of chaos' marked by a rise in ethnic conflict, nationalism, religious fundamentalism, international crime, social inequality and environmental degradation (ibid., 15). Societies are subject to a constant state of change imposed by the market and yet this change has no obvious direction, ideological value or social purpose. In this context, individuals are left in a state of anxiety, malaise and uncertainty facing unknown future perils and dangers: 'uncertainty has become the unique certainty' (ibid., 17). He argues that one consequence of globalization has therefore been a 'rise of irrational thought' as individuals search for meaning, value and identity within religious fundamentalism, political extremism or occultism (ibid., 123). He believes that in this new chaotic world, the threat of ethnic and political conflict and of religious fundamentalism constantly increases.

For Emmanuel Todd, this state of chaos is not an arbitrary outcome of economic processes, but a product of particular social and cultural traditions linked to the Anglo-Saxon world. He defines this in terms an 'absolute individualism' that frees the individual of all collective structures and beliefs and thereby weakens the foundations of political order within society. This individualism, he argues, is a cultural and anthropological predisposition of the Anglo-Saxon type that originates partly in a societal model based on the absolute nuclear family. This familial structure is characterized by an early separation between parents and children which tends to predetermine, more broadly, a relationship of the individual to society. If the contemporary world has been plunged into chaos, this is not the result of 'conscious economic actions' but reflects the impact of an 'unconscious' Anglo-Saxon anthropological type and the impact of an enduring societal model rooted in individualism (Todd, 1998: 20).

Writing the crisis

For free market ideologues, whose theories helped to define the world order over the past 30 years, a crisis is a spontaneous, cyclical or natural phenomenon caused by abstract economic forces that are beyond human control.[6] The economist Joseph Schumpeter, an oracle of Chicago School teaching, argued that economic crisis was part of the 'creative destruction' of capitalism which allowed it to renew and strengthen itself. While every market crash produced 'collateral damage' – in the form of public sector redundancies or weakened infrastructure and social services – this was ultimately beneficial, as it led to greater economic growth and innovation. The solution to economic crisis lay not in political interference which only distorted 'natural' market processes, but in the self-regulating market itself which, if left to its own devices, would soon adjust its internal mechanisms and establish a new and harmonious equilibrium. Such doctrine helps to explain the response of many European political leaders to the 2008 economic crisis, who have sought not to pursue structural reforms but instead, to deepen neo-liberal policies, in the belief that this will stimulate the market's own healing processes.

Recent books on the economic crisis by leading French thinkers present a radically different interpretation of these events and recommend a very different path for France to follow. This section looks at books written by three influential French thinkers (Ignacio Ramonet, Frédéric Lordon and Hervé Juvin) who each produced a virulent critique of the causes and consequences of this crisis.[7] The three books considered here can be situated within a renewed criticism of free market economics by French intellectuals in the wake of the crisis and form part of 'an unprecedented mass' of new books, articles and manifestos on this theme (Wieder, 2010). I argue that these writers perpetuate a tendency that was evident in earlier literature on globalization and that sees the crisis in broad civilizational terms. On the one hand, they challenge a neo-liberal conception of the crisis as a temporary economic cycle or adjustment. They present this instead as the collapse of an entire civilization, a hegemonic order and ideological system which has dominated the world for over three decades. Their aim is to expose the political and ideological causes of the crisis and therefore to build a persuasive case for profound structural reform. Each of these writers appeals for radical change and for the construction of an alternative order that would rise from the ashes of a defunct neo-liberalism. On the other hand, some writers perpetuate an essentialist perspective that explains economic processes in relation to cultural determinants. In the wake of the crisis, the relationship between France and the United States is reconfigured in terms of binary couplings based on good and evil, innocence and guilt, victim and perpetrator. Whereas the United States is often cast as the evil perpetrator, driven by malevolent ideological designs, France and Europe are its hapless victims, beguiled by its promises of endless prosperity and ensnared in its tentacles of power. We will see that this perspective tends to obscure the role of French and European leaders in laying the foundations for the economic crisis in Europe.

For these writers, the economic crisis is not a cyclical economic adjustment, but a seismic event, one that has brought an entire neo-liberal order crashing down and that has utterly transformed the face of the world. The crisis has destroyed the foundations of the neo-liberal order, creating a kind of *tabula rasa*, which offers an historic opportunity for deep-seated transformation. Ignacio Ramonet in his book, argues that the crisis marks a definitive historical juncture, signalling 'the end of an era of capitalism' and the transition to a new and markedly different historical phase (Ramonet, 2009: 13). The crisis has plunged the world into 'the most terrible of systemic crises. And the apocalypse is far from over' (ibid.). He describes the crisis not as an economic event, but as something with the dimensions of a natural disaster, a force of nature that has destroyed everything in its path and this is a 'hurricane', 'volcano', 'cyclone' or 'earthquake' (ibid., 22, 24, 89, 90). For Ramonet, the crash of the American banking system has precipitated the fall of the 'hyperpower' of the United States and the transition to a new geopolitical context characterized by American decadence and the rise of China and India as the new economic superpowers on the world stage.

For the leftist economist, Frédéric Lordon, a columnist for *Le Monde diplomatique*, the crisis constitutes a systemic failure that has laid bare a system of capitalist expansion that was built on an obscene accumulation of wealth, the boundless greed of financial elites and new forms of exploitation. For him, this is not a routine event, but a 'crise de trop' that has pushed the limits of financial greed beyond what is socially acceptable or humanly tolerable. He points to deeply rooted rage within public opinion, an anger that has no political outlet and that could lead, he warns, to an unprecedented explosion of social violence. Similarly Hervé Juvin in his book *Le Renversement du monde* (*The Reversal of the World*, 2010),[8] emphasizes the historical significance of the crisis which he compares to the fall of the Berlin Wall, yet here what has collapsed is an entire post-cold war order, built on 'Wall Street and Anglo-American finance' (ibid., 240). The crisis has brought an end to a system rooted in 'absolute individualism' which has destroyed society in the name of market integration and whose most pernicious effect is that of cultural loss. Yet, he warns that France and Europe are now faced with a new cultural threat in the form of a 'globalization of Islam' carried by the rising power of China and India (ibid., 238). The new world order will be marked by a reassertion of cultural, ethnic and religious identities 'a war of peoples, nations and civilizations' which he sees as a just retribution against an American cultural model that suppressed differences and imposed a uniform market system. Juvin has been described as an 'intellectual executive' whose work is influenced by the intertwining worlds of culture and business and his book combines a trenchant leftist critique of neo-liberalism with a traditionally right-wing preoccupation with themes of cultural identity, nation and national borders (Anderson, 2006: 132). Insofar as he can be situated politically, he is close to the centre-Right journal *Le Débat* and its chief editors, Pierre Nora and Marcel Gauchet are the first to appear in the list of acknowledgements in his book.

Each of these writers challenges a neo-liberal view of the crisis as a *deus ex machina*, that is derived from abstract economic laws outside human control. They seek to politicize the crisis by revealing its political and ideological determinants and by inscribing it within an overarching political order. This is a crisis caused not by arbitrary economic forces, but by the conscious decisions of political leaders informed by a dominant neo-liberal ideology. For Ramonet, the economic crisis has been prepared in advance through a specific historical trajectory that has its origins in the 'conservative revolution' in the United States in the 1980s and to a fateful collusion between Wall Street bankers, multinational firms and the United States government which fell into the thrall of Chicago School teaching. He goes on to trace the trajectory of the crisis through its key historic episodes, that of the 1997 Asian crisis, the collapse of the American energy company Enron in 2001 and that of the Italian milk-producer Parmalat in 2003, the rise of American subprime mortgages, the collapse of the Bear Stearns bank in 2007 and Lehman Brothers in 2008. He portrays a system driven by a logic of compulsive greed, frenzied speculation and political corruption which spiralled out of control and eventually brought the whole neo-liberal system crashing down. For him, a decisive episode in this historical trajectory was the decision of the Clinton government in 1999 to deregulate the financial sector by abolishing the Glass-Steagall Act which had separated banking activities into savings and investment and which had been in existence since the Wall Street Crash of 1929. This political decision has given rise to a new model of financial capitalism driven by 'the laws of the jungle' which imposed its influence over the rest of the world with disastrous social consequences (Ramonet, 2009: 78). He clearly designates those responsible for the economic crisis: 'the American political class bears the main responsibility' by approving a deregulation of the financial sector which allowed banks to operate in a context that was free of all legal regulations and ethical principles (ibid., 100).

Similarly, Lordon challenges a tendency to blame abstract financial markets for the crisis and he attributes this instead to an American regime of capitalist accumulation put in place by powerful political and financial elites. Like Ramonet, he traces the crisis to the decision of American political leaders to introduce a new *modus operandi* for the financial sector that transformed the structures, regulations and principles that were already in place. The causes of the crisis, he argues, 'did not fall from the sky' but were part of a coherent ideologically driven system that was put in place by purposeful political decisions (Lordon, 2009: 49). He emphasizes that markets do not have the means to deregulate themselves or to define the conditions in which they operate and that it is political leaders who must do this for them: 'But it was not within the power of private actors to define the rules of the game themselves, only states could do that for them' (ibid., 30). For Lordon, it is crucial to understand the underlying structural and political causes of the crisis because only a profound transformation of these structures and policies can provide a way out of the crisis. In a similar vein, Juvin points to a 'political crisis' derived from specific decisions taken in a particular place at a given moment in time and this was a 'localised, circumstantial and determined crisis' (Juvin, 2010: 6, 14). For him, the decisive historical episode was the explosion in American subprime mortgages which he describes as a ruthless and exploitative regime that encouraged the poorest households to buy property through mortgage loans that they could ill afford and which banks then bought and sold as 'financial products'. Yet Juvin is concerned less with an economic or historical analysis of the crisis than with providing a broad philosophical reflection on the consequences of neo-liberalism for the human condition. For him, the greatest damage wreaked by neo-liberalism is that of cultural loss and this is a system that has destroyed the natural diversity and heterogeneity of humankind. This is not about the free movement of capitalism, but is a war against humanity itself that has wrecked cultural identities, social diversity and national specificities: 'The globalist ideology that characterises neo-liberalism has engaged in a new war against the diversity of human societies, a war in which individualism is the flag and cultural products the heavy artillery, a war against the differences and eccentricities of the world, which is ultimately a war against the world, against its irreducible diversity and its vital antagonisms' (ibid., 8).

If these writers help to challenge the economic determinism of neo-liberal theory and to inscribe the crisis within a specific political and ideological context, some of them provide an essentialist interpretation that sees the workings of a predetermined cultural type behind the crisis. What often emerges is a biased picture which demonizes the United States and obscures the specific role of French leaders in preparing the terrain for the crisis in Europe. For instance, Ramonet is keen to examine the precise historical trajectory of the crisis, yet this is a history from which France is entirely absent or at least, that appears only on the sidelines, as hapless victim or innocent bystander. Whereas the United States is seen as an autonomous actor responsible for its own political decisions, the experience of the crisis from a European perspective is equated with a natural disaster or a pathological phenomenon that is beyond human control. France's only wrongdoing is to have had the misfortune to find itself 'in the eye of the cyclone' and to have been swept along by natural forces that it was powerless to control (Lordon, 2009: 24). Elsewhere, he invokes the crisis as a form of contagion, a disease or virus that attacks the flesh in an arbitrary way: 'Like a plague, this fever contaminated the planet' (ibid., 93).

It is Juvin who goes furthest in portraying an essentialist vision that sees the crisis as the product of a reckless and expansionist American culture, invoked in terms of clichéd images of cowboys, frontiersmen and the Wild West. He seems concerned less with empirical observation or verifiable facts, than with building an overarching cultural theory that sweeps up diverse processes into a single logic of cause and effect. For him, the crisis was not about the objective mechanics of the market but expresses an American 'anthropological project' that seeks to transform the human condition by stripping individuals of their cultural and social affiliations and turning them into abstract consumers and slaves to the market. The crisis is the consequence of an American cultural model based on 'absolute individualism' and that places emphasis on individual rights, freedoms and desires above every other principle. For Juvin, the crisis can be located as a continuation of an American frontier culture of the nineteenth century and which led disastrously to the eradication of native American Indians:

> The planetary diffusion of an historical exception continues, that of the American colonization that emptied a continent of its population, which has conserved the figure of the colonialist as a model and which creates law through force and uses its wealth to legitimize a theft of land and a destruction of its resources. (Juvin, 2010: 77)

In the contemporary context, it is Europe and the rest of the world that has become the new frontier of the Wild West, an open territory that is ripe for American expansionism. Continuing the colonialist metaphor, he argues that American neo-liberalism, by imposing indebtedness on the masses, has resulted in a return of slavery that will be perpetuated into the future as generations to come are burdened by debt. Bizarrely, Juvin sees the crisis as an opportunity to attack all his enemies at once and alongside the United States, he targets the Far Left which, for him, is also responsible for propagating an extreme individualism that is dangerous for cultural identity and social belonging. By seeking to promote individual rights and equality, to eradicate national borders and to challenge discrimination, the Far Left, in his view, has incarnated the same logic as that of neo-liberalism, one that has suppressed cultural differences in favour of creating abstract individuals.

In his lucid and on this point, more objective account, Lordon presents a very different viewpoint, one that emphasizes the 'crushing responsibility' of French political leaders in creating the political and economic conditions that led to the crisis (Lordon, 2009: 50). He reserves his most acerbic criticism for the French Socialists who through their leadership of the European Union introduced successive policies of economic deregulation and financial liberalization that helped to usher the neo-liberal model into Europe. He points to legislation such as the 1986 law on the deregulation of financial markets, the 1988 directive on capital mobility, the 1990 abolition of tax on capital revenues, the 1998 tax alleviation on stock options, the 2001 reform of pension funds, all of which were implemented by French Socialists in an effort to liberalize the French and European economies. The French were not, in his view, innocent onlookers, but willing disciples of a dominant neo-liberal creed and were eager to implement its core tenets within Europe: 'It is a dramatic irony of political history that in France the "Socialists" were the key architects and those who bear the main responsibility' (ibid., 50). He criticizes what he sees as the hypocrisy and duplicity of Socialist leaders who, since the crisis, have been keen to point the finger at American bankers as the sole culprits of a crisis in which they themselves seemingly played no part. This is an 'intellectual whitewashing' by French leaders who were interested not in establishing the underlying causes of the crisis, but in absolving themselves from blame (ibid., 72). If Europe had caught the 'contagion' of neo-liberalism, he argues, this is because it actively encouraged the spread of this disease: 'And the great Europeans seem surprised to discover they have the clap after having prohibited the use of condoms' (ibid., 53).

Each of these writers appeals for radical change and for the construction of an alternative order that could rise from the ashes of a defunct neo-liberalism. Ramonet sees the crisis as a catalyst for change, a revolutionary moment that opens up new historical possibilities: 'This is not a crisis it is a revolution' (Ramonet, 2009: 18). While the crisis is the cause of widespread social suffering, it has also generated hope for the creation of a new and better world. He urges his readers not to 'waste this opportunity' and to help rebuild the world on a more democratic and equitable basis (ibid., 17). Although he emphasizes the utopian possibilities of the crisis, his vision of an alternative model is vague and ill-defined, falling short of the utopian ideal he hints at throughout the book. His conception of a new society is based loosely on a 'disarming of financial power' and a deepening of the democratic power of citizens (ibid., 139). Citizens need to reclaim the power to make decisions about their own lives and to determine their own futures: 'we need above all to give citizens greater control over the strategic resources of states and over the economic decisions that concern their lives' (ibid., 140). Yet, he says little about how citizens, dispossessed by the effects of the crisis, will reclaim this democratic power and how they will go about creating a new world order. Whereas Ramonet's historical treatment of the crisis is rigorous and insightful, his vision of the future lends more to wishful thinking.

For Juvin, the solution to the crisis lies in a reaffirmation of 'human societies' as distinctive cultural, historical and political entities and as the primary defence against destructive market forces. In his view, it is wrong to call for a return of the state in the wake of the crisis, since governments and political leaders are caught up in the apparatus of the neo-liberal economy itself. Instead, he believes that societies need to recover their own sense of collective being, their social foundations and their cultural essence, that have been violated by destructive foreign influences. Europe, he argues, needs to reassert its historical uniqueness and geographical separateness emphasizing what distinguishes its collective identity from that of others: 'Without history, we have no means to be ourselves, know ourselves and favour ourselves, without geography . . . we have no means to situate ourselves' (Juvin, 2010: 194). This return to the collective self is to be achieved through a reinstatement of national borders. He argues that borders are the means to protect Europe from the twin evils of Anglo-Saxon neo-liberalism and immigration, seen equally as symptoms of a hybrid and nomadic world which strips away social and cultural bonds:

> The construction of autonomous societies calls for the return of borders, both as door and as wall, as bond and divide, as a sign of the Other and of self. The quest for autonomy necessitates an urgent reaffirmation of the internal unity of nations which respect their own diversity. (Ibid., 233)

If he provides a trenchant critique of neo-liberal economics, he also panders to a crude cultural elitism that sees the crisis as a product of alien cultural influences which have trammelled France and Europe's purity and innocence. Juvin equates all that is wrong in the world with that which is foreign and all that is virtuous with protected national cultures of European origin.

It is Lordon who goes furthest in elaborating a model for an alternative world order that could replace neo-liberalism and provide the foundations for a democratic and egalitarian society. He suggests that just as during the eighteenth century, when the French masses drew on their experience of oppression and injustice to mobilize into a revolutionary social force, so today, the people, driven by a deep-seated anger against the injustices of the economic order, may rise up against the establishment and lay the foundations for a new society. His vision of an alternative order is inspired both by Marxism and radical democratic theory in a political model that is rooted in democratic ideals, but that gives workers control over the means of production. On the one hand, he proposes a 'minimal programme' of reforms to modify the configuration of financial capitalism in order to protect society from its worst excesses (limits on shareholder profits, regulated external competition, wealth redistribution, socialized forms of credit). On the other, he envisages a radical transformation of the workplace based on collectivization of the means of production, in which all employees would participate directly in decision-making on salaries, production levels and working conditions. Both sets of measures are seen as mutually reinforcing in that a collectivized workplace can only operate in a context in which limits are imposed on the power of financial capitalism. Lordon's project of social transformation, by combining radical change at local level with concrete reforms in the neo-liberal system combines social idealism with pragmatism. Yet, in focusing his new social model on the workplace, he tends to neglect the situation of the unemployed who are the primary victims of neo-liberal economics, but who do not figure in his project of a future society. While these writers all provide a radical critique of neo-liberalism, their analysis of the causes and consequences of the crisis tend to differ markedly. Some writers see the crisis as a new dawn, a moment full of utopian possibilities for radical change, whereas others call for a retrenchment of national and European frontiers as the only means to rebuild cultural identity and to keep others out.

Conclusion

I have argued in this chapter that French intellectuals share a 'civilizational' perspective of globalization and perceive this not in economic terms, but as an assault on France and an entire group of societies. If they mobilized with such intensity and force, this is because they believed that France and Europe, just as during other periods of national crisis from history, were faced once again with a profound and deep-seated external threat. Yet, this civilizational perspective has had contradictory effects on the nature of French intellectual opposition. On the one hand, French thinkers have helped to produce a radical critique that challenged the terms of neo-liberal theory and advanced a countervailing interpretation of the market changes taking place. In the face of a dominant free market ideology or *pensée unique*, they reconfigured globalization as a politically and ideologically determined process, one that emanated from a specific national culture. They have helped to politicize globalization by transforming an otherwise abstract and unseen economic process into a coherent political system, an ideological project and a cultural product. On the other hand, French intellectuals tended to perpetuate an essentialist vision of globalization that equated this with an 'Anglo-Saxon world' defined by a set of dominant cultural traits and characteristics. For them, globalization was not determined by economic processes alone, but reflected a predefined cultural propensity rooted in Anglo-Saxon traditions. The economic dimension of globalization was seen as a mere obscuration for the deeper cultural and anthropological forces at work.

The 2008 economic crisis has generated a fresh wave of criticism from French intellectuals with an outpouring of new books, articles and manifestos that have denounced a neo-liberal ideology held responsible for the crisis. For many leftist intellectuals, this crisis seemed to vindicate what they said all along about the dangers of an unbridled model of global capitalism. In recent books, they provide a trenchant critique that exposes the political and ideological determinants of the crisis. For them, the crisis did not 'fall from the sky' but is a consequence of conscious human decisions taken by specific political leaders under the sway of a dominant neo-liberal ideology. By linking the crisis to a broader political order, an ideological system or civilization, these writers build a persuasive case for the creation of an alternative world order to replace a discredited neo-liberal system. Yet some of these writers also perpetuate an essentialist perspective that explains economic processes in relation to cultural determinants. They revive a binary opposition between Europe and the Anglo-Saxon world that sees Europeans as innocent victims of evil American designs, trapped in an economic machine beyond their control. Whereas determinacy is assigned to the United States, the European experience of the crisis is described in terms of a natural catastrophe, disease or contagion. As Frédéric Lordon points out, this is a form of intellectual hypocrisy that obscures the complicity of French and European leaders in paving the way towards the crisis and in creating the conditions for their own economic demise (Lordon, 2009).

Notes

1 Many of the key intellectuals who formed part of the *nouveaux philosophes* of the 1970s declared their support for Nicolas Sarkozy's presidential campaign and these included André Glucksmann, Alain Finkielkraut, Pascal Bruckner and Bernard Kouchner (a key figure in the French humanitarian movement).

2 Critics tend to see the mobilization of 2005 against the European Constitutional Treaty as the end point of this period of intellectual intervention. For instance, Ignacio Ramonet points out that few notable intellectuals intervened in debates during the riots in the suburbs of 2005 and that there was a marked absence of intellectuals in the 2006 demonstrations against a reform of employment contracts (Ramonet, 2006).

3 More recently, Terra Nova created in 2008 and on the centre-left, brings together researchers, politicians and employers in order to promote an intellectual renewal of social democracy. Its president Oliver Ferrand was a former advisor to Lionel Jospin and it is funded by donations from private sector companies. Unlike other leftist intellectual groupings, Terra Nova has been criticized as being a vehicle for mainstream socialism that is closer to the Fondation Saint-Simon in political orientation than to its leftist equivalents.

4 I have translated all of the titles of these books and the original French titles are cited in the bibliography. There are English translations available for two books: Pierre Bourdieu's *Contre-feux* 1 (Translated by Richard Nice as *Acts of Resistance: Against the Tyranny of the Market*, New Press, 1999) and Viviane Forrester's *The Economic Horror* published in English translation by Polity Press in 1999. I have chosen to use a more direct translation of Bourdieu's *Contre-feux* (*Counter-fire*) because it expresses more clearly Bourdieu's intention to use words and arguments in this book as a form of opposition.

5 During the Nazi occupation of France, Hessel joined the French resistance, was caught, tortured and deported to Buchenwald and Dora concentration camps where he escaped hanging. After the war, he helped to draft the Universal Declaration of Human Rights and later became a diplomat.

6 Naomi Klein examines how the Chicago School's 'crisis hypothesis', developed in the 1980s, was used to inform American policies of aggressive intervention in Latin American in order to impose a liberalization of their economies. Chicago School economists saw market crashes as a catalyst for change, an historic opportunity to impose or deepen neo-liberal reforms. During a crisis, normal democratic practices are temporarily suspended and political leaders are at liberty to take radical measures in response to a perceived national emergency. A market crash was seen to provide the ideal opportunity for 'shock therapy' or a right-wing counterrevolution that can impose American-led neo-liberalism on a disorientated population. See Naomi Klein *The Shock Doctrine* (London: Penguin, 2007).

7 The writers discussed in this chapter should be distinguished from other commentators on the Right who have argued that the crisis is an opportunity to deepen neo-liberal reforms. Hence the liberal economic historian, Nicolas Bavarez, in *Après le deluge* (Perrin, 2009) argues that the crisis is a transitional phase that does not signal the end of neo-liberal globalization but simply accelerates its rhythm. He appeals for a set of reforms to regulate the global economy in order to ensure its continued survival. France, in his view, needs to continue along the path of liberal reforms, if it is to overcome its own immobilism and find a way out of the crisis. Similarly, the economist Jean-Marc Slyvestre who was economic affairs correspondent for the television channel TFI from 1994 to 2010, develops a neo-liberal interpretation in *La France piégée* (*Trapped France*, Buchet/Chastel, 2008) which sees the crisis as an opportunity to modernize France and integrate its economy into a global market place: 'The crisis offers a rare opportunity: that of launching reforms in a context in which we do not have the option to refuse them' (Slyvestre, 2008: 286). He sees Nicolas Sarkozy as a kind of saviour who has helped France to overcome its stagnation and who must now stand firm in the face of plummeting popularity rates and persist in the course of economic reform.

8 Juvin is president of Eurogroup Institute, a European consultancy firm that he helped to create. He writes regularly for the monthly economics newspaper *L'Expansion*.

5

A l'Attac: A new political identity for the Left?

Comment cela s'appelle-t-il, ce moment où un autre monde devient possible? Cela a un très beau nom, camarades. Cela s'appelle l'aurore.

Ramonet, 2002: 21

French activists have been at the forefront of a movement of opposition to globalization that has mobilized across a national and international stage. Defined as *altermondialisme*[1] or alterglobalism by its participants, this movement encompasses a vast and heterogenous network of groupings, parties and ideological currents within different countries, which together seek to challenge the negative effects of economic integration and to create an alternative world order rooted in democratic and humanist ideals. At a time of crisis on the Left, with a decline of traditional ideologies and belief systems, the alterglobalist movement seems to provide a new project of social transformation that takes on the capitalist system as a whole in its new and globalized variant. For Michel Wieviorka, this movement has revived a radical potential on the French Left and helped to restore belief in a utopian vision of social change: 'In less than a decade or so, the struggles that challenge neo-liberal globalization have succeeded in imposing their themes and their ideas on public debates . . . and have liquidated arguments about a social void, generalized individualism or the end of "grand narratives" ' (Wieviorka, 2003: 7). In the face of a dominant neo-liberal ideology, French activists have posited a vision of an alternative world order and argued that there is still room for radical change and that 'another world is possible'. For some, this movement offers the possibility of ideological renewal at a time of crisis, based on a profoundly internationalist vision and it acts as 'the harbinger of a renewal of the Left and a reconfiguration of the French political landscape' (Ancelovici, 2002: 49).

This chapter examines the role of the Association for a taxation of financial transactions in support of citizens (Attac),[2] the most influential, best organized and politically significant French association within a wider movement of opposition to globalization. Described as 'the single most successful movement against neo-liberal globalisation',[3] Attac helped to define the very terms of *altermondialisme* both in France and across an international stage. Created in 1998, Attac was marked, from the outset, by spectacular popular success and it mobilized some 30,000 followers in France at the height of its influence and spawned a network of over 40 branches in Europe and across the world. Originally created to campaign for the introduction of a tax on international financial transactions (Tobin tax), Attac has since become a broad platform for anti-neo-liberal opposition, gaining support from intellectuals, trade unions, ordinary citizens and parties on the Left and Far Left. It acted as a key player in an international movement and was the driving force behind the creation of the World Social Forum that met in its most recent chapter in Dakar, Senegal in February 2011 and mobilized some 75,000 participants from 132 different countries. Similarly, it has played a major role in international counterdemonstrations over the past 20 years that have challenged the power of the G8, the International Monetary Fund, the G20 and the World Trade Organization. Since the 2008 economic crisis, in a context of widespread disillusionment with neo-liberal economics, many of the themes on which Attac campaigned for many years, have been recuperated by mainstream political leaders at international level. Once a lone voice in its campaign for the Tobin tax, this proposal has now received the backing of political leaders across the world. On 8 March 2011 notably, the European Parliament voted overwhelmingly in favour of introducing such a tax within the European Union.

The chapter explores both the political and ideological potential and limitations of Attac's project for an alternative world order. On the one hand, Attac helped to construct a new form of identity for the French Left based on a vision of international solidarity that bridged national frontiers and embraced the interests of humanity as a whole. Attac appealed for a democratic resurgence in which citizens of the world would rise up against the destructive power of capitalism, reclaim democratic freedoms and lay the foundations for a new world society. It sought to challenge globalization not by retreating behind national frontiers, but by transcending those very frontiers, reaching out towards others and helping to create new forms of solidarity across an international stage. Its political vision was grounded in a belief in the basic and inalienable rights of all human beings, the irreducible solidarity of mankind and the power of ordinary people to change the world. On the other hand, Attac was constrained by a French republican culture from which it drew its main political and ideological inspiration. Its founders envisaged Attac as a French association that would affirm nationally defined democratic and humanist principles elsewhere in the world and its co-founder, Bernard Cassen described it as 'a French internationalist organisation and not an international NGO' (non-governmental organization)[4] (cited by Wintrebrau, 2007: 50). Attac did not present a new conception of political action but rather, it reaffirmed ideas and practices that were rooted in French tradition, reactivating these in a context of globalization. If it called for an alternative world order, a brave new dawn, this was one shaped according to nationally defined values and principles. Attac seemed to embrace a profoundly internationalist vision of change, yet its project for an alternative world order was grounded in all the symbols, traditions and principles of French republican culture.

Rise and fall

Recent accounts of Attac portray an association that is facing terminal decline and that has lost its political momentum, its levels of popular support and its capacity to exert an influence in political life. Launched on a tide of popular support and promising that ordinary citizens had the power to change the world, Attac now seemed to have exhausted its utopian impetus. It became commonplace in the French media to speak of a movement in 'deep crisis' that was undergoing a phase of 'depression' and that was no longer capable of mobilizing mass popular support (Zappi, 2006; Vidal, 2006). Academics, such as the French political scientist Eddy Fougier, shared this bleak prognosis and suggested that Attac, which had once occupied the centre stage of French political life, had been reduced to a state of 'powerlessness and marginalization' (Fougier, 2008b). Even former leaders of the association were of the same opinion and criticized a movement that had become politically irrelevant and ideologically defunct. Hence, Bernard Cassen, Attac's co-founder and first president who went on to join a rival association, Mémoire des luttes, remarked that 'alterglobalism is finished with' and that the Left needed to look for other political models. For him, Attac was a spent force ('there is no project that can possibly oppose a systemic neo-liberal model') and it was time to move on to a new phase of post-alterglobalism (cited by Mayer, 2008). Similarly, Jacques Nikonoff, Attac's second president (2002–2006) who left to set up the association, Mouvement politique d'éducation populaire, wrote a newspaper article in August 2009 that described an 'alterglobalism in decline' and he criticized what he saw as a divided, disorienated and politically irrelevant movement. He argued that the main weakness of this movement was its failure to build consensus in relation to the political measures needed to bring about concrete changes in public policy (Nikonoff, 2009).

Attac's apparent fall from grace can be situated in relation to the events of 2006, when the association became embroiled in a bitter scandal linked to the alleged rigging of internal election results. It was revealed in June 2006 that the results of an election to renew the association's national council that had taken place earlier that month, had been falsified in order to give a majority to Attac's incumbent leaders.[5] As a result of this scandal, confirmed by an independent enquiry, Attac's president, Jacques Nikonoff, was forced to resign and four other members of the association's leadership subsequently withdrew. It was in the aftermath of the 2006 events that the association began to run into serious deficit and these financial difficulties were compounded by its declining membership. Once a mass-based organization, Attac lost a third of its members after 2006 and its membership went from 30,000 members at the height of its influence in 2003, to 12,500 in 2007. Its membership levels in 2010 stood at 9,500 members. In reality, this scandal merely brought into the open, tensions which had been bubbling beneath the surface for many years and Attac's leadership, since 2003, had been characterized by 'violent conflicts' over the association's political role and its relationship with the parties (Wintrebrau, 2007: 7). On the one hand, Attac's president and his allies (Jacques Nikonoff, Bernard Cassen and Michèle Dessenne) who held the reins of power, favoured a strong, centralized and disciplined structure and sought to build links with parties and with government. They tended to mistrust the influence of trade unions and the Far Left within the association and rejected all forms of political militancy. Cassen who wielded extensive personal control over Attac and whose ideas helped to determine Attac's political line, sought to transform Attac from an oppositional movement into an established political force. His successor, Nikonoff, who like Cassen was characterized by his autocratic style of leadership, shared a similar vision, seeking to establish for Attac a forceful presence in mainstream politics. On the other hand, some leaders, including Attac's three vice-presidents (Susan George, Gus Massiah and François Dufour), favoured grassroots participation, pluralist representation, direct action, political autonomy and refused to consider any links with mainstream parties. This latter group became increasingly critical of what they saw as a centralized leadership which was imposing its own political views and eliminating differences of opinion within the association. In an open letter written by the three vice-presidents on 7 July 2005 and addressed to all Attac's members, they criticized the 'authoritarian attitudes' of a leadership which saw itself as the 'guardian of truth' and that sought to suppress all countervailing ideas (cited by ibid., 244).

Yet, if Attac's decline seemed swift and dramatic, this was also a reflection of the heights it had once scaled within French public life, the remarkable extent of its popular support and its widespread international following. Attac has been recognized as 'the most public face of the anti-globalization movement in much of Europe' and is undoubtedly the most politically significant and best organized of all recent anti-neo-liberal movements (Klein, 2002: 194–5). Attac has its origins in the context of political and social radicalism that prevailed in France after 1995 with, on the one hand, a renewal of protest by movements and trade unions and on the other, by a widespread political engagement of left-wing intellectuals in opposition to neo-liberalism. Attac was launched in 1998 by journalists close to *Le Monde diplomatique*, a newspaper that had been at the very centre of the intellectual backlash against neo-liberalism. In December 1997, Ignacio Ramonet, then chief editor of this newspaper, published an editorial ('Disarming the Markets') in which he denounced conditions of economic decline and a democratic deficit created by globalization: 'The globalisation of financial capital is placing populations in a state of generalized insecurity' (Ramonet, 1997). He called for a new tax to be imposed on international financial transactions (the Tobin tax, named after the American economist and Nobel Prize winner, James Tobin), which could be used to regulate international economic exchanges and to promote social and human interests. In the weeks that followed, *Le Monde diplomatique* was inundated by thousands of letters of support from associations, trade unions and ordinary citizens, all of whom favoured the idea of setting up a new organization to press for the introduction of a Tobin tax. In fact, it was the scale of this response within public opinion that prompted the newspaper's editors to take steps to set up a new association. In the words of Bernard Cassen, the newspaper's director general (and subsequently president of Attac): 'We were completely taken aback by the scale of the response to this appeal which surpassed all our expectations'.[6] On 16 March 1998, *Le Monde diplomatique*'s editors organized a first meeting to bring together a diverse range of leftist political groupings, trade unions, publishing houses and intellectual clubs, with the aim of launching a new political movement. Its objective was not only to call for the introduction of the Tobin tax, but to engage in a broad political struggle against 'all aspects of domination by the financial sphere' (Attac, 2002a: 11). Within six weeks, the organizations involved had agreed on the statutes, a political programme and a provisional leadership for the new grouping. Attac was born.

From the outset, Attac's origins within a major newspaper of the intellectual Left was critical in defining the character of this association and the role it would later assume within political life. Unlike other protest groupings that were formed within the fragmented networks of left-wing militancy and populated by movement activists, political dissidents and trade unionists, Attac emerged within the higher echelons of the left-wing press and was backed by some of France's leading intellectual elites. This was a unique experiment whose founders sought to convert abstract discourse into political practice, to translate theoretical ideas into social change on the ground and to transform general principles into a model of political action, capable of mobilizing a mass following behind it. *Le Monde diplomatique* had established a solid reputation for high-brow criticism and debate on international affairs and for many years had acted as a mouthpiece for the left-wing intelligentsia.[7] This was 'a newspaper produced by and for an elite' and many of France's leading left-wing thinkers had, at various points, filled the column inches of this newspaper including figures such as Pierre Bourdieu, Cornelius Castoriadis, Noam Chomsky and Gisèle Halimi (Szcepanski-Huillery, 2003: 3). Although it only acquired full independent status from its sister newspaper *Le Monde* in 1996, it had for many years pursued an anti-liberal and anti-American stance, publishing articles on the dangers of neo-liberalism, American cultural imperialism and the ravages of free market economics. Alongside other newspapers and journals, it participated in the wave of intellectual criticism of this period, forming part of a 'committed press' ('presse engagée') which attacked the *pensée unique* and challenged the foundations on which neo-liberalism was based. When Attac was created, it therefore benefited from the solid intellectual foundations provided by a respectable newspaper. It did not need to carve out a new political or intellectual space for itself, as the arguments it presented had for many years been elaborated on the pages of *Le Monde diplomatique* and had already found a solid resonance within a section of public opinion. Pierre Tartakowsky, former secretary general of Attac explained this point clearly: 'What distinguishes Attac is that an established intellectual current gave rise to a new association. There are few cases in France where a newspaper actually produces an association and it is usually the other way around. The major historical precedent is of course the Dreyfus Affair and the creation of the Human Rights League from Emile Zola's appeal in the pages of *L'Aurore*'.[8] Attac began life with a concrete ideological framework, becoming an incarnation in organizational form of the political views expressed in *Le Monde diplomatique*: 'Without *Le Monde diplomatique*, there would never have been Attac' (Cassen cited by Losson & Quinio, 2002: 131). Far from being a fledgling organization struggling to find its feet in a hostile political world, we can see that Attac already held the keys to the French political establishment: those of intellectual status and influence. It stood apart from other protest groupings in France and elsewhere, in terms of its social origins, its cultural capital and the intellectual resources it had at its disposal.

Attac had the advantage of being able to draw on an existing pool of leftist activists and intellectuals who were active in different political and social struggles at that time. Many of the organizations that responded to *Le Monde diplomatique*'s original appeal and that rallied behind Attac had been at the forefront of political militancy in the period since 1995 and had mobilized to defend the rights of public sector workers, the unemployed, homeless and undocumented immigrants or to oppose privatization and economic liberalization. The first meeting organized by *Le Monde diplomatique* on 16 March 1998 was intended to bring together all those interested in creating a new association. Alongside journalists from *Le Monde diplomatique*, who originally launched the grouping, its founding members included representatives from trade unions (SUD-PTT, FSU, Groupe des dix, branches of the CGT and CFDT), protest groupings (AC!, DAL, DD!!, CADAC, Confédération paysanne), the left-wing press (*Charlie Hebdo, Politis, Témoignage Chrétien, Alternatives économiques*), and some public intellectual figures who were included for symbolic purposes (e.g. René Dumont, Susan George, Gisèle Halimi, Manu Chao). In fact, part of the strength of the new grouping stemmed from its role as a point of convergence for existing networks of militancy, bringing together activists from different political factions and organizations and mobilizing them around a single unifying objective. Pierre Tartakowsky remarked in this respect: 'All these people around the same table with a desire to work together. This shouldn't be underestimated because these people have never worked together before and there is no precedent like this in France'.[9]

The outcome of this meeting was an agreement among those present to lay the foundations for a new association that would 'promote and pursue actions of all forms in order to allow citizens to reclaim the power which the financial sphere exercises on all aspects of political, economic, social and cultural life throughout the world' (Attac 2002a: 162). At a constitutive general assembly held in June 1998, the statutes of the association were accepted and four structures were put in place: a College of Founders composed of the founding members of the association; a bureau and administrative council which would assume executive power; a general assembly representing all members of the association; and a scientific council responsible for research and publication. Bernard Cassen, director general of *Le Monde diplomatique* was to become Attac's first president and act as the chief architect of the new association.

Those who would go on to become leaders within Attac were typically dissident political figures, acting on the fringes of the Left, who had been marginalized by more mainstream organizations and who discovered in Attac a channel for their political views and an alternative institutional platform. For instance, Christophe Aguiton who became head of Attac's international section, had been expelled from the trade union confederation, the CFDT, in 1988 and went on to form SUD-PTT and later AC!. Pierre Khalfa, founding member of Attac and part of its national bureau, had also been expelled from the CFDT, in the late 1980s and was active within the new trade unionism, representing the Groupe des dix. Annie Pourre, also a founding member of Attac, had been expelled from the Communist Party in 1982 and went on to set up the protest grouping Droits devant!! Even Bernard Cassen, undeniably the most influential figure behind the new association, was director of a newspaper that until the 1990s, remained on the fringes of the press establishment and was overshadowed by its sister newspaper, *Le Monde*. These leaders had experience as activists and members of a diversity of parties across the Left. Bernard Cassen had close ties with the Mouvement démocratique des citoyens (MDC) and its leader Jean-Pierre Chevènement and he was a member of his ministerial cabinet during the 1980s. Christophe Aguiton was a long-standing member of the Trotskyist party, the Ligue Communiste révolutionnaire, while Pierre Khalfa had links with the Green Party. Pierre Tartakowsky was a member of the Communist Party until he left in 1991 and is a representative of the Communist-led trade union UGICT-CGT. Jacques Nikonoff, Attac's subsequent president (2003–2006) was a member of the Communist Party and was on that party's national council until October 2001.

Yet, what distinguished Attac from many other protest groupings formed during this period, was that it had the backing of large numbers of intellectuals drawn from university, press and political circles. At the time when Attac was created, many leftist intellectuals in France were beginning to call for new forms of opposition to economic globalization that would challenge its theoretical and discursive basis. Among the most prominent and outspoken of these was Pierre Bourdieu who called for a new synergy between intellectuals and political activists in which the fruits of research would be placed at the service of political causes: 'It is necessary to invent new forms of communication between researchers and activists, or a new division of labour between them' (Bourdieu, 1998: 63). Attac seemed to fulfil this ideal as an association that integrated the intellectual and political dimensions of activism within French society and which mobilized them for purposes of challenging neo-liberal globalization. Attac was characterized, from the very beginning, by the presence of large numbers of intellectuals within its ranks. Alongside journalists from *Le Monde diplomatique* who launched the association, its founding members included left-wing newspapers and journals, research groupings and publishing houses. All of Attac's leaders had previously published books on key political or social issues (Cassen, Tartakowsky, Aguiton, Nikonoff, Coutrot) or were public intellectuals of international renown (Attac's first vice-president, Susan George). Many had close ties with the university sector, in their capacity as researchers or lecturers (e.g. Cassen helped to found the 'open faculty' of Vincennes, now the University of Paris VIII). Attac's subsequent president,

Nikonoff, had an intellectual and political profile typical of many of Attac's leaders. Of working-class background and employed for many years as a welder, Nikonoff was a key figure within the Communist-led trade union, the CGT, before becoming a professor of economics at the University of Paris VIII and the author of three books. Similarly, Thomas Coutrot, co-president of Attac since 2009 (with Aurélie Trouvé), is a left-wing economist who works in the Ministry for Work and Employment. He was a member of the Communist Revolutionary League until 1988, a social movement activist and is the author of four books.

Within Attac, intellectuals assumed an active and decisive role, shaping the political orientation and rationale of the association. Alongside the intellectual figures who joined Attac's leadership, intellectuals were also recruited to the association's 'scientific council', a structure set up specifically to pursue research and publication within Attac. The original 20 odd members of the scientific council were all left-wing economists who were committed to using the science of economics for political ends and were opposed to what they saw as a prevailing neo-liberal orthodoxy. Some had been involved in earlier initiatives such as the 'Appeal against the *pensée unique*' launched by 300 economists in the wake of the 1995 strikes. François Chesnais was one of the economists who came to Attac from this appeal: 'Attac was born in a climate of political and intellectual radicalism after 1995 and was nourished by a growing frustration with Lionel Jospin and the drift towards liberalism within the Plural Left government. I had published regularly in *Le Monde diplomatique* and was naturally one of the *intellectual workers* solicited by Bernard Cassen at the beginning of August 1998. I was asked to contribute to various economic studies concerning matters such as international financial markets and the Asian crisis. Along with other members of the scientific council, I had been involved in the "Appeal against the *pensée unique*" which met regularly in 1996 and 1997 and brought together economists concerned with the relationship between economic matters internationally and the functioning of democratic societies'.[10]

The strong presence of economists within Attac reflected the overall orientation of this association in which the science of economics was used to contest a prevailing neo-liberal model and to explore alternative possibilities. The first president of the scientific council was René Passet, professor of economics, later succeeded by Dominique Pilhon, also an economist. Yet Attac's leadership made concerted efforts to attract researchers from a more diverse range of subject disciplines and the current composition of the scientific council includes political scientists, sociologists, legal experts, alongside a core of economists. A letter written by Bernard Cassen and Dominique

Pilhon on 29 April 2002 to Attac's leadership emphasized the need to widen the composition of the scientific council:

> The enlargement of the scientific council to disciplines other than economics has become a priority in order to allow Attac to produce information in the new domains opened up by the struggle against diverse aspects of liberal globalization and in the formulation of alternatives to serve in political debate and struggles. (cited by Wintrebrau, 2007: 83)

The presence within its ranks of large numbers of intellectuals, coming from different backgrounds, gave Attac a unique power and authority within French political life: here was an association whose propositions were backed by a substantial body of evidence, by rigorous analysis and by the work of established and respected scholars. In putting forward its political demands, it could lay claim to all the objectivity and impartiality offered by science in itself. Although drawing on a left-wing agenda of republican and socialist inspiration, Attac was able to couch its arguments in a language of pure scientific rationality. French political tradition has always accorded a special status to intellectuals in the public sphere, which has no direct equivalent in other European countries. In fact, republican tradition was predicated

> on a generalized belief that the possession of a certain level of professional authority in a given cultural field was in itself a sufficient qualification for public intervention in the political world. This was and indeed remains, one of the distinctive features of the structure of political life in France. (Hazareesingh, 1994: 52)

Formed within intellectual circles close to *Le Monde diplomatique* and supported by public intellectuals from across the French Left, Attac was elevated to a privileged status, denied to other protest groupings that were formed during the same period. We will see that the preponderance of intellectuals within Attac helped to give this association a unique purpose, that of educating French citizens in order to generate a widespread mobilization against neo-liberalism.

An educated citizenry

Whereas other leftist groupings formed in France during the same period were often inspired by Marxist or Trotskyst ideas, Attac drew its ideological and political resources from French republican culture. It can be situated within an enduring leftist republican project that seeks to reaffirm a historical legacy of democratic principles in the present and in particular, in response to the new challenges posed by contemporary globalization. While Attac looked outwards across an international stage and sought to construct an alternative world order, it also turned inwards towards national political culture and tradition. Attac's leaders identified themselves with an Enlightenment tradition that emphasized the importance of knowledge, education and reason in the public sphere. Such ideals in the aftermath of the French Revolution were bound up with a broader republican culture which saw education as a means to overcome the ignorance and servility of the past, to inculcate moral and social values and to help create good citizens. Attac's leaders defined its central mission as that of 'popular education', to diffuse knowledge in the public sphere, to contribute to public discussion and debate and to help create an educated citizenry.[11] They located its historical antecedents in the republican education leagues of the mid-nineteenth century and in particular, the Ligue d'enseignement created in 1866. In the face of globalization, Attac's aim was to revive the educational role of these leagues by creating a 'popular education directed toward action' in which knowledge would become once again a tool of democratic change, social progress and human emancipation (Attac, 2002a: 7).

Whereas during the Third Republic, education was intended as a means to challenge popular prejudices linked to religious dogma, Attac reactivated this principle in order to confront what it saw as a new form of indoctrination, that of neo-liberal ideology. For Attac's leaders, neo-liberalism was above all, an ideological apparatus, a system of thought which had insidiously taken hold within European societies and which was seen to suppress free and critical thought. Bernard Cassen described this as a 'liberal virus', which had infected people's minds and prevented them from thinking clearly: 'Our heads have been stuffed with neoliberalism, its virus is in our brain cells, and we need to detoxify them. We have to be able to start thinking freely again' (Cassen 2003: 56). This neo-liberal doctrine, Attac's leaders argued, was backed by powerful international organizations and national governments and had therefore been elevated to a hegemonic position within public debate. It had assumed the guise of a dominant ideology or *pensée unique* that was rarely open to question or debate. For Attac's leaders, this dogma was the principal cause of France's social ills, as it undermined social progress and dragged society backwards towards premodern conditions. In the absence of free and rational thought which was the engine of modernity, such conditions had been allowed to re-emerge in the contemporary period. Attac's fundamental aim was therefore to 'decontaminate people's minds', to dispel ignorance, to stimulate critical thought and thereby to further the goals of democracy (Cassen, 2003: 56). It set out to reassert a conception of democracy grounded in human reason, in which education became a means to affirm democratic and humanist ideals and to help emancipate humanity itself.

For Attac, it was the communication of ideas, arguments and information which was paramount in the struggle against economic globalization and much of its energies were devoted to this task. The importance of intellectual production is revealed by the place of the scientific council, a unique structure within Attac, whose role is to 'ensure the scientific rigour of documents produced and diffused by Attac'.[12] Grouping together researchers, public intellectuals and activists, this is a veritable powerhouse, producing a prolific output of reports, analyses and scientific evidence that gives Attac the intellectual authority it needs to intervene in the public domain. Within the scientific council there are currently 150 researchers within 20 working groups, which focus on different themes such as international financial institutions, privatization, health, pensions, economic democracy and multinational corporations. Each group produces a working report, which is presented to the scientific council as a whole and discussed by its members. This may then form the basis of a public campaign or concrete proposal put forward by Attac. René Passet, former president of the scientific council, defined its role in the following terms:

> Its objective is to produce information which is accessible to everyone, in all forms, on aspects of the international financial sphere and to communicate it mainly to local committees and members of the association. In addition, the council has the task of formulating concrete proposals which can form the basis of a public campaign. (Passet, 2000: 1)

On the one hand, it produces information of an accessible and informative nature that is aimed towards the association's members and its network of local committees. On the other, it produces specialized documentation that can be used to formulate proposals or to lobby government via Attac's representatives in parliament. For instance, the scientific council has produced reports on the Tobin tax, on the 35-hour working week, pensions and genetically modified goods which have provided the basis for a formal discussion within the French National Assembly.

The existence of a scientific council responsible exclusively for research and publication, sets Attac apart from most other left-wing protest groupings in France or elsewhere. Unlike these, Attac's actions in the public sphere are the result of careful and studied preparation, of exhaustive research and analysis and of considered reflection and debate. Attac had the distinct advantage of having a critical discourse and a weight of scientific evidence at its disposal and this gave it a special legitimacy in the public sphere and in its dealings with national government. Yet, Attac's research output is not intended for narrow intellectual elites and is aimed at the general public and as wide an audience as possible. Attac's leaders argue that if ordinary citizens are to make informed choices and to participate fully in political decisions, then they need to be able to decodify and appropriate a discourse of neo-liberalism for themselves. Attac therefore seeks to popularize often complex and abstract economic processes and to encourage a critical awareness among citizens who are often disorientated by the logic of neo-liberalism. Intellectual activity is conceived as having a broad civic purpose and is directed towards the goals of social and political transformation.

To this end, Attac achieves an extraordinary publishing output, producing books, reports, newsletters, information sheets and also organizing public events such as seminars, workshops and conferences. The publishing house linked to Attac, Mille et Une Nuits, produces cheap, pocket-sized books intended to educate a general public about key international developments. It produces a monthly newsletter, *Lignes d'Attac* and an electronic information sheet, *Le grain de sable*. At the same time, Attac is at the centre of a vast communication network that links, via the Internet, members in France and supporters scattered across the world. The Internet plays a crucial role within Attac, fulfilling its mission to diffuse information, inform public opinion and create a 'virtual community' linking all those interested in 'the struggle against the dictatorship of financial markets' (Trautmann, 2001: 10).

Within Attac, activists are expected to be fully informed about the political issues in which they are engaged and collective action is always to be preceded by reflection and debate. Members are encouraged to educate themselves, to pursue their 'thirst for learning' by studying the documents, analyses and reports produced by the association (Attac, 2002a: 33). According to Bernard Cassen 'militants must be well-informed, intellectually equipped for action. We don't want people turning out on demonstrations without really knowing why' (Cassen, 2003: 45). Indeed, for collective action to succeed, 'the necessity for rigour must be permanent' (Attac, 2002a: 110). Attac sees itself as a type of 'popular university' informing and educating all those who belong to the association and an important part of its activity is directed towards this end: it organizes 'summer schools' on different themes; it produces internal reports and explanatory notes; it encourages local committees to organize seminars and conferences.

Attac's role has been described as one of 'counter-expertise' in that it draws on its own intellectual resources to provide an alternative critical viewpoint that contests an 'official expertise' of government. It aims to develop a critical discourse within the public domain, to create a language of opposition and to contest a hegemonic vision of the economy. The notion of counter-expertise which has been adopted by some recent social movements and protest groupings in France can be defined as 'the production of knowledge in relation to an issue or cause . . . which acts as a critique of a "dominant system of thought" (notably that formulated by political power) and as an alternative to this' (Crettiez & Sommier, 2002: 351). For social movement activists, knowledge and expertise can act as critical instruments of social and political contestation and a means of confronting a monopoly on public information held by official experts and government representatives. In the face of globalization, Attac revived a republican tradition that laid emphasis on education as a force for social progress and appropriated this tradition for its own purposes. It challenged neo-liberalism as a form of biased thinking that had been imposed on the French people and which prevented them from thinking freely. Through 'popular education', Attac would emancipate the people from their prejudices and misconceptions and help to lay the foundations for an alternative world order.

Un autre monde

At a time of crisis on the Left with a decline of grand narratives, Attac helped to construct a new language of opposition, a project of social transformation and an alternative political identity which were attuned to a modified context of neo-liberal globalization. Its political vision was profoundly internationalist in character, aspiring towards a new world order that would embrace the interests of humanity as a whole. Its project can be described as a 'post-Marxist alternative to liberalism' that creates a different conceptual framework for understanding the world and its problems (Ancelovici, 2002: 429). Here 'globalization' took the place of 'capitalism' as the overarching structural context for situating social and political relations in the contemporary world. Instead of the State as a unified target for opposition, Attac challenged a diverse array of supranational institutions stretched across an international stage. In the place of the 'employers' or 'bourgeoisie' of Marxist analysis, Attac opposed multinational corporations acting outside the level of nation and society. Instead of references to 'exploitation' within a system of production, Attac signalled new forms of social domination produced by distant and unseen economic forces. Attac did not call for a class resurgence but for a new international solidarity that would bring together citizens across the world in order to defend fundamental rights and to challenge the destructive power of financial capitalism. It helped to provide a conception of political identity in which the fate of French citizens was inextricably bound up with that of other people in different countries across the world, in a vision that broke with traditional relationships based on class or nation. Attac believed that it was by overcoming their differences, by bridging national frontiers and by affirming their common humanity that people could help to create a different world.

For Attac, globalization is a dominant conceptual framework, taking the place of capitalism as the structural context for situating leftist opposition and articulating social grievances in France today. They see this as a 'second capitalist revolution', a qualitatively new phase in the development of capitalist societies that breaks with existing modes of social and political organization (Ramonet, 2002: 13). Attac sets out to provide the 'mediating interpretive tools' to help us understand this transformed social and political world and to allow us to 'recognize the enemy clearly' (Starr, 2000: 2). For Attac, globalization constitutes a systemic change that has its origins in the fall of the Berlin Wall, the break-up of the Soviet Union and the shift to neo-liberal economics under the leadership of Ronald Reagan in the United States and Margaret Thatcher in Britain. The rise of a hegemonic neo-liberal model, during this period, is seen to have transformed the nature of social and political relations and to have precipitated a distinctly new phase in modern capitalism. The salient feature of this new phase is that private capital has acquired a freedom, legitimacy and authority that is without precedent in the history of modern capitalist societies. Capital has broken free of its ties with a given system of production and is no longer subordinate to the authority of the nation state: 'The Earth is experiencing a new phase of conquest, like during the era of exploration or of colonisation' (Ramonet, 2002: 13). Globalization is seen as much more than a simple phase of economic restructuring – this is a 'historical cycle', a grand political scheme, a distinctive ideological vision that has caused profound changes to the structure, cohesion and functioning of contemporary societies (ibid., 17). In this new international order, the fate of French workers is connected with that of peasant farmers in Mexico, factory workers in China or the unemployed in the United States. Their grievances cannot be considered separately at the national level, as they have all fallen victim to an international structure of power which increasingly determines the conditions of everyday lives.

Attac presents us with a modified vision of political relations and state power compared with traditional Marxist analysis. Whereas Marxism challenged the State as the representative of 'dominant bourgeois interests' in society, Attac confronts multiple and competing sites of power that lie beyond the borders of the nation state. It points to a decentered and deterritorialized system in which power is dispersed across an international stage and vested in unelected independent structures that have no democratic accountability and that are located beyond the reach of citizens (such as the World Bank, International Monetary Fund, World Trade Organization). These institutions serve the needs of private corporations imposing the 'right to free trade' above all other democratic and social rights. In the face of this perceived attack on democracy and society, Attac calls for a reaffirmation of state power – the state alone is seen as capable of resisting and constraining rampant market forces and of protecting democratic values and a notion of the common good. Bernard Cassen, saw the state as a rampart against neo-liberalism and he called for a return to the principles of national sovereignty and state economic control, based on the example of some leftist governments in Latin America.[13]

In its political campaigns, Attac targets international institutions as the new site for leftist opposition and struggle. A key moment in the rise of alterglobalism in France and 'a founding moment' in the emergence of Attac itself, was the mobilization against the Multilateral Agreement on Investment (MAI) round of international negotiations which began in December 1997 (Mouchard, 2005: 321). Protestors who took part in this movement challenged the way in which the MAI negotiations – in which France was directly involved – were being conducted in secret by distant international elites, far away from the glare of public scrutiny. Under the terms of these international agreements, private corporations would have the power to sue national governments and bring them before international tribunals, where their laws were seen to interfere with the principle of free trade. It was in reaction to the seemingly undemocratic and secretive nature of these talks that a widespread mobilization took place in France, involving film-makers, leftist activists, trade unionists and intellectuals. As a result of this opposition, France pulled out of the talks in October 1998 and Canada quickly followed suit, leading to the collapse of the MAI. For many protestors, this was 'a history of victory' giving renewed legitimacy and vigour to a nascent alterglobalist movement (ibid.).

For Attac, globalization has redefined social relationships, so that the dominant forces are no longer the 'employers' of the Marxist scheme, but corporations or 'footloose' capital that act outside and beyond society itself. Here any notion of a cohesive society in which individuals are bound to one another in relations of social class has collapsed. The power of corporations is seen to stem precisely from their freedom from social and national ties, their ability to act outside social norms and to operate above national laws and regulations. In a world driven by transnational market forces, capital is dissociated from its link with social class and becomes an anonymized and free-wheeling entity, with a shift 'from human to non-human ownership' (Starr, 2000: 26).

Attac conjures up an image of an atomized and fragmented society in which all threads of social cohesion and all civic bonds have been dissolved: 'In its current neo-liberal phase, capitalism transforms everything it touches into merchandise; it disintegrates old forms of community and disperses human lives into a "solitary crowd" ' (Ramonet, 2002: 17). The relations of production that characterized the Marxist scheme have unraveled and citizens now stand alone in the face of powerful and destructive market forces. A significant part of Attac's activism is centered on challenging the actions of multinational corporations and signaling their destructive social effects. For instance, Attac was the first association to support a boycott against products made by the French multinational Danone, where company bosses decided in March 2001 to close two of its production sites and thereby make 570 employees redundant in France. Attac denounced what it saw as a ruthless profit-making logic that increasingly seemed to determine social relations in a globalized world. The company bosses had reached this decision not because the company was experiencing losses – it was in fact experiencing healthy levels of growth – but because it predicted a future downturn in the economy: 'The Danone affair and the closure of a production site not because it was losing money but because it wasn't gaining enough, shows that capitalism assumes a new guise in the context of financial globalization' (Attac, 2002a: 132). At a time of globalization, Attac argues, profit is increasingly separated from the act of production itself and from the world of work and is determined by a speculative logic alone in which employees are treated as one disposable economic instrument among others.

Attac seeks to expose and lay bare the mechanisms of social inequality produced by globalization and to make explicit the causal relationships that link global economic processes with inequalities in the everyday. How was the fate of say, French rail workers or factory employees determined by the actions of multinational corporations? To what extent are the lives of the unemployed conditioned by the decisions made by supranational institutions? For Attac, the expansion of financial capital across an international stage has exacerbated inequalities on an unprecedented scale: 'Inequalities have become one of the key structural characteristics of the era of globalization' (Ramonet, 2002: 19). However, Attac's conception differs markedly from the Marxist notion of exploitation and globalization is seen to have produced new forms of social domination and control that have their origins both within and outside the workplace. The 'new inequalities' are no longer a product of class relationships within a given system of production, but stem from the distant, subtle and complex forms of capitalist power which prevail within all spheres of human existence. Attac's discourse is characterized by a realignment of the terms of Marxist analysis whereby grievances are re-interpreted and connected with a new system of meaning, in a systematic alternation 'that radically reconstitutes for participants what is going on' (Snow, 1997: 219).

Attac sees itself as the pioneer of a 'new internationalism' that mobilizes citizens across the world in a democratic movement that seeks to 'reclaim together the future of our world' (Attac, 2002a: 24). Its aim is to realign the grievances of French citizens with those of other people across the world in a way that seems to challenge a strictly Marxist conception of social class. Attac pursues an ideal of international solidarity rooted in a belief in the inalienable rights of human beings, the fundamental solidarity of all mankind and the primacy of democratic and humanist values. It sees the citizen as an agent of democratic transformation who, by mobilizing with other citizens across the world, can assume the power to change the world. Attac's political action is directed less towards addressing specific grievances at national level than towards challenging sources of inequality or injustice at international level. Hence the revenue accrued from its proposed Tobin tax ('this world solidarity tax') is intended to redistribute wealth in order to provide development aid, to promote education and public health in poorer countries and to foster sustainable forms of development (Attac, 2002a: 10). Much of Attac's political intervention is intended to foster links between citizens and activists across the world and to create new forms of international activism. Hence at the anti-World Trade Organization demonstrations in Seattle in 1999, at the first World Social Forum in Brazil in 2001, at the counterdemonstrations against the G8 summit in Germany in 2007 or at the World Social Forum in Senegal in February 2011, French activists demonstrated side by side with other activists from across the world in order to challenge global financial power.

Yet, if Attac helped to construct an alternative political identity for the Left, one that transcends national frontiers and crosses the divisions of social class, its project is also imbued with all the values and ideals of national political culture. In displacing the terms of Marxist theory, Attac tends to reach instead for the ideological and symbolic resources of French republicanism. It is in relation to the French Republic, its traditions, values and institutional model that Attac articulates its role on an international stage. Attac expresses its goals not in revolutionary Marxist terms, but in relation to core democratic values of equality, solidarity and justice. For Attac, the foundational values of the Republic can provide a blueprint for an alternative world order, one in which the interests of human beings take centre stage. It envisages a society in which democratic and social principles would become the cornerstone of human relationships and determine all other political and economic arrangements in 'a new economy . . . that places the human being at the centre of its preoccupations' (Ramonet, 2002: 21). Attac situates itself in a line of historical continuity with the past, fulfilling an ongoing democratic project that was defined over two centuries ago at the time of the French Revolution: 'Yes, perhaps Attac does represent a turning-point. The demand for justice and equality which, like a groundswell, crosses the history of humanity, re-emerges with us' (ibid., 20). Its aim is to secure a 'new generation of rights' that will democratize all aspects of political, economic and social life and these new rights will include the right to peace, the right to nature, the right to information, the right to childhood and the right to development (ibid., 10).

Attac's purpose is not simply to mobilize the French public, but to create a 'société solidaire' that will unite all citizens of the world and break the chains of global capitalism (Attac, 2002b: 62). Just as in the past, when the Republic saw itself as a force of emancipation destined to liberate humanity from the tyranny of nature, so Attac believes that it is helping to liberate mankind from the 'dictatorship of markets' and to project democratic ideals in order to ensure 'human emancipation from all forms of domination and oppression' (Attac, 2003: 5). It sees itself as a beacon of democratic values, reigniting 'the flame of international contestation' in order to create a 'new space for world representation' (Ramonet, 2002: 20). Such a democratic resurgence is necessary because globalization is seen to attack the very foundations of democracy:

> The power of globalization is such that is forces us to redefine the fundamental concepts on which the political and democratic edifice of the 18th century was based, concepts such as nation state, sovereignty, independence, Republic, democracy, *Etat-providence* and citizenship. (Ibid., 17)

Some of Attac's discourse seems to share the messianic character typical of republican universalism and its ambition is 'to fight across space and time' and create a movement 'in the image of the world we want to construct' (George, 2002: 30). While helping to construct a new political identity that bridges national frontiers and aspires towards a new world order, Attac's project is shaped by nationally defined political values and traditions. If it envisages an alternative order that will break with neo-liberal globalization, this is an order moulded by the principles and ideals of the French Republic.

Political impact

Along with a myriad of other protest groupings formed in France during the late 1990s, Attac set out to challenge the status quo, to produce alternative ideas and to demand radical social change. This was a social movement in the sense that it aimed 'to change society in the name of a generalized belief' and to contest the political establishment at a most fundamental level (Turner 1986: 92). More specifically, Attac formed part of an alterglobalist movement that criticized the economic policies of government, denounced trends towards privatization, questioned market principles and defended social and human rights. Yet, while challenging the political establishment and its practices, Attac succeeded in gaining unique access to that very establishment. What is striking about Attac is its considerable success within mainstream political life in the space of just a few years. Where other protest groups formed at the same time were mostly overlooked by political leaders and marginalized by the parties, Attac quickly acquired a presence for itself within the institutions of government. Moreover, parties publicly embraced Attac and were eager to associate themselves with a group that held intellectual authority and commanded considerable popularity within society. Attac quickly moved, in the words of one journalist, from a stance of 'contre-pouvoir' to one of 'pouvoir' (opposition force to established power): 'In the space of two years of being an opposition force, anti-globalisation protest has practically become a power in itself' (Monnot, 2001a).

Barely a year after the creation of Attac, in June 1999, a group of députés set up an Attac committee in the French National Assembly to forward the demands of that group within parliament. Launched by five deputies from the ruling Plural Left coalition, the committee initially mobilized 60 deputies of which the majority were Socialists (36), Communists (13), with some Green party representatives (4) among others. Having representation in parliament, Attac now had the means to lobby government directly, to make concrete proposals for reform and to press for the introduction of a Tobin tax. Conversely, the deputies belonging to the Attac committee in parliament could now claim a popular legitimacy as mediators of an important civic and democratic cause, as defenders of the common good and of the interests of the people. In the words of one deputy, they were fighting to 'reclaim the political power abandoned to financial markets, to international institutions' (ibid.). Alongside its representation within the National Assembly, committees were also set up within the Senate and European Parliament. In April 2000, an international parliamentary forum was created bringing together 650 deputies from around the world who supported Attac's aims. Yet, as we shall see, many activists were bitterly opposed to this gradual shift into the mainstream political domain and believed that Attac, in doing so, was betraying its fundamental principles and underlying ethos.

At the same time, the French government seemed to be increasingly well-disposed towards Attac and eager to listen to its demands. Where other protest groupings had struggled for political recognition, but failed to make any genuine breakthrough into mainstream politics, Attac was openly embraced by the parties of government. In September 2001, the French Minister for the Economy, Laurent Fabius received a delegation from Attac to discuss the feasibility of introducing a tax on international financial transactions. This meeting, according to Bernard Cassen, marked 'a change in the government's stance' in relation to the Tobin tax and a clear expression of support with the association's aims.[14] This support was later confirmed when the then Prime Minister, Lionel Jospin sent 'a very kind letter' to the leaders of Attac on 18 October 2001, stating: 'the questions raised by your movement are close to the concerns that this government tries to highlight in its international discussions and in most cases with success'. He went on to assert the government's willingness to work closely with Attac, declaring 'the members of my cabinet are of course ready to have a discussion with you' (Monnot, 2001b). One month later, Attac succeeded in the very political aim it had set itself at the time of its creation: on 19 November 2001, the French National Assembly voted in favour of a change in French law to introduce the principle of the Tobin tax (on condition that other European countries made a similar legislative commitment). While this victory (later reversed by the French Senate) was purely symbolic in that the Tobin tax could only effectively operate in a European and international context, it does reveal the willingness of the French political establishment to listen to Attac and to respond to its demands. French politicians have continued to give vocal support to Attac and to express a commitment to its demands. In January 2002, for instance, Bernard Cassen received an invitation to the Elysée palace to meet some of Chirac's advisors. Jean-Pierre Raffarin's right-wing government also supported the World Social Forum, jointly organized by Attac, and three government ministers attended the 2003 forum held in Porto Alegre, Brazil. Again on 14 January 2003, Bernard Cassen met government representatives at Matignon where he requested funding for the European Social Forum to be held in Paris later that year. That Cassen should openly solicit financial support from a government that had vigorously pursued the very neo-liberal policies that Attac opposed, met with a furore among some Attac activists and with criticism in sections of the French press. As we will see, Attac's success in imposing itself as a credible force within mainstream politics has met with forthright resistance and hostility within certain currents of the movement.

In the meantime, Attac was courted by parties on the Left and Right and criticism of globalization had in fact become 'a success on the Left, the Far Left and also on the Right, since even the President of the Republic, Jacques Chirac, now indulges in this' (Monnot, 2001b). Political leaders seemed eager to pander to a rhetoric of alterglobalism and these themes increasingly became *de rigueur* for any party wishing to inspire support among a flagging electorate. Socialist representatives in particular, went to great lengths to line up behind Attac, working in close cooperation with Attac's leaders on areas of policy and on political campaigns. These were 'the new messengers' of Attac, representing its cause and articulating its demands within the corridors of power (Weill, 1999). In fact, the willingness of Socialist representatives to pursue an alliance with Attac led one journalist to remark: 'But what has got into the Socialists who are falling over themselves to get close to the anti-globalists?' (Lebègue, 2002). Some Socialist representatives (Jean-Christophe Cambadélis) went so far as to urge other party members to exercise greater caution and to avoid pandering to the latest political trends. The right-wing French president, Jacques Chirac, suddenly became a champion of the anti-globalization cause on the international stage and his successor, Nicolas Sarkozy has continued to defend the alterglobalist cause, so that one journalist questioned whether, he had in fact become 'Attac's new muse' (Maris, 2009). In his speech to the International Labour Organization in June 2009, Sarkozy declared that the Tobin tax was an excellent idea and he argued that all countries should be obliged to respect 'elementary rules in relation to the environment, the right to work and public health' (ibid.). At the same time, local party sections flocked to join Attac and become official members of this new grouping. In the first two years, 55 parties joined Attac at local level, mainly Communists, Trotskyists and Greens, but with some right-wing parties as well. Local councils, often Communist-led also joined and there were 71 localities within the association by the end of 2002.[15] Two Socialist regional councillors in Brittany even took steps to set up their own Attac committee within the region.

Yet, many activists were fiercely opposed to these growing links with the parties and this continues to be a source of considerable internal conflict within the association. Some activists argued that Attac's agenda was being hijacked by the parties and manipulated for short-term electoral gain (what the French describe as *récupération*). This position was summed up by one activist in the following terms: 'the discrediting of politicians is at the very origin of Attac's development. The more elected representatives there are within the association, the more we risk being discredited as well' (cited by Losson & Quinio, 2002: 141). Activists urged the association to protect its autonomy and freedom of initiative at all costs. It was in response to these growing criticisms, voiced mainly by local activists, that Attac's leaders decided to take decisive action: in July 2000, Attac's administrative council decided to freeze all membership of Attac by political parties (in December 2002, only eight local party sections remained members of Attac). At the same time,

Attac's leaders issued an explicit statement, hoping to reassert its independence in relation to the parties and stem the tide of criticism emerging from local committees: 'Attac produces politics, Attac is interested in politics, but Attac, its national representatives, its leaders – at whatever level – are not influenced by anyone'.[16] In a similar vein, Attac's committees within parliament were renamed as 'coordinations of elected representatives' in order to distinguish them from local Attac committees and Attac's leaders whether national or local were henceforth prohibited from standing in public elections.[17] The quarrel over Attac's relationship within its leadership seemed to intensify after 2003, dividing those who favoured autonomy, grassroots democracy and pluralism, against those who sought to build links with the parties and to transform Attac into an established political force (Wintrebrau, 2007). This issue was raised in the run-up to the 2004 European elections, when a proposal backed by some of Attac's leaders, to put forward alterglobalist candidates in these elections, was bitterly contested by others and was later abandoned. Again during the 2007 election campaign, Attac and other movements on the non-institutional Left failed to agree on a unitary candidate to represent a broad anti-liberal platform. For some, this represented a significant blow for a leftist movement (*gauche de la gauche*) which had been mobilizing for many years and which now seemed incapable of making the transition into the mainstream. The election of Nicolas Sarkozy on a campaign of ultra-liberal reforms, seemed to weaken the legitimacy of Attac and of a wider alterglobalist movement which had built its campaign on popular opposition to neo-liberalism.

But Attac has also exercised a forceful influence within political life, situating itself in relation to national events, presenting new arguments and ideas and shaping the discourse of parties and political leaders. Activists took part in key political campaigns in France from the late 1990s onwards, defending workers' rights, the role of the public sector, state pensions and opposing job redundancies and growing instances of privatization. Activists campaigned against the sinking of the oil tanker *Erika* off the Brittany coast (January 2000); they supported a boycott of Danone products following a threat of massive redundancies at the company (June 2001); they denounced the imprisonment of José Bové (one of Attac's founding members) and opposed the 2003 proposals for pension reform, denouncing this as 'a campaign of disinformation' (Attac, 2003). Attac played a decisive role in the campaign for a 'No' vote in the run up to the 2005 referendum on the European Constitutional Treaty and was the most active non-governmental association within this campaign. The victory of the 'No' vote in this referendum was considered by many in the French press as a political victory for Attac. In the period before the 2007 election campaigns, Attac published a set of 102 proposals (*Le Manifeste altermondialiste*) which was intended to place the question of an alternative to neo-liberalism at the centre of the election campaign. However, faithful to its vocation to remain autonomous from party politics, Attac refused to back any particular candidate and did not declare its support for the anti-liberal candidate, José Bové. Attac also played a central role in opposing Nicolas Sarkozy's 2010 pension reform and together with Fondation Copernic, launched a petition movement ('Voicing Citizen Demands on Pensions') that was backed by parties on the Far Left, the Greens and part of the Socialist Party.

Attac is also a key player on the international stage and forms part of a wider alterglobalist movement that mirrors and opposes the actions of powerful international organizations and multinational corporations. Whenever world business leaders meet, wherever international political summits are held, whenever trade rules are negotiated, Attac participates in counter-demonstrations that challenge and contest the political and symbolic power of those in authority. Thus, an Attac contingent took part in the Seattle anti-World Trade Organization demonstrations in December 1999; it participated in a 'counter-summit' in Göteborg, Sweden in July 2001; demonstrators took part in social protest in Genoa in July 2001 at the time of the G8 summit and again in Barcelona in March 2002 at the time of the European Council summit and Attac was active during the demonstrations against the G8 summit in Germany in 2007. Attac was the main organization behind the creation of the World Social Forum that was set up to challenge the market-led ethos of global elites gathered at the World Economic Forum (held at the same time in Davos, Switzerland). Bernard Cassen, Attac's founder, originally came up with the idea of creating a social forum that would 'make a symbolic rupture with Europe and Davos' and that would be held 'on the same day and the same month of the year' as the Economic Forum as a way of challenging its perceived monopoly on global discussion and debate.[18] While Davos has in the past, played host to business leaders such as Bill Gates of Microsoft, Douglas Dast of Coca-Cola, Philip Condit of Boeing and Hollywood actors such as Richard Gere and Julia Ormond, left-wing intellectuals such as Noam Chomsky, Arundhati Roy and Tariq Ali have addressed the crowds at the World Social Forum. The last social forum was held in Dakar, Senegal in February 2011 and gathered participants from some 132 countries who crowded into seminars and workshops, held marches and demonstrations and tackled the idea that 'another world is possible'.

While Attac once seemed like a lone voice in the wilderness in its campaign for the introduction of a Tobin tax, since the 2008 economic crisis, this has been supported by many political leaders across Europe and the world and has also been embraced by many sections of public opinion. For instance,

Nicolas Sarkozy, anxious to assume a strong denunciatory stance in relation to the crisis, led a campaign for the introduction of such a tax. The demand for an international tax was also supported by other world leaders and at the G20 finance ministers summit in November 2009, Nicolas Sarkozy and Gordon Brown both called for the introduction of a 'global financial transactions tax'. In Britain, the campaign for a 'Robin Hood' tax was launched in February 2010 by a network of charities and non-governmental associations and has been endorsed by economists, politicians and celebrities. Crucially, on 8 March 2011, the European Parliament voted massively in favour of introducing a tax on financial transactions (529 voices in favour and 127 against) and which is intended to generate up to 200 billion euros every year within the European Union alone.

Attac sees itself as part of an international civic movement that pits itself against a tide of economic liberalism and seeks to put the interests of people before those of private enterprise. Yet it is characterized by its moderate and restrained stance in relation to other more radical groupings and it shirks away from the political violence often associated, in the media at least, with alter-globalist protest: 'Attac is seen as a "well-behaved" organization in relation to some of its foreign counterparts' (Monnot, 2001a). Some Attac leaders have sought to project an image of a respectable and disciplined association that can work alongside mainstream parties. For instance, during the demonstrations against the G8 in Genoa in 2001, with an escalation of street violence, Bernard Cassen demanded that Attac withdraw from the demonstrations and was fearful that this might damage the association's reputation. Yet, both the French and Italian Attac contingencies refused to do this and criticized in turn, Cassen's 'stalinist methods' (cited by Wintrebrau, 2007: 190). After 2001, Attac's leaders always sent members of its national council to international events in order to monitor and restrain any potential militancy among Attac members.

Conclusion

Attac's critical role was to construct a new framework for leftist opposition, a project for society and an alternative political identity which were profoundly internationalist in character. In the face of globalization, Attac sought to transcend categories of nation and class, in favour of a conception of international solidarity that bridged national frontiers, crossed social divisions and embraced, in principle at least, the interests of humanity as a whole. It argued that the fate of French citizens was inextricably bound with that of other people across the world, who had all fallen victims to a hegemonic economic order, one that stretched across all four corners of the globe and transformed the conditions of everyday life. Attac set out to create a line of causality between the grievances of French citizens and an overarching and modified structure of power that was located at international level. To confront this new order, Attac argued, French citizens needed to mobilize with others around the world in order to challenge the new sites of power. Here it is the citizen rather than the worker who is viewed as the central agent of social transformation. But he/she is not an isolated individual and is bound to others across the world by virtue of a common humanity and an irreducible set of democratic rights. By acting together, citizens had the power to change the world, to construct an alternative world order and to reclaim 'the power that the financial sphere exerts on all aspects of political, economic, social and cultural life throughout the world.'[19] Attac envisaged an alternative globalization in which the power of financial capitalism would be constrained and in which the interests of people would take precedence over profit motives. In its early years, Attac's political message found a deep-seated resonance within public opinion and it became the single most important association in a wider movement of opposition to globalization at international level. Since the economic crisis of 2008, Attac's demands have also been backed by many political leaders and its proposed Tobin tax has been approved by an overwhelming majority of deputies within the European Parliament.

Yet, if Attac's project was internationalist in character, it carried with it all the values and traditions of national political culture. While Attac looked beyond French national borders and sought to change the world, its political and ideological resources were defined within a strictly national context. It was in relation to the French Republic, its values, traditions and institutional model that Attac defined its mission on a national and international stage. Attac did not seek revolutionary change, but sought to reassert democratic and humanist principles at the centre of the international order. It did not call for a rupture with the past, but sought to fulfill an ongoing democratic project defined over two centuries previously. It did not aim to conquer the state or seize the means of production, but to diffuse democratic values throughout the world. Attac defined its central mission as that of 'popular education', a concept that had its origins in Enlightenment ideas and that was later espoused by the education leagues of the nineteenth century and that saw knowledge, education and reason as tools of citizenship and social progress. Whereas during the Third Republic, education was conceived as a means to dispel the popular prejudices linked to religious dogma, Attac revived this idea in order to confront a new form of prejudicial thinking: neo-liberal ideology. Attac's leaders saw globalization as a form of dogma that impeded free and critical thought and thereby endangered the project of modernity itself. Attac's aim was to diffuse knowledge in the public sphere as a means of overcoming ignorance, furthering citizenship and emancipating the whole of humanity. At a time of globalization, it sought to revive the spirit of the Enlightenment in relation to the new threats to rationalism that seemed to come from beyond France's borders. We will see in the following chapter that in the face of globalization, social movements such as the Confédération paysanne also reached for forms of political symbolism derived from national culture and in particular, those rooted in French peasant traditions.

Notes

1   The term *altermondialisme* was first used by Arnaud Zacharie, the leader of Attac-Belgium in 1999 and was adopted by activists instead of the term 'anti-globalisation' which had been widely used by the press to describe the movement. Activists argued that they were not opposed to globalization and did not seek to destroy international relationships, but to modify their nature, so that greater emphasis was laid on democratic and humanist ideals. In France, the term *altermondialiste* became popular among activists after 2002 and was widely used by the French press during the European Social Forum in Paris in November 2003. The term is also used in other European countries, *movimiento altermundialista* in Spain, *movimento altermondialista* in Italy and *movimento alterglobalização* in Portugal. Its English translation, alterglobalism is rarely used and the term anti-globalization tends to be used instead (Fougier, 2008a). The 'Battle of Seattle' in November 1999 which mobilized thousands of activists across the world in protest against trade negotiations being led by the World Trade Organization is considered as the founding moment of this movement. Yet, some French political scientists have questioned the supposed newness of alterglobalism and suggest that, in the French case, this movement has its origins in well-established political and ideological networks. They suggest that the 'prehistory of alterglobalism' can be located in earlier movements, including the post-1968 libertarian Left, the movement against Third Word debt, anarchism, Christian solidarity networks, peasant militancy, trade unionism and the leftist critical media. (Agrikoliansky et al., 2005: 12).

2   In March 2009, Attac's members approved a new set of statutes and the association's title was changed to 'Association pour la taxation des transactions financières pour l'action citoyenne' (Association for a taxation of international transactions for citizen action).

3   This quotation was made in the 'Programme notes' of the *New Left Review*, introducing Bernard Cassen's article in that issue (*New Left Review*, 19 Jan–Feb 2003).

4   During the period when Attac's political role was being discussed, Bernard Cassen wrote an article in *Le Monde diplomatique* (March 1998) entitled 'The Nation against Nationalism' in which he emphasized the importance

of reasserting the nation as a rampart against economic globalization: 'The nation is still a new idea: a space for democracy, solidarity and resistance against the law of markets and at the same time, it is a platform for true international cooperation' (cited by Wintrebrau, 2007: 50).

5   Following the suspicions of some of Attac's leaders that the results of the internal election of early June 2006 which gave a clear majority to the incumbent leadership (centered around Jacques Nikonoff, Bernard Cassen and Michèle Dessenne) had been tampered with, an independent enquiry took place and concluded that 'The material proof of a fraud in favour of the outgoing leadership has been established' (*Libération*, 7 October 2006). The new elections, held in December 2006, gave a majority to the leadership's rivals and two co-presidents were elected (Aurélie Trouvé and Jean-Marie Harribey). Jacques Nikonoff and his supporters bitterly contested the results of this second election arguing that Attac had been hijacked by 'leftist, communitarian and sectarian currents' (George, 2007). In August 2009, the case against certain Attac members was dismissed through lack of evidence and the concluding judgement was that while it was likely that a fraud had been committed, it was yet to be proven. For a detailed discussion of the background to this scandal, see Wintrebrau, 2007.

6   Interview with the author, 10 February 2003.

7   *Le Monde diplomatique* was originally created as an impartial source of reference on international affairs, but its political line changed with the arrival of Claude Julien as general editor in 1973. Bernard Cassen and Ignacio Ramonet also joined the newspaper during the 1970s and helped to shape its new editorial line. The newspaper increasingly assumed a critical leftist stance on world affairs publishing articles on American foreign policy, anti-colonial struggles and the Third World. *Le Monde diplomatique* was one of the first newspapers to criticize the policies of economic deregulation being pursued by Ronald Reagan in the United States and later in Britain under Margaret Thatcher, taking a critical stance in relation to what was not yet known as neo-liberalism. It was in the early 1990s that the first articles appeared which questioned the role of international financial institutions (International Monetary Fund, World Bank, World Trade Organization) and the impact of 'global financial markets' on social inequalities and on the countries of the Third World.

8   Interview with the author, 6 February 2003.

9   Interview with the author, 6 February 2003.

10   Interview with the author, 7 February 2003.

11   Although the term 'popular education' is referred to in many documents produced by Attac, it was only included in the association's statutes in their revised version approved by Attac members in 2009 and which added that the association's goal was 'to promote popular education' (Nouveaux statuts d'Attac, article 1). This concept was first elaborated by the republican philosopher Marie de Condorcet who in his 1792 report *The General Organisation of Public Instruction* argued that education was critical in order to dispel the prejudices and ignorance of the past and to promote a conception

of citizenship based on the flowering of human reason. He recommended two types of education: (i) primary school education; and (ii) life-long learning that was intended to bring knowledge to the masses and to help create active and responsible citizens. The secular education leagues which flourished in the nineteenth century and in which Attac identifies its historical antecedents, sought to bring literacy and education to the people as a means of propagating democratic ideals and deepening citizenship. The notion of 'popular education' has undergone a revival in contemporary France and has been embraced by Attac and more recently by the Mouvement politique d'éducation populaire, created in 2008 and led by two former Attac members, Jacques Nikonoff and Michèle Dessenne. This association defines its role as the politicization of French society through a diffusion of knowledge and critical ideas.

12 Statuts d'Attac, article 12 (Attac, 2002a: 168).

13 Cassen sees the governments of Evo Morales in Bolivia, Hugo Chavez in Venezuela and Lula da Silva in Brazil as examples of socialism for the twenty-first century which could provide models for European countries. This is central to his campaign for 'post-alterglobalism' within the association Mémoire des luttes, for which he currently acts as secretary general.

14 See *Le Monde,* 15 September 2001, 'Laurent Fabius a reçu une délégation d'Attac'.

15 Internal document. Attac (2003) Etat des lieux, 31 December 2002.

16 Rapport d'activité du Conseil d'administration. Assemblée générale d'Attac à Tours, 3 novembre 2001.

17 'Attac et la sphère politique' Complément au premier document d'orientation du Conseil d'administration, 7 juillet 2003.

18 Interview with the author, 10 February 2003.

19 Statuts d'Attac, Article 1.

6

Agriculture and identity: The Confédération paysanne

In his speech in Poligny (Jura) in October 2009, where he addressed an audience comprised mainly of local farmers, Nicolas Sarkozy affirmed that agriculture had a significance within French society that went beyond economic or material considerations alone and that it concerned the very nature of Frenchness itself: 'French national identity is constituted by a distinctive relationship between the French and the land.' The value of agriculture, he suggested, could not be quantified according to economic variables or statistical ratios because it held a visceral and spiritual place within people's hearts: 'France has a carnal relationship with agriculture' (Puljak, 2009). Announcing financial aid of 650 million euros for French farmers, he argued that his government would defend farming, not simply out of economic interest, but because this was a fundamental moral obligation. Sarkozy's remarks appealed to well-entrenched French beliefs about the role and importance of agriculture within public life (Rogers, 2000). In France, agriculture has long represented an essential component of national identity and is seen to represent what Jules Michelet referred to as 'the soul of the nation', reflecting a set of traditions and cultural attributes that are indissociable from Frenchness itself. Indeed, the influence of agriculture today seems to stem as much from its economic and demographic importance, as from its representational and symbolic capacity.

During a period of globalization, agriculture has been revived as a powerful symbol of identity and a means to confront the challenges and uncertainties of a rapidly changing world. On the one hand, it offers a collective myth, a canvas on which to project hopes and fears, a means to escape unpalatable realities and to reconstitute the world differently. In the face of a threatening world, it conjures up a rural idyll that is reassuring, stable and wholesome, free of all the vicissitudes of the present and it seems to offer a place that 'stays warm however cold the winds outside' (Bauman, 2001: 15). On the other hand, it provides a model of resistance and in particular, resistance to modernizing change. Many French farming unions have invoked agriculture as a symbol of opposition to globalization that is increasingly used to affirm a particular set of collective values and beliefs and to invalidate the claims of neo-liberalism. Agriculture summons up a world governed by distinctive organizing principles, in which the ideals of community, public good, honest labour and cultural heritage are seen to take precedence over crude profit motives. It provides a discursive means to challenge a dominant free-market ideology, by affirming the primacy of community over economics and of people over profits, as expressed by the Confédération paysanne's slogan 'the world is not for sale' (Bové & Dufour, 2000).

This chapter examines the case of the Confédération paysanne and explores the nature and causes of its remarkable success within French society. On the surface, the Confédération seems to be a force that is at odds with the political and socioeconomic realities of contemporary France. It is a marginal farmers' union representing the vested interests of a tiny and shrinking minority and is cut off from the concerns of the general population. It is characterized by a traditional and nostalgic outlook, one that extols the virtues of family farming, of rural village life, of agrarian traditions and local customs. Moreover, the Confédération flies in the face of all the dominant trends towards economic integration. Whereas France is increasingly globalized and integrated into an international economy, the Confédération calls for a withdrawal from international markets, a closure of borders to trade and a massive increase in state protection. It envisages a return to a traditional closed society, one that is protected by the State and sheltered from external influences. The Confédération rejects the very idea of open markets as a system for organizing modern society and favours instead, an ideal of the small-scale community-run economy. Yet if the Confédération appears to be marginal or anachronistic, it has not been overlooked or pushed onto the margins of French society. On the contrary, at the height of its influence, the Confédération was hailed as a champion of the 'general interest' and it commanded deep-seated support across French society. Politicians from both Left and Right rallied to its side and declared their vociferous support for its cause. When José Bové took part in a hunger strike in January 2008 in protest against the French government's failure to prohibit genetically modified crops, he was visited by the Socialist presidential candidate, Ségolène Royal who praised his courage and his willingness to defend the common good of all French citizens. Beyond its own interests, the Confédération seems to speak for all ordinary French men and women, embracing their anxieties and fears and articulating them within the public sphere.

If the Confédération enjoyed extraordinary popular success, this is because it was able to transform itself from an obscure farmers union from the Midi into a force of opposition to globalization that was waging a broad crusade against a malevolent external threat. Its influence had little to do with conventional political or institutional patterns, with the impact of apparatus or structure, but stemmed instead from its symbolic power. For Pierre Bourdieu, power is not limited to formal political or institutional means but assumes an essential symbolic dimension as well and this involves a capacity 'to produce and impose representations . . . of the social world' and thereby to shape consciousness and the way people understood social reality' (Bourdieu, 1991: 127). He argued that at times of profound crisis, otherwise weak groups could challenge the established order and impose their own representations of the social world. In order to succeed, all political opposition required a cognitive subversion ('a conversion of the vision of the world') which could serve to challenge or subvert established representations or schemes of classification (ibid., 128). Drawing on Bourdieu's notion of 'symbolic power',[1] I argue that the Confédération used its symbolic and discursive skills to reinvent its own cause as one of opposition to globalization. By redefining its enemy as neo-liberal globalization, the Confédération was able to acquire a new status, recognition and popular support within French society. On the one hand, it was able to transcend narrow farming circles and reach a mass public audience, giving expression to deep-seated tensions and anxieties within French society. Indeed, its discourse against globalization instantly found resonance within a population fearful and anxious about the nature of globalizing change. On the other, the Confédération was able to posit itself as the defender of a traditional cultural identity, laying claim to a whole symbolic universe linked to peasant farming. In its rhetoric, the Confédération skilfully juxtaposed peasant farming against all the perceived ills of a globalizing world, so that it seemed to offer a defence against present changes and contingencies. What explains the Confédération's success was its ability to transform a narrow economic cause into a broad cultural mission and to posit itself as the defender of a fragile and precious identity under attack from the ravages of a globalizing world.

Agriculture and identity

In contemporary France, agriculture continues to act as a potent and highly charged symbol of identity, belonging and community. If the tricolour flag is the standard bearer of national identity, it is rivaled by the much older and unofficial symbol of *le coq gaulois* (the French cockerel) representing the qualities of courage, strength, pride, fertility and expressing France's deeply rooted peasant origins.[2] The pervasive influence of French agriculture today seems to stem as much from objective material realities and from the economic importance of farming, as from symbolic and representational factors. As an economic activity, agriculture and in particular small farming, has shrunk over the past half century to a tiny proportion of the status that it once occupied within the national economy. Whereas agriculture continued to employ a third of the nation's workforce at the end of the Second World War, today it employs between 7 per cent and 10 per cent and in the case of small farming, less than 3 per cent. Moreover, the nature of agriculture has been utterly transformed from the model of peasant farming which still prevailed until the mid-twentieth century and which provided an enduring historical model of national identity. The shift to a productivist mode of agriculture in the 1960s, based on the rise of large-scale, intensive and mechanized farming was extremely successful in terms of production outputs and ensured that France became and still is, the second largest exporter of agricultural produce in the world, after the United States. Yet, it had devastating effects on small peasant farming, triggering the collapse of a traditional peasant economy and the rapid disappearance of small farms from the French landscape. During the period from 1955 to 1990, the average size of farms doubled and the number of people working on farms fell from 5 million to 1.5 million (Clout & Demossier, 2003). Today, small farming survives principally as a marginal and subsistence activity and small farmers as a social category have been characterized by declining living standards, social isolation and crippling indebtedness. Meanwhile, French agriculture has been sustained by European funding under the Common Agricultural Policy (CAP) which protected both large market-driven farms and small family-run holdings. The progressive withdrawal of such funding in recent decades and the increased exposure of French farmers to open market conditions has become a source of ongoing and often violent protest in the French countryside (Thompson, 2003).

French observers, from historians, to sociologists and anthropologists have documented the dramatic transformation of agriculture in the post-war period and its profound implications for French society as a whole. The French sociologist Henri Mendras, in his prophetic study, *La fin des paysans* (*The End of*

the Peasantry, 1967),[3] suggested that the modernization of French agriculture during the post-war years, based on an increasingly widespread use of
the tractor, a concentration of farm size, greater production efficiency and a
migration from the countryside to towns, had brought the French peasantry
to 'vanishing point' (Mendras, 1970: vii). He equates economic modernization with a negative market-driven logic which was brutally imposed on a
traditional and fragile way of life characterized by rural village communities,
family-based relationships, traditional and slow-moving production methods
and an equilibrium between man and nature. Modernization, in his view, had
precipitated the collapse of a whole civilization, a way of life, a cultural tradition and social structure that defined French society itself:

> The eternal 'peasant soul' is dying before our eyes, just as is the patriarchal
> family domain founded on subsistence polycultivation. It is the final battle
> of industrial society against the last stronghold of traditional civilization.
> What we are undertaking here, then, is not simply a study of a new
> agricultural revolution but a study of the disappearance of traditional
> peasant civilization, which is a fundamental element of Western civilization
> and Christianity, and its replacement by the new modern technological
> civilization, which will often take on different forms in the country than it
> assumes in the city. (Ibid., 14)

Mendras presents a bleak prognosis of a society that had chosen to sacrifice,
on the altar of economic modernization, a precious and irreplaceable culture
that was now faced with extinction. He contested a prevailing modernist logic
that saw an extension of market forces into the French countryside as an
indisputable good and presented this instead in terms of a profound social
and cultural loss:

> But in reconstructing a new society on the dismantled structures of family,
> farm, and village, they sound the knell of the last vestiges of the peasantry
> in France, who will not survive their generation. Thus, with them, the
> peasantry will itself be extinguished. And what will a world without
> peasants be like? (Ibid., 246)

The timing and effects of the decline of the French peasantry was and still
is a subject of great controversy. For instance, the historian Eugen Weber's
central work, *Peasants into Frenchmen* (1970) situated the decline of the
peasantry much earlier at the turn of the century (1870–1914) and linked this
to the impact of state-led modernization and centralization (railroads, schools,
military service, markets) which gradually integrated rural communities into a

common national culture.[4] Whereas Mendras saw modernization as a negative process of capitalist appropriation, Weber compared this to an internal conquest or colonization, but saw this in a positive light as a source of emancipation and progress.

Despite the realities of a rapid decline in farming, themes of agriculture, the peasantry and rural village life have acquired in contemporary France, the status of a collective myth exerting a deep-seated influence within public consciousness. Their importance stems from their symbolic and interpretative potential and their capacity to conjure up a magical 'fairy-tale world', far removed from the realities of the present.[5] Agriculture may be used to invoke a common past and a precious heritage of traditions, customs and rituals that are seen to define national identity. It is a means to express symbolically the continuity of past and present and to reaffirm the cultural integrity of the community in the face of its apparent subversion by the forces of change. Agriculture may also symbolize the ideal of rural village life in which personal and family relationships are paramount, in which people still interact with each other as 'whole persons' in a social context in which 'everyone knows everyone else in all his aspects' (Mendras, 1970: 7). Here modernity has not disrupted interpersonal relationships and the family remains the basic unit of social life in a world in which there is 'no distinction between economic and family life' (ibid., 76). Agriculture also expresses the cultural specificity and rootedness that is linked to a particular place and that is expressed by the notion of *terroir*. The localities and regions of the French countryside are each seen to possess a particular blend of soil, climate and tradition that is unique and identifiable and that anchors the individual to a particular place. Finally, agriculture evokes a set of moral and cultural codes that reflect the 'eternal order of the fields' and that are characterized by fortitude, self-determination and resilience. These values are often linked with the figure of the peasant who, because of his use of traditional methods and his unique connection with nature, is seen as intrinsically virtuous: 'The good peasant is courageous' (ibid., 164). It is not surprising that Nicolas Sarkozy drew on agricultural symbolism as part of his campaign to restore national identity during his presidency and this was the subject of a number of his key speeches, including his speech at Salon Space in Rennes in December 2007, at the Salon d'Agriculture in February 2008 and at Daumeray (Maine-et-Loire) in February 2009. We have seen that it was in his speech at Poligny in October 2009 that he made an explicit connection between agriculture and French national identity.

However, the significance of agriculture as a symbol of identity is not static or permanent, but reflects changing contingencies in society at any one time. For the American social anthropologist Susan Carol Rogers, agricultural images act like 'persistently empty vessels that can be filled with the concerns of the moment' and reflect underlying tensions within society at any given period (Rogers, 2000: 61). She notes that such imagery can be found at different points in history, such as in nineteenth-century paintings, in the political discourse of the interwar period or in fiction of the 1950s. Like all markers of identity, agriculture tends to become important at times of profound national crisis. Another social anthropologist, Anthony Cohen makes this point clearly: 'It has long been noticed that societies undergoing rapid, and, therefore, destabilizing processes of change often generate atavistically some apparent traditional forms, but impart to them meaning and implications appropriate to contemporary circumstances' (Cohen, 1985: 46). If agriculture has become such a pervasive symbol of identity in France today, this is because globalization seems to have unsettled and disrupted established modes of identity and belonging. The increased openness of markets, technological innovation, the speed of financial flows, cultural interconnectedness and the rise of supranational institutions have all served to undermine the traditional boundaries of community. Globalization has been experienced in France as an 'assault on social encapsulation' that destroys cultural specificities, uproots territorial attachments, levels out differences and engulfs society in a great transformative tide (ibid., 44). In the face of this challenge to identity, agriculture has been revived as a powerful symbolic defence, a means to ward off outside threats, to preserve the past and to subvert present realities. In contemporary France, agriculture has been reconstituted in opposition to globalization as a kind of symbolic other, a binary opposite to a changing and uncertain world. Whereas globalization is experienced as rapid transformation, agriculture represents a world of stability, timelessness and security. Whereas globalization uproots individuals and communities, agriculture seems to anchor the individual in the soil and to bind him/her to a specific locality or place. Whereas globalization homogenizes cultural differences, agriculture represents a specific and unique cultural identity that seems immune from change. Agricultural symbolism today is characterized by an 'invention of tradition'[6] that reactivates the myths of the past in relation to changes in the present. Indeed, this symbolism is defined as much by French history, by an enduring set of traditions and practices, as by the impact of globalization in the present.

Peasantry

Perhaps the most potent and enduring symbol linked to French agriculture is that of the peasant who is seen to embody certain timeless and irreducible qualities that are bound up with national identity. Susan Carol Rogers notes that the peasant survives in France today, less as a social category that can be quantified or empirically observed, than as an abstract cultural ideal on which certain values and ideas are projected: 'In France, it is the *peasant* farmer who has long stood for the *soul* of the nation, evoking the deep-rooted cultural traditions and implantation in the national territory which define France, and the equilibrium which guarantees the health of society' (Rogers, 2000: 62). On the one hand, the peasant is viewed as a gatekeeper to the past, preserving an 'ancient knowledge' and handing it down from one generation to the next (Mendras, 1970: 202). By virtue of this unique relationship with the past and a deep-seated connection to the French soil, the peasant is seen to possess certain timeless qualities such as fortitude, resilience, wisdom, honesty and openness. He/she is a symbol of virtue and purity preserving a lost innocence in a decadent modern world. On the other hand, the peasant is more than a simple receptacle for France's past and is also a figure of resistance who actively refuses change, who rejects the supposed values of modernity and fends off outside influences. The peasant is seen to be fiercely attached to the land, proud of his heritage, steadfast in his values, uncompromising in his methods. In contemporary France, farming unions and rural leaders have reactivated the image of the peasant as a symbol of resistance to globalization. Hence, José Bové seemed to internalize and act out aspects of the peasant persona and he studiously cultivated his image as an archetypal peasant complete with checked shirt, pipe and gallic moustache. His aim was to present himself as a leader who incarnated values of the soil, those of tradition, self-determination and honest labour and who rejected the perceived evils of the outside world. Similarly, Régis Hochart, leader of the Confédération paysanne since 2005 emulates a typical peasant style as a means to reflect a set of collective beliefs and to express his resistance to neo-liberal globalization.

Landscape

Agriculture is bound up with the theme of landscape and is seen to delimit the boundaries of the national territory, to express the geographical and physical contours of identity and to bear the indelible mark of the French national character. Many historians have linked French national identity to the physical attributes of the land which seem to provide a permanent backdrop to national history, shaping and determining human actions over time. For Fernand Braudel, French identity was defined by the land: the geography of France had determined early patterns of human settlement, forms of economic activity, social customs and continued to exert a decisive influence on human actions in the present day. Similarly, Armand Frémont sees the land as a quintessential site of memory which reflects France's specific history, geographical diversity and cultural traditions. For him, French identity is etched into a national landscape which stretches back to the beginning of time and preserves traditional customs and practices in the present:

> The land in France is not only the most extensive realm of our history and which is everywhere the most present, it is also the deepest. The land possesses all the values of a peasant civilization whose roots are stretched across the ages and which is still present in contemporary landscapes. (Frémont, 1992: 54)

The French preoccupation with landscape and in particular with cultivated landscape is a central dimension of national identity. Concerns about cultivated landscape date back to the late nineteenth century when it was feared that unoccupied territory would leave France vulnerable to attack from the enemies surrounding it (Rogers, 2000). Farming was a means to lay claim to the land and to appropriate it as part of the national space. Similarly the need for cultivated landscape reflects fears about wilderness and about nature left to run wild expressing 'a deep-seated abhorrence of uninhabited space within the national territory' (ibid., 57). The image of cultivated landscape, bearing the mark of human intervention and appropriated for collective purposes, is essential to the notion of civilization itself. Indeed, uncultivated landscape is regarded as being distinctly unFrench: 'wild spaces, everything that lies outside the control of peasants only constitutes a very limited part of the national territory' (Frémont, 1992: 19). It is interesting that globalization is often represented as an incursion of foreign influences on French national soil. In their study of a protest movement in the Languedocian village of Aniane against the plans of the Californian wine producer Mondavi to purchase local land to build a new winery, Diane Barthel-Bouchier and Lauretta Clough show how the terms of this dispute were reconfigured by some local activists as that of Asterix and Obelix against the invading Romans. A defence of local wine production was reconfigured as a defence of the integrity of French national territory and of the nation itself.[7]

Produits de terroir

Different studies have shown how in the French case, food such as cheese, wine, foie gras, chocolate are endowed with symbolic and cultural properties that transcend their economic value alone.[8] These foodstuffs, when produced locally or regionally according to traditional methods, are regarded not simply as tradable merchandise or products for consumption, but are seen as essential markers of identity that reflect a unique rural heritage and set of cultural tastes. In contemporary France, produits de terroir have been subject to a surge in popularity and this has been explained in terms of a generalized desire to recover the past, to reactive traditions and to reassert roots. Unlike mass-produced foodstuffs, these products are seen to possess a distinctive character that is linked to a particular rural setting, to the transmission of traditional methods and to locally defined cultural practices. Eating produits de terroir is not simply about consumption, but is a means of 'imbibing memories' and of 'symbolically integrating a forgotten culture' (Demossier, 2000: 151). In his extensive study of French identity, Pierre Nora includes wine and wine production as key sites of memory that are seen to capture the essential elements of national identity. Historian Georges Durand, in his chapter on wine in Nora's volume, notes that although wine, when consumed in excess could induce forgetfulness, it is in fact a quintessential object of memory summoning up a rich historical lineage that stretches back to the origins of French civilization itself. He observes that wine is venerated in French culture as a sacred, ancestral, mystical and communal object that is part of France's past and that also defines its common destiny:

> Through this experience of two millennia of the history of the vine and of wine, we can see the extent to which the art of winegrowing and this attachment of the people of France to a product from our land makes wine an integral part of our national destiny. The vine and its branches have woven with our people, a common history. Brought by the Greeks and the Roman conquerors, vine and wine are contemporaneous with the origins of our civilization which allowed us to participate in Greco-Latin Europe. (Durand, 1992: 803)

Yet, produits de terroir can also serve as instruments of protest that signify an opposition to globalization and to the spread of mass-produced and industrialized food. Hence rural activists link produits de terroir with a set of ideological principles, those of cultural diversity, public health, small-scale economics and environmental sustainability that challenge a commercially driven logic represented by 'le Big Mac'. While these are objects of tradition, they are also symbols of the resistance of 'culture against transnational capital' (Heller cited by Williams, 2008: 5). It was for this reason that José Bové and his fellow activists, when traveling to Seattle to take part in protest against the World Trade Organization, took with them on the plane 350 kilograms of Roquefort cheese as 'a gift to the people of Seattle'. What he was defending was not merchandise but a whole way of life, a set of values and a vision of social change (Capdevielle, 2001).

In from the margins

During the mid-1950s, Pierre Poujade, a shopkeeper from the village of Saint-Céré in the department of Lot in southern France, organized a protest against tax inspectors who had come to verify the income of another shopkeeper in the village. This act of protest soon escalated into a broad movement of opposition to economic modernization and to 'the system', that rallied support from groups as diverse as shopkeepers, artisans, peasants and winegrowers. Describing the victory of Pierre Poujade in the parliamentary elections of 1956, the historian Jean Touchard wrote: 'For the first time in the history of France, a man finds himself brought to the first rank by his obscurity itself.'[9] Had he lived to the present decade, Touchard might have thought that history was repeating itself. In 2007, José Bové, a sheepfarmer from the Massif Central, but also an activist and erstwhile leader of the Confédération paysanne, stood as a candidate in the French presidential elections. His purpose, as set out in his manifesto, was not to represent the specific interests of sheep farmers like himself, but rather to defend the 'general interest' of all French citizens at a time of globalizing change. Indeed, Bové had 'accepted' the invitation to stand for France's highest political office on behalf of the French people as a whole in order to protect their collective values, their distinctive social model and their well-being. France's interests, he declared, lay in a defence of social gains or 'acquis' (in welfare, pensions, health and education) and in a vigorous rejection of neo-liberal globalization, seen as responsible for a whole host of social ills from unemployment and precariousness, to racism and social exclusion: 'It is time to launch an electoral insurrection against economic liberalism' (Bové, 2007: 173).

Bové's decision to stand for French president was a culmination of the meteoric rise of himself and the Confédération paysanne during the course of the preceding decade. Following the 'McDonalds affair' of August 1999, when a group of 300 farmers led by Bové, dismantled a McDonalds construction site in the town of Millau in southern France, this small and once obscure farmers' union had been catapulted to the centre of public debates and Bové, its unofficial spokesperson was hailed a national hero. During their protest, farmers had loaded bits of roof, prefabricated walls, light switches and doors from the McDonalds site onto their trailers and dumped it all outside the offices of the sub-prefecture while chanting in local dialect 'McDo defora, gardarem Roquefort' ('Out with McDonalds, let's keep Roquefort'). Following this action, five activists were arrested and Bové was given a short prison sentence. The protest attracted many weeks of sympathetic coverage from the French media and gained for the Confédération the support of a majority of French citizens. In a poll taken at the time of Bové's trial in June 2000, 45 per cent of people said that they 'supported' or 'felt sympathy' for him and 51 per cent said they agreed with his position on economic and financial globalization. Large majorities said they agreed with Bové on the issues of defending small farming and avoiding 'la malbouffe' (Gordon & Meunier, 2001). Meanwhile, the Confédération's cause inspired the vocal support of party leaders from across the political spectrum and also from intellectuals, celebrities and trade unionists. Following José Bové's arrest, political leaders across the Left rallied to his side and called for his immediate release. In September, the French president of the time, Jacques Chirac, visited Bové and François Dufour at the Salon d'Agriculture where he was offered a signed copy of their book. Bové was subsequently invited to a much publicized dinner at a Parisian restaurant by the Prime Minister, Lionel Jospin. This popularity was evident again in November 1999, when Bové flew to Seattle to lead the French contingent during the protest movement against the World Trade Organization. On 27 of November, when Bové addressed a citizens' forum in Seattle, he received a standing ovation from its 3,000 participants.

When José Bové and François Dufour's book *Le Monde n'est pas une merchandise (The World is Not for Sale)* was published in 2000, it was an instant best-seller with 92,000 copies sold in the space of just a few weeks and with translations published in several languages. The book extended further the growing reputation of Bové and the Confédération outside of France and in particular, within a burgeoning movement of opposition to neo-liberal globalization. From its inception, the Confédération had in fact fostered international links with other farmers' associations: this was a means to exert influence within international decision-making and at the same time, to reinforce the status of an otherwise marginal farmers's union. Confédération leaders helped to create the Coordination paysanne européenne in 1986 which aimed to represent the interests of small farmers in European policy-making. The Confédération was also a founding member of Via Campesina in 1993 which continues to represent farmers' associations from across the world.[10] This movement now claims 50 million members representing 69 organizations from 37 different countries. If the McDonalds affair was a media coup in France, it also found resonance within public opinion across an international stage. In October 1999 an image of Bové, smiling with raised handcuffed fists was published on the front page of a number of foreign newspapers, including the *New York Times* and the *Washington Post*. Furthermore, the Confédération's actions found widespread support among international farming associations and it was in fact the American National Family Farming Coalition which helped raise the bail necessary to secure Bové's release from prison. On his release, Bové declared outside the Montpellier courthouse, in front of an eager press audience that his intention was to construct a new international movement which would challenge the supremacy of markets over politics. On the 12th June 2000, *Business Week* ranked Bové among the 50 personalities most likely to shape the new Europe.

Bové's growing popularity was evident again in 2003 when 250,000 people gathered on the barren plateau of Larzac deep in south-western France on the weekend of 8 August in response to Bové's call for a mass rally against globalization. Described in the French press as 'a historic turning-point' for anti-globalization protest, Larzac was intended to strike a blow against 'a system of capitalist barbarism' and to reclaim democratic control over governments.[11] This event included participation by 150 activist associations from across France, but also drew speakers from across the world, such as Evo Morales, later to become president of Bolivia, Indian academic and activist Vandana Shiva, author Arundhati Roy and Lori Wallach from Public Citizen in the United States (Williams, 2008). In their public statements during this event, the Confédération identified itself with a broad and universalist project of social transformation, one that transcended the borders of France alone and embraced the interests of humanity itself. Its ambition was nothing less than to challenge a prevailing ideology of neo-liberalism and to affirm the rights of people before profits. It sought to reclaim the world from the grasp of greedy multinationals and to refashion it along democratic and humanist lines. Moreover, its cause was not one of economic or material interests but of higher irreducible principles: 'We are fighting for values of humanism, equity and solidarity'.[12] It was a question of defending fundamental democratic values and traditions in the face of the globalizing forces that assailed them.

Following his decision to stand down as leader of the Confédération in 2003, Bové went on to become a prominent figure in leftist politics in France (the 'gauche de la gauche'), leading the movement of opposition to the European Constitutional Treaty in the run-up to the referendum of 29 May 2005. It was the success of this campaign and the subsequent victory of the 'no' vote that led Bové to announce his candidacy for the French presidential elections in an interview with *Libération* in June 2006: 'I am a candidate to the Left of the PS who brings together an anti-liberal, ecological, anti-productivist and alterglobalist Left. I am prepared to go to the Elysée Palace'.[13] Bové hoped to lead a new leftist alliance bringing together all those outside mainstream parties, including social movements, Far Left parties and trade unions who opposed neo-liberalism. However, divisions within the Far Left and the failure to agree on a common candidate to represent them, resulted partly in Bové's weak score in those elections (1.32 per cent and tenth position out of 12 candidates). Undaunted by this setback, Bové has continued to pursue his political career and responded to the 2008 collapse of world financial markets with virulent and outspoken criticism, calling for a new international tribunal to judge the 'financial criminals' who were responsible.[14] More recently, Bové was nominated as a candidate in the 2009 European elections as part of the Europe Ecologie group.

When looking at the Confédération, we are faced with a puzzling contradiction. On the one hand, the Confédération achieved massive popular support, was widely identified with the general interest and aligned itself with a universalist project of social transformation. On the other, it was and still is, a politically and institutionally weak organization with limited political resources, poor representativity and few material strengths. The Confédération is typical of what Pierre Bourdieu would describe as a 'dispossessed' group that is without 'political capital' and which lacks the structural means to exert power or influence within French society (Bourdieu, 1991: 174).

While the Confédération appealed in its rhetoric to the whole of the nation, in reality it continues to represent only a tiny and shrinking minority on the very fringes of French society. When the Confédération was created in 1987, its chief purpose was to provide representation for peasant farmers 'les paysans', a group undergoing severe demographic and social decline, who had fallen victim to the 'productivist' mode of agricultural modernization and who had been pushed onto the margins of French society. It set out to defend farmers' material interests, protect their incomes and promote an alternative agricultural model. This new union was born out of a concrete material situation affecting a particular social group and it sought to alert public opinion to the catastrophic fate confronted by small farmers and to the imminent demise of family farming within the national context, a situation that Régis Hochart, the Confédération's current president referred to as 'the sinking of the French peasantry' (Hochart, 2007). From its inception, the Confédération therefore spoke not from a position of popular support or mass representation, but one of vulnerability and marginality and lacked the 'instituted political interests' that might characterize a more powerful organization (Bourdieu, 1991: 175). It denounced the poor conditions faced by family farmers, their declining living standards, their indebtedness, their dwindling numbers and the collapse of a traditional way of life.

The Confédération occupies a marginal position in the 'political field' and this is a dissident leftist union on the fringes of a powerful agricultural lobby. From the outset, the Confédération was marred by 'isolation and financial crisis' and lacked the institutional or material means to influence government policy or make itself heard (Bruneau, 2001: 21). In 1986, the French government under the new agricultural minister, François Guillaume, introduced a system of majority representation for farming unions which meant that only the larger more representative unions were granted national recognition and by extension, public funding and inclusion in policy-making processes. As a minor farmers' union, the Confédération was denied national status and recognition. It was and still is overshadowed by the dominant farmers' union, the FNSEA which continues to represent the majority of French farmers and enjoys a close relationship with political power and a role of 'co-gestion' (joint management) in the formulation of government policy. At the 1989 chamber of agriculture elections, two years after its creation, the Confédération gained 18 per cent of the votes among French farmers, against 64 per cent gained by the FNSEA. In 2001, when it was at the height of its popular influence, the Confédération paysanne's support rose to 27 per cent in the chamber elections against 52 per cent for the FNSEA. In the wake of the presidential elections and Bové's weak score, this support fell to 19 per cent in the 2007 chamber elections and it lost its position as the second farmers union in France to the right-wing Coordination rurale. Marginal, weak and unrepresentative, the Confédération paysanne lacked the 'objectified political resources' needed to exert power and influence within the political field (Bourdieu, 2001: 181).

At its peak, the Confédération was identified as a champion of the general interest, defending the common good of French society as a whole. Yet, from the outset, it was characterized as a highly particularist organization that defended the vested interests of one group against all others. For Jacques Capdevielle, the success of the Confédération manifested the rise of a new corporatism at a time of globalization: 'José Bové is not only the hero of traditional values. He allows all particularisms that feel threatened to identify with his struggle' (Capdevielle, 2001: 148–9). The Confédération defined its central project as 'l'agriculture paysanne' which it saw as an alternative model of agricultural production, but also as a model for society. This project was first outlined in a Confédération report dating from 1987 and has since been reformulated as a set of ten principles for an alternative agricultural model. As part of this project, the Confédération argues that small farming should be accorded a privileged status within French society and be given special recognition from the State. Farming, it suggests, is different from any other economic activity ('agriculture is not an activity like others') in that it is intrinsic to the well-being and vitality of the French nation. Unlike any other category of worker, the farmer is responsible for feeding the nation and for maintaining the countryside for the good of all. On these grounds, the Confédération argues for greater protectionism, a redistribution of public subsidies, fixed prices for agricultural produce, a renationalized market and control over imports. It envisages a highly regulated model of agricultural production in which the State would be responsible for regulating farm size, levels of production, pricing on agricultural produce and the degree of intensification: 'We demand an agricultural policy that regulates markets, that redistributes the means of production and that protects the most vulnerable in the name of national solidarity' (Confédération, 2007a: 2, 5). In addition, the State would engage in a policy of farm creation setting up new small holdings, so that farmers could establish themselves on the land. The Confédération believes that farmers' incomes should not be determined by market forces, but should be guaranteed from year to year through fixed prices on agricultural produce. While assuming the mantle of the collective good, the Confédération seems to call for a defence of the particular and for the special status of small farmers against other interests.

In its political aims, the Confédération appears to swim against a tide of socioeconomic change and its demands seem to be at odds with those of the general population. Although France is increasingly integrated into a world economy and is now the second exporter of agricultural produce in the world, the Confédération calls for a return to a closed economy and a withdrawal from the international market. From the outset, the Confédération was characterized by a virulent opposition to unregulated market forces which it saw as destructive, predatory and invasive. Jean-Philippe Martin has situated the Confédération within a leftist anti-capitalist current on the margins of the French farmers' movement, with its origins in the late 1960s ('la nouvelle gauche paysanne'/ 'the new peasant Left') (Martin, 2005). At the beginning, its target was a 'productiviste' model of agricultural modernization and it engaged in a radical critique of this model. It saw productivism as an economic activity which aimed to maximize production and profit at the expense of social need or environmental cost: 'to produce for the sake of producing' (Bové & Dufour, 2000: 106). Beyond its impact on agriculture, productivism was linked to a broad set of social problems (environmental decline, poor food quality, declining social conditions and increased health risks) and was seen to undermine the very fabric of French society: 'it is the destruction of an entire social fabric that is at work' (Confédération, 1989: 9). But this discourse was also inspired by a broader post-1968 leftist critique of consumerism that called into question the value and ends of economic production. Productivism was seen to create a concentration of economic resources in the hands of a few multinational agribusiness firms bent on producing exports for the global economy, while small farms were forced out of business. Since the mid-1990s, however, the Confédération has increasingly shifted the focus of its opposition from state-led productivism to an economic globalization that has its origins outside France's borders. Globalization is portrayed as a profound threat to the economic interests of small farmers by intensifying market competition and leading to an influx of cheap products that usurp locally produced goods. In its public discourse, it denounces globalization as a vast imperialist project that seeks to impose American power across all four corners of the world and this is described as 'the dictatorship of markets' or as 'American imperialism'. The source of France's ills no longer stemmed from the capitalist state or from nationally driven modernization, but from external markets that were imposing their model on France, undermining economic and cultural interests and threatening the French nation itself.

Critical to its response to globalization has been the notion of 'food sovereignty' which it helped to devise in 1996 and which has since become a key principle for the international farmers' movement. According to this notion, farmers would have a fundamental right to 'protect their agriculture from cheaply priced imports' and would have exclusive access to their own local and national markets (Confédération, 2007a: 2). Trade between countries would only take place in strictly controlled circumstances: 'Only the surplus should be traded, and that only bilaterally' (Starr, 2005: 57). In addition, governments would be required to reorientate their policies in favour of family farmers through a system of 'public financial support' that confirms their vocation as 'guardians of the land'. At a time of increased economic liberalization, the Confédération seemed to fly in the face of the dominant trends and favour a completely opposing model of economic development based on market regulation, state protection and a closed economy.

Cheese and hamburgers

In *Language and Symbolic Power*, Pierre Bourdieu argued that power in modern societies was not confined to formal institutional means, but assumed an essential symbolic dimension as well. This 'symbolic power' involved a capacity to produce meanings, norms and representations in the public domain and thereby to shape consciousness and the way people understood the world:

> a power of constituting the given through utterances, of making people see and believe, of confirming or transforming the vision of the world and, thereby, action on the world and thus the world itself, an almost magical power which enables one to obtain the equivalent of what is obtained through force. (Bourdieu, 1991: 170)

Symbolic power was derived partly from a capacity to express, make visible and objectify otherwise latent and unexpressed sentiments within society. Here power is exerted by expressive, interpretive and representational means that operate outside the formal mechanisms of apparatus or structure. Yet, symbolic power was not a mystical or obscure disposition, but a potent

means of extending power within society and of fulfilling instrumental or political ends. Bourdieu's intention was to expose and analyse the often hidden
mechanisms behind this symbolic power and to examine the way it could be
used to further vested interests: 'we have to be able to discover it [power] in
places where it is least visible, where it is most completely misrecognized'
(ibid., 163). For him, power in modern societies is seldom exercised as overt
physical force but is instead transmuted into a symbolic form and thereby
endowed with a legitimacy that it would not otherwise have. Symbolic power
is in fact an 'invisible power' that is all the more forceful because it is rarely
recognized as such and this is a 'gentle, invisible violence, unrecognized as
such' (Bourdieu, 1991: 127).

If the Confédération lacked institutional strength, had limited political influence and weak representation, the key to its success lay elsewhere in its
symbolic potential and its capacity to draw on representational and discursive
resources to further its own interests. Through a use of vivid images, clear
rhetoric and colourful symbols, the Confédération was able to impose its own
representation of the social world and thereby transform its position within
French society and the meaning ascribed to its actions. At a time of crisis, it
used its symbolic resources to redefine its purpose within French society,
to assume a new and compelling mission and to mobilize widespread popular support. Jean-Philippe Martin has noted that the Confédération, from the
beginning, laid emphasis on symbolic forms of intervention and that this was
a conscious strategic choice on the part of its leadership who sought to com-
pensate for weak electoral influence and limited organizational resources.
Symbolic action became a privileged means for the Confédération to transcend its own limitations and to reach a wide public audience: 'This constant
proliferation and search for new means of action is linked to the weak implantation of the union which does not have recourse to a solid network' (Martin,
2005: 213). Indeed, José Bové favoured a style of political action that was
symbolic and representative in nature that sought to communicate a message
to society rather than make a physical display of force: 'action always involves
the staging of a cause' (Bové, 2000).

Critical to the Confédération's success was its capacity to reconfigure its
own narrow economic cause as part of a broad crusade against globalization.
Ezra Suleiman has referred to the way in which certain French interest groups
invoked globalization for instrumental ends, as a way of transforming otherwise sectional interests into a higher universal cause (Suleiman, 1999, 2007).
For the Confédération, globalization offered a powerful symbolic tool, an 'illu-
minating metaphor', a means to transform the nature of its struggle and assign
itself a new and critical vocation. First, this allowed the Confédération to transcend farming circles and to appeal to as broad a public audience as possible.

By invoking globalization, the Confédération was able to tap into widespread societal concerns and a major source of anxiety and tension within French society. At a time of social upheaval, cultural dislocation and widespread malaise, its invective against globalization instantly found resonance within public opinion. Secondly, this was a means for the Confédération to aggrandize its own cause and open it up to new layers of meaning and interpretation. It was no longer a question of routine matters of trade and market competition, of issues that were of interest to farmers alone. The Confédération had assumed a new and urgent mandate, one that implicated all French citizens and that concerned the whole of French society.

The Confédération's transformation from obscure farmers' union to champion of resistance to globalization was sudden and dramatic, the outcome of one specific episode of symbolic action or what Pierre Bourdieu would describe as an 'act of symbolization and representation' (Bourdieu, 1991: 191). The events of 12 August 1999 when a group of farmers affiliated to the Confédération paysanne dismantled a McDonalds construction site in the small town of Millau in Southwestern France are well known and I do not intend to reconsider them in detail here.[15] Instead, I will consider this episode as an example of the Confédération's symbolic power and the way in which it was able, through a skilful use of symbols and rhetoric, to transform a routine protest about trade sanctions into a wider mission to defend France against globalization. The importance of this episode lay not in what objectively took place or in the actual course of events, but in the meaning that was later ascribed to them. This was a high symbolic moment or what Kenneth Burke has described as a 'mystic moment' that provided 'a stage of revelation after which all is felt to be different' (Burke, 1952: 305). It allowed the Confédération to transform its status within French society and assume a power and an influence which it did not possess in organizational or material terms.

Ivan Bruneau has shown that the action of 12 August 1999 was a continuation of grassroots protest carried out by local activists over the previous decade and whose stakes were purely material and were confined to questions of economic interest, market competition and trade position. For those involved – members of the local branch of the Confédération paysanne and the sheep farmers' union (SPLB) – it was experienced as 'une action comme les autres', little different to others carried out over many years and involved a defence of product sales on foreign markets (Bruneau, 2004: 123). However, the Confédération's choice of symbols on this occasion and in particular, the juxtaposition of two culturally charged symbols (McDonalds versus Roquefort) served to open up this action to new layers of meaning and interpretation. Through their action, the Confédération created a 'semiotic ground', a space in which new meanings and representations could be constructed (Apter, 2006: 221). In the aftermath of this event, and the intense media attention that it attracted, the Confédération's leaders were eager to present their version of events and to impose their own interpretation of what had occurred. During frequent press interviews, television appearances and orchestrated media appearances, José Bové and others argued that this event was about something of far greater urgency and universal import than the specific interests of farmers caught up in yet another skirmish over trade. Rather, the 'meaning' of the episode was about challenging 'globalization' by making McDonalds a symbol of 'globalization by money to the detriment of the rights of people, their health and democracy' (Laval, 1999a).

In their public discourse after 12 August 1999, the Confédération's leaders constructed a new 'interpretive repertoire' that recapitulated the events and transformed their meaning in a number of fundamental ways (Apter, 2006: 220). First, this was no longer about the particular interests of farmers caught up in a dispute over trade. Rather, it was a question of the 'general interest' and the need to safeguard French society from the health risks posed by globalization. By attacking McDonalds, the Confédération argued that it was striking a blow against mass-produced, industrialized, hormone-filled food that was sapping the health, vitality and well-being of the French nation. Here globalization is portrayed as a pernicious, toxic force that seeps silently across borders and contaminates everything that it touches: 'we suddenly realised that globalization was forcing us to ingest hormones' (Bové & Dufour, 2000: 23). José Bové used the term 'malbouffe' ('junk food') for the first time on the 12 August 1999 to denounce the poor quality standardized food epitomized by McDonalds hamburgers. They were counterposed against Roquefort, which became its symbolic opposite, pure, earthy, traditional and healthy. As he remarked: 'it's Roquefort against hormone-injected beef' (Belmont, 1999). In their discourse, Confédération leaders repeatedly affirmed the traditional role of farmers as guardians of the well-being of the nation. Through their actions, local farmers were in fact reasserting this primordial mission to defend public health and vitality. For instance, in a dramatic speech made by José Bové outside a Montpellier courthouse on 17 August, following an offer of release on bail, he avowed that he would remain in prison to continue his struggle and to safeguard the integrity of French agriculture and hence the good of the whole nation: 'If the struggle against the World Trade Organization, if the struggle for a healthy and clean agriculture require peasant farmers to stay in prison, then I will stay in prison' (Laval, 1999b). Bové had become the eternal peasant-citizen sacrificing his own freedom to protect the French people and to defend their interests at their hour of need.

A second aspect of this discursive strategy was to present their action not as one of economic defence but one of cultural necessity. By attacking

McDonalds, Confédération leaders argued that they were taking a stand against the American cultural model that threatened France's identity, its traditions and a whole way of life. A protest about trade sanctions was therefore reconstituted as an 'anti-American cultural struggle' (Grosrichard, 1999). McDonalds was portrayed as a symbol of an Americanized popular culture imposing its bland and uniform model across the French territory. In fact, the creation of new branch of McDonalds in Millau seemed to confirm the image of a cultural onslaught stretching into every corner of deepest rural France. Thus, the Confédération was defending France from a threat far greater than that posed by market competition which was 'the standardization of tastes', conceived as an assault on French tastes, high culture and distinctive traditions (Besset, 1999). Here food takes on its full resonance as a maker of cultural identity. In its rhetoric, the Confédération emphasized the importance of food as an intrinsic cultural act, whereby one affirms one's own identity and communes with past generations. Fast food, by contrast, was portrayed as a form of cultural decadence signifying a loss of identity, roots and family ties: 'it represents both a loss of family relationships and of roots linked to the land and to a place of life. This way of living does not correspond to an anchorage, a land or a culture. In fact, people are disconnected from the soil.' By explaining its actions by reference to the dangers of globalization, the Confédération was able to transform its own cause into one of cultural defence and into an expression of 'the land against the power of a multinational' (Bové & Dufour, 2000: 81, 7). This was likely to garner far greater popular support than an appeal to the material interests of peasant farmers.

Thirdly, this episode did not concern economic or material interests, but involved higher irreducible principles. According to this scenario, activists were impelled by a desire to safeguard democratic principles and freedoms. Here McDonalds is portrayed as a 'symbol of economic imperialism' and the vanguard of a system of global capitalism that was fundamentally at odds with French democratic traditions. By targeting McDonalds, the Confédération was protecting the French way of life and its civilization from the corrupt and barbaric forces that were gathering strength at its borders. In its rhetoric, the Confédération identified globalization with images of imperialist and totalitarian power that was endangering democratic freedoms and this was 'the tyranny of markets' which was imposing a market-controlled system across the entire French territory: 'it is the hegemonic desire of trade that seeks to devour everything' (ibid., 24, 93). In the face of globalization, the Confédération posited itself as the voice of democracy and freedom. Its mission was nothing less than to reclaim the world from the grasp of greedy multinationals and to refashion it along democratic and humanist lines. Meanwhile, José Bové was recast in the media as a sort of reincarnated Asterix defending French

territory against barbaric invading hoardes. He was the 'hero of traditional values' defending France's democratic soul and engaged in a David and Goliath
struggle against the might of powerful corporations (Capdevielle, 2001: 148).
Hence, a dispute over trade sanctions was recast as a Manichean battle of
good against evil with the Confédération lined up squarely on the side of
virtue and righteousness. The Confédération presents itself as a champion
of rights and for José Bové, the purpose of activism is to 'rebuild the world
on the basis of rights' (cited by Williams, 2008: 134). They struggle against a
neo-liberal globalization that is seen to destroy a precious democratic legacy
by turning public goods such as water, the earth and food into commodities.

  The McDonalds affair marked a triumph for the Confédération's symbolic
power, bringing rewards equivalent to those that might be gained by other
more conventional political means. This episode represented a 'moment of
rupture' that utterly transformed the Confédération's status within French
society and the meaning ascribed to its actions, leading to its 'public rebirth'
as a force completely different to the one created over 10 years previously
(Bruneau, 2006: 66). Bourdieu has argued that political agents are involved
in a symbolic struggle aimed at 'imposing the definition of the social world
that is best suited to their interests' (Bourdieu, 1991: 167). By reconfiguring
their cause as one of opposition to globalization, the Confédération articulated and gave expression to deep-seated anxieties within French society
and at the same time, it assigned itself a new and universal mission. From
an obscure and marginal farmers' union, it became a symbol of the general
interest, speaking for all French men and women concerned about the nature
of globalizing change.

Peasants against markets

If the Confédération paysanne articulated widespread fears and anxieties
about globalization, it also offered a refuge from them, a retreat into a world of
tradition, rootedness and belonging. Critical to the Confédération's power was
its capacity to reconstitute peasant farming as a symbol of French identity at
a time of globalizing change. We have seen that in France, peasant farming
assumes a significance far beyond its economic importance alone and it survives as a 'highly charged and manipulable symbol' that represents tradition,
cultural identity, national heritage and the social good. Yet, as Rogers has
shown, such symbolism is not static, but responds to external contingencies
in society at any one time. Peasant farming has in fact been revived at various
points in French history as a means to resolve tensions in society and to man-
age processes of change: 'it is no wonder that peasants should be made to

disappear and reappear over time as change is managed, controlled and interpreted' (Rogers, 1987: 56, 60). What explains the Confédération's success is
that it revived such symbolism at a time of globalization, widely experienced
by the French as social upheaval, cultural dislocation and ultimately, as a threat
to identity. Unlike previous periods of socioeconomic change, globalization is
not seen to come from within the national territory, but from external forces
that are often viewed as fundamentally illegitimate. It is at this critical juncture
that the Confédération has been able to capture one of the nation's most
enduring myths, laying claim to a whole symbolic universe linked to peasant
farming. Anthony Cohen has shown how communities tend to reconstruct
identity symbolically when faced with outside pressures for change:

> Indeed, the greater the pressure on communities to modify their structural
> forms to comply more with those elsewhere, the more are they inclined to
> reassert their boundaries *symbolically* by imbuing these modified forms with
> meaning and significance which belies their appearance. (Cohen, 1985: 44)

The Confédération did not simply revive a well-established repertoire of symbols
and images, but rather, posited this as an *antidote* to all the evils of a globalizing
world. The force of such symbolism lay in its oppositional value and the way it
was used to counterpose the dominant tendencies of globalization. It became
a refuge, an anchor, a bulwark against a world of ceaseless change and uncertainty. What characterizes the Confédération's discourse is a symbolic game
of opposites, whereby peasant farming is aligned with all that is virtuous, traditional, authentic and globalization is recast as its irreducible opposite, evil, predatory and alien. In its discourse, the Confédération skilfully juxtaposed peasant
farming against a dominant image of global society, so that it became its cultural
nemesis, a place in which identity is reaffirmed, tradition is preserved and social
bonds are restored. It used symbolic power to pursue, in the words of Bourdieu,
'the possibility of changing the social world by changing the representations of
this world which contributes to its reality' (Bourdieu, 1991: 128).

Identity

Where globalization is seen as an alien, homogenizing force, one that oblit-
erated cultural specificity, peasant farming was presented as a symbol of
national identity that was pure, distinctive and unchanging. In its monthly magazine, *Campagnes solidaires*, the Confédération sets out an economic case
for the protection of small farming by presenting objective facts and figures,
concerning for instance, the declining numbers of local cheese producers or

pig farmers in certain regions, the decimation of farming incomes, the unfair distribution of production quotas or the dwindling percentage of European funding allocated to small producers. Yet, these economic arguments are conflated with broader cultural themes that transcend farming circles and implicate French society as a whole. In a recent edition devoted to the wine industry entitled 'Le vin n'est pas qu'une marchandise'/ 'Wine is not simply a commodity', an image of a typical French vineyard was depicted alongside an image of a traditional French peasant pulling a horse-drawn carriage through the fields (Confédération, 2007b: 9). The message here is that wine is not simply a product that can be bought and sold at the cheapest possible price. Rather, like cheese, milk or pâté, it embodies all the virtues of 'terroir', the special qualities of local soils, specific places and cultural traditions that cannot be replicated elsewhere: 'Wine growers who have chosen to make quality wines according to the fundamental notion of *terroir* are all threatened by the reform of the CAP' (Confédération, 2006: 4). This reflects a wider discourse within the Confédération which argues that small farming should be protected not only on economic grounds, but on the basis of cultural necessity. It is a question of preserving a sacred and fragile world, one embedded in tradition and which is an essential part of being French:

> Yet cultural identity is also agricultural identity, even if they are not peasants or do not live in the countryside, even if they live in cities, these people have peasant roots, roots that connect them to all of the French regions. Europe and globalization cannot take this power away from us. (Bové & Dufour, 2000: 39)

Globalization is therefore seen to represent a threat far greater than that of market competition, which is that of impending cultural loss.

Yet, this is not identity as a submissive or docile state, but as a form of cultural resistance and in particular, resistance to change. The Confédération's evocation of peasant farming as a symbol of identity is most striking in the personality of José Bové. Through a carefully honed physical appearance and an orchestrated media campaign, Bové cultivated an image as the eternal French peasant who was proud, steadfast and resolute. The press commented endlessly on his image, his 'moustaches gauloises', his pipe, checked shirt and corduroy trousers, seen to characterize the timeless qualities of the French peasant:

> This descendant of Robin Hood is warmly received because he incarnates a fundamental right to cultural diversity and he does this in relation to one of our most important collective myths, that of the peasantry, the

true peasantry, consisting of men proud of their land, their animals, their work. (Viard, 1999)

Yet, Bové also personifies the peasant who is fiercely attached to the land, to local traditions and customs and who stubbornly refused all external pressures. One of the most publicized images of Bové, depicts him smiling with raised handcuffed fists outside a court in Montepellier where he had announced his intention to stay in prison to continue his struggle. This photographed image was published in newspapers in France and across the world and became a symbol of resistance for all those who felt threatened by neo-liberal globalization and who refused to accept its terms. For Bové, peasants, just like the working class during the industrial period, had become a critical force for resistance in the twenty-first century, leading the struggle against neo-liberalism: 'Peasants resist because they are the last rampart against the cultural homogenization of the world' (cited by Losson & Quinio, 2002: 75).

Tradition

Where globalization is experienced as ceaseless change and upheaval, peasant farming is presented as a symbol of tradition and continuity, one that anchors the French to their past and to a shared cultural legacy. Peasant farming is posited as a model of simplicity, timelessness and purity that is untainted by the evils of modern society, by ever-expanding markets and by mass agricultural production. It is counterposed against an image of globalization as all-encompassing change, a neo-liberal tide that transforms, uproots and destroys everything in its path. The Confédération has made ample use of images to evoke a traditional and nostalgic rural world, with symbols of horse-drawn carriages, ploughs, village festivities, peasant farmers toiling in the fields. In its discourse, it extols the virtues of traditional farming methods, favouring 'techniques used by our parents, crop rotation, use of varied fodder and keeping a permanent meadow' (Bové & Dufour, 2000: 91). These, it argues, are essential to preserve the environment but also to maintain a precious link with past generations. Deploying traditional methods, the peasant farmer is portrayed as a guardian of the land, safeguarding a shared heritage and ensuring the transmission of a precious culture from one generation to the next. In *Campagnes Solidaires*, the Confédération encourages farmers to abandon modern intensive methods and to embrace the traditional methods of their forefathers. The magazine regularly features families who have 'taken the plunge' and made the decision 'to return to the soil' and to traditional family farming. One couple decided to abandon intensive cereal farming and devote themselves to regional cheeses produced using artisanal methods ('the couple decided to make cheese like their grandparents'). This allowed them to rediscover the joys of family life and to work 'alongside their children who are always ready to lend a hand' (Confédération, 2007c: 16–17). This return to traditional farming is portrayed as a courageous act, an acknowledgement of the debt that we all owe to past generations.

Community

Where globalization is portrayed as a profit-driven machine that erodes social bonds, peasant farming embodies a traditional model of social relationships characterized by close familial ties and rural village life. If the Confédération paysanne defends farmers' economic interests, it also claims to protect a whole way of life rooted in small family farms, fêtes de village and agrarian ceremonies. It projects an idealized image of society in which familial and social bonds are preserved and where the family farm is handed down from one generation to the next: 'the peasant family should remain in control of its economic activity and if possible remain, or assume responsibility for all its means of production'. The Confédération argues that economic modernization destroyed not only farmers' livelihoods but a model of social relationships that is the cornerstone of French society: 'it involved the reversal of an old world represented by the peasants' (Bové & Dufour, 2000: 89, 96).

The Confédération's particular style of protest is steeped in a world of village solidarities and kinship relationships. In fact, the very idea of creating this farmers' union originated, according to its leaders, during a village celebration at a local farm where a couple were celebrating their 25th wedding anniversary. Over a banquet laid out in the hen-house, local farmers and activists chatted 'amongst friends' and came to reflect on 'the peasant condition': 'With joy and good humour, the guests celebrate the couple by spending an entire day feasting around a table laid out in the hen-house. During the course of two meals, some began exchanging ideas about the peasant condition.' In fact, the Confédération's politics can be characterized as a mixture of radicalism and village festivity where local farmers get together to affirm their rights, but also to share local produce and celebrate village traditions. François Dufour described one protest action as a kind of giant picnic where farmers chanted slogans, proclaimed their rights, but also passed around local cheeses and enjoyed the odd glass of wine: 'We organised picnics, tasting of traditional produce, barbecues outside around forty McDonalds restaurants' (ibid., 45, 70). With close family relationships and a solid social structure, peasant farming offered a reverse mirror image of an alienating and unfamiliar globalizing world.

Conclusion

Over the past decade, the Confédération and its former leader, José Bové have been at the forefront of a national and international movement that challenges neo-liberal globalization and proposes an alternative model for society. At the height of its influence, the Confédération commanded widespread public support, was widely identified with the general interest and aligned itself with a universalist project of social transformation. I have suggested here that the Confédération's remarkable success was derived from its symbolic power which it used to transform its position within French society and the meaning ascribed to its actions. In *Language and Symbolic Power*, Pierre Bourdieu argued that at times of profound crisis, otherwise marginal groups could assume a symbolic power that was normally reserved for established elites:

> But the constitutive power of . . . language, and of the schemes of perception and thought which it procures, is never clearer than in situations of crisis: these paradoxical and extra-ordinary situations call for an extra-ordinary kind of discourse, capable of raising the practical principles of an ethos to the level of explicit principles which generate (quasi-) systematic responses and of expressing all the unheard-of and ineffable characteristics of the situation created by the crisis. (Bourdieu, 1991: 168)

In France, globalization constituted just such a crisis and was widely experienced as upheaval, dislocation and transformation. Unlike earlier periods of modernization, it was viewed as an external process that originated outside French borders and that was alien and dangerous to French interests. In this context, the Confédération intervened to construct new meanings and symbols and to impose its own representation of the social world. It transformed an otherwise complex, distant and intangible process of globalization into a symbolic game of opposites between two opposing universes. On the one hand, the French model, symbolized by Roquefort cheese, with its cultural distinctiveness, democratic traditions and social cohesion and on the other, globalization represented by McDonalds, a world of ceaseless change, cultural dislocation and savage greed. In so doing, the Confédération articulated deep-seated fears, tensions and anxieties within French society, bringing them out into the open and giving them concrete expression and visibility. It seemed to speak on behalf of all French men and women concerned about the nature of globalizing change and was widely identified with the 'general interest'.

Yet, the Confédération did more than simply express these tensions, it also offered a refuge from them, a retreat into a world of tradition, timelessness and security. At a moment of crisis, the Confédération revived a traditional symbol of identity, one that captured the essence of a lost Frenchness and 'a stable core of self, unfolding from the beginning to end through all the vicissitudes of history without change' (Bauman, 2001: 17). The Confédération's particular skill was to counterpose peasant farming against a prevailing image of neo-liberal globalization, so that it became its very antithesis. Where globalization was seen to threaten or homogenize identity, peasant farming embodied an identity that was culturally specific and rooted. Where globalization was viewed as ceaseless change and uncertainty, peasant farming represented a world of tradition and timelessness. Where globalization was seen to destroy social bonds, peasant farming offered an ideal of community rooted in rural village life. This became an antidote to all the evils of a malevolent globalizing world, one in which identity was reaffirmed, tradition preserved and social bonds restored.

Notes

1 Based on Pierre Bourdieu's *Language and Symbolic power,* I define symbolic power in the following way: (i) a capacity to use symbolic and discursive resources to construct new meanings and representations; (ii) the power to articulate and make visible latent sentiments and tensions within society; (iii) a capacity to use symbolic resources to generate power and influence within society (Cambridge: Polity Press, 1991). Bourdieu first developed the notion of symbolic power in the context of analysing kinship relationships in Kabyle society and he went on to use this concept to examine the educational system, the political field and gender relationships. This research in presented in the following books: Pierre Bourdieu, *The Logic of Practice* (Cambridge: Polity Press, 1990); *La noblesse d'Etat* (Paris: Minuit, 1989); *Language and Symbolic Power; La domination masculine* (Paris: Seuil, 1998).

2 The symbol of the French cockerel dates from the medieval period, but it was during the Renassiance that it became linked with the idea of the French nation. Its etymological origins are in the Latin term *gallus*, which signifies both cockerel and Gallic. It became a popular symbol of national identity during the period of the French Revolution, but was replaced under Napoléon Bonaparte by the symbol of the eagle, seen to better symbolize the strength of the French Empire. By contrast, the tricolour which is the official symbol of the French nation dates from the period after the French Revolution (1794) and represents the three colours of liberty championed by the revolutionaries. The *coq gaulois* is included as one of the items in Pierre Nora's extensive study of realms of memory that are deemed to encapsulate French identity. See Michel

Pastoureau 'Le Coq gaulois', in P. Nora, *Les Lieux de Mémoire*, Volume III, Les France, pp. 506–39.

3 Henri Mendras (1967) *La Fin des paysans. Innovation et changement dans l'agriculture française* (Paris: Sedeis). The title of the English translation of Mendras' book, *The Vanishing Peasant. Innovation and Change in French Agriculture* (translated by Jean Lerner Cambridge and London: MIT Press, 1970) suggests an ongoing process and does not have the same sense of finality as the original French title. Other key texts documenting the demise of the peasantry and its broad social and cultural implications include Roland Maspetiol *L'Ordre éternel des champs: Essai sur l'histoire économique et les valeurs de la paysannerie* (Paris: Librairie Médicis, 1946) and Jean-François Gravier, *Paris et le désert français* (Paris: Flammarion, 1947).

4 Eugen Weber, *Peasants into Frenchmen: The Modernization of Rural France, 1870–1914* (Stanford: Stanford University Press, 1976). For a discussion of Weber's book, see the special issue of the journal *French Politics, Culture and Society* dedicated to this work (vol. 27, no. 2, Summer 2009).

5 Schneider emphasizes the emotive and irrational character of modern myths: 'Modern myths do not consist of something accessible to reason but something that acts as a stimulus and is taken in emotionally' (Schneider, 1988: 31).

6 See E. J. Hobsbawm & T. Ranger, *The Invention of Tradition* (Cambridge: Cambridge University Press, 1983). In his introduction, Eric Hobsbawm defined 'invented traditions' as follows ' "Invented tradition" is taken to mean a set of practices, normally governed by overtly or tacitly accepted rules and of a ritual or symbolic nature, which seek to inculcate certain values and norms of behaviour by repetition, which automatically implies continuity with the past. In fact, where possible, they normally attempt to establish continuity with a suitable historic past. . . . However, insofar as there is such reference to a historic past, the peculiarity of "invented" traditions is that the continuity with it is largely fictitious. In short, they are responses to novel situations which take the form of reference to old situations, or which establish their own past by quasi-obligatory repetition.' (Hobsbawm, 1983: 1f.).

7 In 2000 to 2001, the Californian winemaker Robert Mondavi tried to buy land in the village of Aniane in order to build a new winery that would produce high-quality wine. Barthel-Bouchier and Clough note that the company's representatives underestimated the symbolic importance of their attempt to purchase land and they were seen as representatives of an American-owned multinational corporation in a stand-off that became known as *l'affaire Mondavi*. Ironically, when French film superstar Gérard Depardieu later purchased a vineyard in the village, it was interpreted very differently and welcomed by most locals as a reinforcement of a shared cultural patrimony (Barthel-Bouchier & Clough, 2005).

8 See Robert C. Ulin, *Vintages and Traditions: An Ethnohistory of Southwest French Wine Cooperatives* (Washington DC: Smithsonian Institution Press, 1996). On the symbolic importance of bread, see Steven L. Kaplan, *Le retour du bon pain: une histoire contemporaine du pain, de ses techniques et de ses hommes* (Paris: Perrin, DL, 2002) and *Le pain maudit: retour sur la France*

des années oubliées, 1945–1958 (Paris: Fayard, 2008). On chocolate, see Susan J. Terrio, *Crafting the Culture and History of French Chocolate* (Berkeley: University of California Press, 2000), and on cheese, see Pierre Broisard, *Le Camembert, mythe national* (Paris: Calmann-Levy, 1992). Laurence Bérard and Philippe Marchenay define produits de terroir in the following way: 'local agricultural products and foodstuffs . . . whose qualities cross time and space and are anchored in a specific place and history. Products such as Epoisses de Bourgogne or foie gras are defined by the fact that they depend on the shared savoir-faire of a given community and culture' (Bérard & Marchenay in S. Blowen, M. Demossier & J. Picard eds. 2000, 154).

9 Cited by Sean Fitzgerald, 'The Anti-Modern Rhetoric of Le Mouvement Poujade', *Review of Politics*, 32 (1970), 168.

10 Via Campesina was launched in Belgium in May 1993 and set out a number of key objectives: food sovereignty, food safety, agrarian reform, overhaul of the World Trade Organization, biodiversity, biotechnology, sustainable development and opposition to genetically modified food. Three years later, at an international meeting of Via Campesina attended by 69 different associations from 39 different countries, these principles were formally incorporated into the association's statutes (Losson & Quinio, 2002).

11 Raphaëlle Besse Desmoulières and Gaëlle Dupont, *Le Monde* (12 August 2003). Larzac has been a symbolic site of protest in France ever since the 1970s when local peasant farmers fought against the extension of the plateau's military camp and the expropriation of their farms. The 2003 rally in Larzac was held 30 years after the first mass gathering on the plateau and served to confirm its status as a symbol of resistance against forces of oppression and power. See Williams, 2008.

12 'Larzac 2003 – José Bové: en avril 2004, j'arrête d'être porte-parole' *L'Humanité* (11 August 2003).

13 'Je suis prêt à assumer d'aller à l'Elysée' *Libération* 14 juin 2006.

14 'Bové souhaite un tribunal international pour faire la chasse aux "criminals financiers"', *Agence de Presse*, 10 octobre 2008.

15 This action was prompted by high import duties imposed by the US authorities on certain European products (including Roquefort cheese) in retaliation at the European Union's decision to ban American hormone-treated beef. For farmers within the Massif Central region who sold ewes' milk to the Roquefort firms and who depended for their incomes and livelihoods on the sale of Roquefort cheese on foreign markets, this decision posed a specific threat to their interests. See Bové & Dufour (2000) and Williams (2008).

7

Conclusion

For free-market ideologues whose theories helped define the world order over the past 30 years, globalization is about 'the integration of economic activities, via markets' and this is a rational, 'natural' and progressive process that brings universal benefits to all (Bisley, 2007: 19). The market is seen as a great unifying force that overcomes barriers, smoothes out differences and reconciles all people in relation to the freedoms and opportunities of the economy. In the wake of the 2008 economic crisis, despite a massive public outcry and intense political backlash, such views were reasserted and many argued that the solution to the crisis lay not in state intervention, but in the self-regulating market itself, which if left to its own devices, would soon re-establish a new and harmonious equilibrium.

We have seen that in France, globalization has often been perceived in a radically different light. Here, globalization has not been considered as a benign market reform, but as a form of tyranny that crushes democratic rights and freedoms and threatens the very foundations of French and European societies. It has not been seen as a source of progress, but as a nightmare of regression, a 'conservative revolution' that drags France backwards to a premodern *ancien régime* where no common rules exist, where rights are trampled upon and where each person turns on his/her neighbour. It has not been seen as a force for unity, but as the cause of bitter conflict and tension, exacerbating divisions within French society and widening the gap between rich nations and the world's poor. Such views are widely diffused throughout French society and have been articulated by political leaders, intellectuals, activists, trade unionists, peasant farmers and ordinary people. This has meant that France, compared with its European counterparts, has had an exceptionally conflictual relationship with globalization. We have seen that France has been at the forefront of opposition to neo-liberalism on an international stage and has gone further than any other European country in denouncing the effects of unbridled capitalism, calling for regulatory controls and appealing for an alternative model for the world economy.

This book set out to examine the nature and causes of French opposition to globalization. Why does France produce greater resistance to globalization than any other country? How is globalization represented and conceptualized within the French public sphere? My key argument is that French opposition transcends the economic realm and touches on more complex, deeply rooted and irreducible questions of identity. At stake are not questions of economic calculus, trade advantage or market position, but the fundamental means by which the French define themselves and their place in the world. If France was marked by a deeper hostility to globalization than elsewhere, this is because it was here that globalization came into sharpest conflict with the terms of national political culture and identity. In France, globalization is rarely perceived as a piecemeal market change or economic reform, but is viewed instead as an assault on an entire civilization grounded in immutable ideological principles and a set of institutions that have been defined over two centuries. In political life, French leaders have denounced globalization as a danger to France and to the French way of life and this is 'a sea of globalization' that threatens to engulf the Hexagon and make it disappear entirely from view. France's mission at a time of globalization was not to integrate and adapt to changes happening elsewhere, but rather, to assert its own identity, to defend its institutions and to project its values in the world. In intellectual life, globalization is portrayed as a cataclysm, an impending disaster or a horror that threatens France and the world with irreversible change. Some intellectuals argued that France, just like during other periods of history, was faced again with a profound external threat, a 'neo-liberal invasion' and that resistance was the only recourse available to those who wished to save France and democracy itself. Similarly, social movements expressed the dangers of globalization in terms of the foundational values, structures and traditions of French political culture. For Attac, neo-liberalism was an attack on human reason and on a tradition of rationalism with its origins in the Enlightenment. Its leaders saw education as a critical means of resistance and a way to challenge the indoctrination that it linked with a hegemonic neo-liberal model. For the Confédération paysanne, globalization was a vanguard for American imperialism that was endangering both public health and France's unique cultural identity. In French public debates, opposition to globalization tends to eschew economic arguments in favour of more urgent and compelling metaphors of 'tyranny', 'barbarism', 'invasion' and 'chaos'.

A key aim of this book was to examine how French identity has been renegotiated at a time of globalizing transformation. The question of what French national identity is and what it signifies today is a source of exhaustive and ongoing scholarly debate and has also become more recently, a sub-ject of intense political controversy. Leading French historians including Jules Michelet, Fernand Braudel and Pierre Nora set out, through their exten-sive national histories, to discover the authentic core of French identity, to safeguard it from changes in the present and to preserve it for all poster-ity. For them, identity was largely an essence, something precious, organic and pre-given that was transmuted unchanged from the past and preserved from one generation to the next. They believed that it was by looking back-wards towards the specific national historical experience, towards long-term structural transformations over time, that the genuine core of French identity could be unearthed. In this book, I have favoured a constructivist approach to French identity that is influenced by recent work by critical historians such as Suzanne Citron, Gérard Noiriel and Anne-Marie Thiesse. For them, identity is not an essence, but a construct that is constantly reinvented in response to the changing preoccupations and needs of the present moment. These writ-ers emphasize the constructed, imagined and invented nature of identity and the way that it is determined both by present contingencies and by a recon-structed past. Identity tends to become important at times of crisis when a community or nation is faced with profound transformation or external threat. At such times, identity becomes a means to resolve tensions in society, to rebuild the threads of community, and to reaffirm a sense of belonging, cohe-sion and rootedness. While identity may, to some extent, be inherent within a community and reflect the impact of a common heritage, shared institu-tions, collective values and culture, it is also something that is fabricated and which may be imposed on society from above. These historians emphasize the malleable nature of identity and the way in which it can be invoked by political leaders in order to further their own instrumental goals. At times of crisis, politicians may exploit widespread fears and anxieties in society, taking advantage of what Alain Badiou refers to as a state of generalized disorienta-tion in order to present themselves as guardians of a national identity under attack (Badiou, 2007). National identity becomes a tool that is manipulated as a way of mobilizing popular support and fulfilling political goals.

If identity has become such an important concern in France today, this is because globalization has been experienced as an external threat, one that challenges the foundations of the political order, violates collectively defined values and that turns the whole pattern of national identity upside down. We have seen that globalization challenges French identity in a num-ber of fundamental ways. Firstly, it calls into question the foundational val-ues on which the French Republic is built, values that are seen to be valid for all people and all time and which are held as sacred and absolute. Whereas economic goods in a globalized society may be subject to negotiation and exchange, ideological principles are not and to transgress these is to call into question the very substance of national identity. Secondly, globalization challenges the French republican model and the role of the state as representative of the 'general interest' of the people. The rise of supranational institutions and the transfer of sovereignty from national to international institutions is seen to diminish the capacity of the French state to represent its citizens and therefore to undermine a fundamental aspect of democracy itself. Thirdly, globalization threatens France's social model and the capacity of the state to protect its citizens from the vagaries of market forces. It is associated with a decline in state intervention, reduced public spending, rising inequalities and the spectre of an American-style ghettoization of French society. We have seen that the French social model is viewed as much more than an instrument for ensuring equality or redistributing wealth and it is also perceived as a cornerstone of national identity. Fourthly, globalization challenges France's international stature and therefore an enduring aspect of the nation's self-image. In fact, fears about globalization are often bound up with fears about national decline and the prospect of a diminished status in relation to the United States and to rising economic power of China and India. Fifthly, globalization challenges French cultural identity and the belief in an exceptional culture with an influence beyond national borders. Instead of radiating its culture elsewhere, France seems to have been submerged by a commercialized, uniform and inferior culture of American origin which is threatening a collective sense of being.

In the face of globalization, contemporary France has been marked by an intense reaffirmation of identity. It is at the level of identity that the French have confronted globalization and negotiated their place in a changing international order. For Zygmunt Bauman, identity is an essential means of creating safety in an insecure world:

> It is like a roof under which we shelter in heavy rain, like a fireplace at which we warm our hands on a frosty day. Out there, in the street, all sorts of dangers lie in ambush; we have to be alert when we go out, watch whom we are talking to and who talks to us, be on the look-out every minute. In here, in the community, we can relax – we are safe, there are no dangers looming in dark corners. (Bauman, 2001: 2)

French identity today is expressed in complex and multifaceted ways and assumes a diversity of symbolic and representational forms. These expressions of identity can be situated at a conjunction between past and present and they are shaped both by a legacy of national history and by the pressures of globalizing transformations in the present. On the one hand, identity reactivates the past, projecting the myths, traditions and collective ideals that are seen to define Frenchness itself. Identity turns backwards in search of itself, looking for foundational myths that can help provide a stable and unchanging sense of self that transcends the vicissitudes of time. On the other hand, identity is always a response to a novel situation and is defined in relation to new challenges to community or belonging. Identity is character-ized by an 'invention of tradition' in which the past is invoked as a symbolic resource, a means to defend the cultural integrity of the community at times of threat, either imagined or real (Hobsbawm & Ranger, 1992). In contem-porary France, identity increasingly provides an antidote to all the perceived evils of a globalized world, conjuring up a 'utopia before the eyes of those who longed for a way out of the confusion of modernity and the rush of time' (Drescher et al., 1982: 4). Frenchness is re-imagined as a fairytale world far removed from the harsh realities of the present, a place in which identity is intact, tradition is preserved and social bonds are restored.

How has French national identity been conceptualized at a time of glo-balizing change? In contemporary France, identity has been symbolically expressed through a multiplicity of representational forms. Firstly, by the return of the Republic as a unifying symbol of national belonging, one that garners support across the Left and Right and throughout civil society. Different observers have pointed to a resurgence of republican identity fol-lowing a period after 1968 when this had fallen into disuse within mainstream political discourse (Bernstein, 2007; Schnapper, 2008). Republican identity today is shaped by the legacy of a national past and by historical references such as the Enlightenment, the French Revolution and Third Republic; by foundational values linked to the 1789 Declaration of the Rights of Man and in particular those of equality, solidarity, justice and human rights; and by a set of republican institutions identified with *L'Etat providence* or the Welfare state. Yet, republican identity today also constitutes an explicit response to the challenges posed by globalization. The Republic is increasingly held up as a besieged fortress or a rampart and as the sole defence against a glo-balizing tide that threatens to sweep France away. Some on the Left have appealed for a return to the French Revolution whose teachings alone can provide a solution to contemporary ills and help to lead the world out of crisis. They argue that the French Revolution is still incomplete and can fulfil its own intrinsic goals by spreading its democratic message in today's complex and divided globalized world (Ferrand, 2007; Peillon, 2008). Others on the Right have posited the Republic is a model of order, stability and authority in the face of the 'immoral capitalism' of globalization (Sarkozy, 2009b). Faced with all the pressures of globalization, the Republic is reinvented as a pure ideal that is increasingly disconnected from its links to concrete historical events, that is freed of all conflicts and divisions and presented as the antithesis to a disorderly, immoral and chaotic globalized world.

Secondly, by the resurgence of colonial identity that acts as a repository for references to past grandeur, international influence, *rayonnement* and national purpose. For Dino Costantini, French identity today is inextricably linked with a historical legacy of colonialism which continues to shape perceptions of France's role and status in the world. Nicolas Sarkozy's presidency was marked by a quest to rehabilitate the positive legacy of French colonialism and to integrate this within a unified concept of national history. Colonial identity reaches for the past and for the myths of national greatness that were linked, in particular, to the Third Republic's project of imperial expansion. Yet, this has also become a critical means of negotiating France's relationship with globalization and political debates on this question are steeped in references to France's colonial past. While Lionel Jospin suggested that France's role was to 'tame' the 'jungle' of globalization, Jacques Chirac sought to 'humanise' financial capitalism by eliminating its more primitive and destructive elements. Meanwhile, Nicolas Sarkozy defined France's vocation as a 'civilizing project' whereby it would once again radiate its values elsewhere in the world, provide a model for others to follow and steer other nations towards a more enlightened path. Faced with a reality of diminishing international influence, colonial identity was a means to subvert reality and to conjure up an image of a nation that was still at the hub of the universe whose civilizing influence stretched across all four corners of the world.

Thirdly, by the rise of rural identity and of a rich symbolic universe linked to images of the peasantry, the land, village life and agrarian traditions. This identity manifests distinctive features of French history and in particular, the country's enduring peasant roots and the historical importance of agriculture as economic activity, cultural practice and way of life. Yet, in contemporary France, rural identity has been reactivated explicitly as a means of negotiating France's relationship with globalization. On the one hand, it serves as a bulwark against globalization, opening up a traditional, wholesome and stable world, one that binds the French to their past and that is immune from changes in the present. In a world of ceaseless change and dislocation, it offers a model of rootedness, timelessness and community, a gateway to 'communal innocence, pristine sameness and tranquillity' (Bauman, 2001: 18). We know that rural imagery has been reactivated throughout French history as a means of dealing with periods of great social, economic and cultural change, so that the figure of the peasant is constantly being brought to life and laid to rest again in response to changing needs and contingencies (Rogers, 1987). On the other hand, it provides a model of resistance and in particular, resistance to change. The figure of the peasant has been revived as a symbolic means to affirm French identity and to reject the changes linked to globalization. Hence, José Bové cultivated his image as the archetypal peasant who was fiercely attached to the land, resolute in his principles and who refused to bow to external pressures. He argued that neo-liberalism was illegitimate because it placed profit over people and undermined the notion of the public good which had historically defined the relationship between French peasants and the people. Rural identity provided a powerful resource for channelling French fears about globalization, for invalidating the claims of neo-liberalism and for expressing the distinctive nature of French identity.

Fourthly, by the rise of a conception of identity rooted in Enlightenment tradition. French identity has long been influenced by the core ideals of the Enlightenment and in particular a belief in human reason, science and the progress of the human race itself. These ideals underpinned the Third Republic's objective to bring learning to the people by introducing a universal and secular system of primary education. Yet, these principles have been revived in contemporary France as a means of expressing and legitimizing opposition to globalization. Hence, leftist intellectuals have criticized globalization not solely on economic grounds, but because it is seen to run counter to the ideals of the Enlightenment and the belief in a political order grounded in values of progress and rationalism. Globalization is portrayed as fundamentally irrational, a system unconstrained by the bounds of human reason, driven by erratic and disruptive market forces. For instance, Attac identified itself with an Enlightenment belief in education as a force for dispelling popular prejudices and ignorance and for improving the human condition as a whole. It saw globalization as an attack on rational thought which it viewed as the cornerstone for modern society itself. Its ambition was to 'detoxify' people's minds and thereby to help liberate all human beings from the chains of neo-liberal dogma.

Does French opposition provide a transformative project that reaches beyond French borders and offers an alternative model for the world economy? Or is it a defensive reaction to change, one that rejects the outside world and that exalts an idealized sense of collective self? I have argued that the French have experienced globalization at the level of identity, but that this identity-based response has had deeply contradictory effects on the nature of French opposition. This opposition tends to reach outwards beyond national borders towards a vision of democratic transformation on a universal scale and also turn inwards, reinstating borders and taking refuge behind the high walls of national identity. France's response to globalization is both progressive in that it aspires towards a world order in which democratic and humanist values prevail, and at the same time regressive, in that it only accepts change on its own terms and seeks to bend the world to its vision.

We have seen that France has acted as a progressive force on the world stage, challenging the key assumptions of neo-liberalism, asserting democratic and humanist ideals and calling for regulatory controls on market forces. Zygmunt Bauman has noted that the trouble with our contemporary world is that it has stopped questioning itself:

> The price of silence is paid in the hard currency of human suffering. Asking the right questions makes, after all, all the difference between fate and destination, drifting and travelling. Questioning the ostensibly unquestionable premises of our way of life is arguably the most urgent of the services we owe our fellow humans and ourselves. (Bauman, 1998: 5)

At a time when the neo-liberal model seemed triumphant, when market transformations were widely viewed as natural and inevitable and economic liberalization was often accepted unquestioningly by national governments, France was one of the few countries to ask these fundamental questions. French politicians, thinkers and activists, in the face of an overwhelming consensus in relation to free market ideology, transformed the economy into an object of controversy, conflict and debate. In international settings, French leaders denounced the destructive effects of neo-liberalism and called for radical reform. They introduced innovative measures to regulate market forces and to redistribute wealth, such as the Tobin tax and the airline solidarity tax. They acted as an advocate for poorer countries, emphasizing the effects of globalization on world poverty and creating new mechanisms for wealth redistribution. French intellectuals helped to renew the parameters of leftist opposition, constructing new analytical tools and critical instruments that helped to lay the foundations for a movement of opposition to globalization on an international stage. In the face of market transformations that seemed complex, distant and unseen, they helped to make visible and identifiable a system of power and thereby to provide a clear target for leftist opposition. They argued that globalization was not the product of abstract market forces that lay outside of human control, but the outcome of specific decisions made by particular political leaders at a specific place and time. Meanwhile, French social movements are integrated into vast international networks that bring together activists from across the world and they have been a critical force in international opposition at the World Social Forum and at demonstrations against the G8, World Trade Organization and International Monetary Fund.

In expressing their opposition to globalization, the French have turned to the political and ideological resources of their own national culture and identity. A notion of 'Frenchness' rooted in symbols of the Republic, rural France or the Enlightenment, provided a counter model to neo-liberalism, a means to challenge its claims and to posit an alternative model. We have seen that politicians, intellectuals and activists drew on the positivist values of republican tradition to articulate their hostility towards globalization. They argued that these values were the cornerstone of European civilization and could provide a blueprint for an alternative world order, one that placed the human being and not money at its centre. French identity also offered a countervailing institutional model in which the state took precedence over market forces and was responsible for protecting citizens from the vagaries of the market. This republican model helped to inspire the concept of 'mondialisation maîtrisée' which provided an alternative model to neo-liberalism at international level. Some have suggested that in the wake of the 2008 economic crisis which discredited neo-liberalism, this French-inspired model could gain fresh legitimacy and influence (Abdelal & Meunier, 2010).

If French identity provided a means to construct a transformative internationalist project, it was also a pretext to reaffirm borders and to take refuge in a narrow and idealized sense of collective self. Identity is highly manipulable and can be harnessed towards very different ends, both progressive and regressive. At a time of globalizing transformation, the French seem to have taken refuge in their past and in national myths and ideals that project a fictionalized identity. Anthony Cohen has shown how the past can be used as a means to reinforce the cultural integrity of a community at times of profound change:

> Symbols of the 'past', mythically infused with timelessness, have precisely this competence, and attain particular effectiveness during periods of intense social change when communities have to drop their heaviest cultural anchors in order to resist the currents of transformation. . . . It is the very imprecision of these references to the past – timelessness masquerading as history – which makes them so apt a device for symbolism and, in particular, for expressing symbolically the continuity of past and present, and for reasserting the cultural integrity of the community in the face of the apparent subversion by the forces of change. (Cohen, 1985: 102–03)

This vision of French identity served purely to restore national pride, reaffirm a sense of distinctiveness and flatter a sense of *amour propre*. French critics have emphasized that the theme of national identity can be appropriated by political leaders to advance purely instrumental goals. For Gérard Noiriel, identity is always inseparable from a broader political project and it is a means to reinforce the goals of nationalism. He argues that at a time of crisis, Nicolas Sarkozy exploited popular fears and anxieties and presented himself as a saviour of the people who alone could defend national identity, heal the wounds of the nation and restore national pride (Noiriel, 2007).

I have argued in this book that paradoxically, identity was used by French leaders as an instrument for furthering economic globalization. The appeal to a strong, independent and proud nation was not intended to slow down or obstruct processes of market liberalization, but rather to allow them to happen on an unprecedented scale. The peculiar strategy of French political leaders was to reinvent national identity as a polar opposite to globalization and therefore as a means to cushion and offset its worst effects. It allowed them to maintain the illusion of a France that was still a leader on the world stage and that remained true to its own traditions, while all the while implementing profound structural changes in the economy. It is ironic that an idealized identity which repudiated outside change created the discursive context in which that very change could take place. France's relationship with globalization resembles an elaborate vanishing act, in which economic realities are made to disappear behind repetitive and persuasive invocations to national greatness and intransigence. Anne-Marie Thiesse has shown how historically, national identity has provided a potent symbol of continuity at times of profound transformation and provided a precondition for changes to take place and in particular processes of economic modernization (Thiesse, 2001).

We have seen that while French intellectuals helped to launch a radical critique of neo-liberalism, they also pandered to cultural stereotypes that demonized France's perceived enemies and venerated France as the quintessential site of civilization. While challenging the economic determinism of neo-liberal theory, they tended to replace this with their own form of cultural determinism that reduced complex economic processes to a pre-given cultural essence, identified with the 'Anglo-Saxon world'. For Emmanuel Todd, the economic dimension of globalization was a mere obscuration for deeper cultural and anthropological forces that predetermined the relationship between France and the Anglo-Saxon world. In his view, globalization manifested the inherent characteristics of an Anglo-Saxon model that he traced back to its English and Calvinist roots and which was characterized by an 'extreme individualism'. He described France's relationship with globalization in terms of an 'anthropological opposition' between a progressive egalitarian French model and a regressive Anglo-Saxon individualism (Todd, 1999). Similarly, Hervé Juvin, in examining the 2008 economic crisis, developed an essentialist vision that saw this as a product of a reckless and expansionist American model, evoked in terms of clichéd images of cowboys, frontiersmen and the Wild West. He situated the economic crisis within an anthropological project of American origin that sought to transform the human condition, by stripping people of their political and cultural attachments and turning them into slaves to the market. France and Europe are cast as innocent bystanders in the face of cataclysmic forces that are beyond their control and which have left them powerless to act (Juvin, 2010). As Frédéric Lordon makes clear, such a perspective tends to ignore the specific role of French politicians and in particular, Socialist leaders, in ushering in neo-liberal reforms and thereby creating the conditions for the crisis in Europe (Lordon, 2009). For the above writers, all that is wrong with France comes from outside its borders and France should respond by creating a fenced-off and walled-up nation, one that more clearly separates 'them' from 'us'.

If France's identity-based response to globalization has helped to exert a democratic influence on the international stage, it has by contrast, had damaging consequences within French society itself. The preoccupation with an idealized national identity has created a dangerous chasm between the real and the ideal, one which is open to distortion and manipulation. On the one hand, French identity has been elevated to a pure myth, an expanse of boundless imagination that is completely disconnected from concrete realities on the ground. On the other, France, in reality, is integrated into an international economy and its fate is increasingly determined by forces outside of national control. To sustain the myth of French identity requires battle lines to be drawn and an idealized Frenchness is forever in need of vigilance, fortification and defence. This gap between the real and the ideal allows political leaders to impose their own version of reality, one that is suited to their particular political designs. In contemporary France, political leaders have tended to channel widespread discontent about the effects of neo-liberalism away from economic processes and towards more visible and identifiable targets:

> Strangers are unsafety incarnate and so they embody by proxy that insecurity which haunts your life. In a bizarre yet perverse way their presence is comforting, even reassuring: the diffuse and scattered fears, difficult to pinpoint and name, now have a tangible target to focus on, you know where the dangers reside and you need no longer take the blows of fate placidly. At long last, there is something you can do. (Bauman, 2001: 145)

French critics have identified a direct causal relationship between economic globalization and a rising xenophobia (Sieffert, 2006; Badiou, 2007; Noiriel, 2007). Unlike the deeds of multinational corporations which are often kept out of sight and when in public view, are often poorly comprehended, immigrant communities are a visible and recognizable presence within French society. They are increasingly targeted as the source of France's manifold ills from national decline, social disorder to moral decadence. While Nicolas Sarkozy, in the wake of the economic crisis, accorded greater freedoms to market forces, he imposed tough new restrictions on the freedoms of immigrant communities living in France. These, he suggested, and not multinational companies were the real source of France's problems and their freedoms needed urgently to be curtailed. While keen to pursue the dream of an open economic space, free of all restrictions, he sought to erect new borders and walls to restrict freedom of movement within France and to stop outsiders from coming in. France's identity-based response to globalization is indeed highly ambivalent and has been both a force for democratic and progressive transformation and a means to justify the most repressive and hard-line policies pursued in the name of an endangered Republic.

Bibliography

Abdelal, R. & Meunier, S. (2010) 'Managed globalization: doctrine, practice and promise', *Journal of European Public Policy*, 17(3), 350–67.

Achar, G. (2006) *The Clash of Barbarisms. The Making of the New World Disorder*. London: Paradigm Publishers.

Actualité (2006) 'Sarkozy nous protège de la mondialisation', le 23 novembre. Available at: www.libres.org/francais/actualite/archives/actualite1106/mondialisation a3 4 . . .

Agence Presse France (2007) 'Chirac, un "animal politique" aux multiples visages.' 16 mai.

Agrikoliansky, E. & Sommier, I., eds. (2005) *Radiographie du Mouvement altermondialiste*. Paris: La Dispute.

Agrikoliansky, E., Fillieule, O. & Mayer, N. (2005) *L'Altermondialisme en France. La Longue histoire d'une nouvelle cause*. Paris: Flammarion.

Aguiton, C. & Bensaïd, D. (1997) *Le Retour de la question sociale. Le renouveau des mouvements sociaux en France*. Paris: Editions Page deux.

Aguiton, C. et al. (2011) *Tous dans la rue. Le mouvement social de l'automne 2010*. Paris: Seuil.

Ancelovici, M. (2002) 'Organizing against globalization: the case of ATTAC in France', *Politics & Society*, 30(3), 427–63.

Anderson, B. (1991) *Imagined Communities*. London & New York: Verso.

Anderson, P. (1999) 'Fernard Braudel and national identity', in S. Clark, ed. *The Annales School. Critical Assessments* (Vol III). London & New York: Routledge, pp. 268–93.

—(2006) 'The world made flesh' (review of H. Juvin's *L'avènement du corps*), *New Left Review*, 39, May–June, 132–9.

—(2009) *The New Old World*. London & New York: Verso.

Appel des résistants à la jeune génération de mars 2004. Available at: http://jerpel.fr/spip.php?article21

Applebaum, A. (2007) 'Farewell, Jacques Chirac: a leader with a deep scorn for fostering democracy', *The Washington Post*, 8 May.

Apter, D. E. (2006) 'Symbols in action: Willy Brandt's kneefall at the Warsaw memorial', in J. L. Alexander, B. Giesen & J. L. Mast, eds. *Social Performance: Symbolic Action, Cultural Pragmatics and Ritual*. Cambridge & New York: Cambridge University Press.

Arthuis, J. (2007) *Mondialisation. La France à contre-emploi*. Paris: Calmann-Lévy.

Attac (2002a) *Tout sur Attac 2002*. Paris: Mille et Une Nuits.

—(2002b) *Attac au Zénith*. Paris: Mille et Une Nuits.

—(2003) *Lignes d'Attac*, 25, jan/feb.

Audier, S. (2010) *La pensée solidariste. Aux sources du modèle républicain.* Paris: Presses universitaires de France.

Badiou, A. (2007) *De quoi Sarkozy est-il le nom?* Paris: Lignes.

Barber, B. J. (1995) *Jihad vs. McWorld.* New York: Times Books.

Barthel-Bouchier, D. & Clough, L. (2005) 'From Mondavi to Depardieu. The global/local politics of wine', *French Politics, Culture & Society*, 23(2), Summer, 71–90.

Bauman, Z. (1998) *Globalization. The Human Consequences.* Cambridge: Polity.

—(2001) *Community. Seeking Safety in an Insecure World.* Cambridge: Polity Press.

—(2006) *Liquid Fear.* Cambridge: Polity.

Bavarez, N. (2003) *La France qui tombe.* Paris: Perrin.

—(2007) 'Pourquoi je vote Nicolas Sarkozy', *Le Point,* 12 avril.

—(2009) Après le déluge. La grande crise de la mondialisation. Paris: Perrin.

Belmont, C. (1999) 'Le Monde paysan envahit les McDo', *Le Figaro*, 1 September.

Bennhold, K. (2007) 'Sarkozy urges French to play "the game of globalization"', *The New York Times*, 31 August.

Bernardin, J.-F. (2008) *Pour une vision réaliste et plurielle de la mondialisation.* Paris: Conseil économique, social et environnemental.

Bernstein, S. (2007) 'L'Idée de la République. Les caractéristiques de la culture républicaine', *Cahiers français*, 336, jan–fev, 8–13.

Bernstein, S. & Rudelle, O., eds. (1992) *Le modèle républicain.* Paris: Presses universitaires de France.

Berthet, S. (2007) 'Constat à l'aimable', in E. Ferrand, ed. *Quelle République pour le 21ᵉ siècle?* Paris: L'Harmattan, pp. 47–55.

Besset, J.-P. (1999) 'Le Robin des bois du Larzac se livre à la justice', *Le Monde*, 21 August.

Binet, L. (2008) 'Supporting Europe and voting no', in M. Maclean & J. Szarka, eds. *France on the World Stage. Nation State Strategies in the Global Era.* Basingstoke: Palgrave Macmillan, pp. 111–26.

Bisley, N. (2007) *Rethinking Globalization.* Basingstoke: Palgrave Macmillan.

Blowen, S., Demossier, M. & Picard, J., eds. (2000) *Recollections of France: The Past, Heritage and Memories.* New York & Oxford: Berghahn.

Boltanski, L, & Chiapello, E. (1999) *Le Nouvel esprit du capitalisme.* Paris: Gallimard.

Boniface, P. (2007) *Lettre ouverte à notre futur(e) président(e) de la République sur le rôle de la France dans le monde.* Paris: Armand Colin.

Bonney, R. (2008) *False Prophets. The 'Clash of Civilizations' and the Global War on Terror.* Oxford: Peter Lang.

Booth, K. (1997) 'Huntington's homespun grandeur', *The Political Quarterly*, 68(4), 425–8.

Boudon, R. (2004) *Pourquoi les intellectuals n'aiment pas le libéralisme.* Paris: Odile Jacob.

Bourdieu, P. (1989) *The Logic of Practice.* Cambridge: Polity Press.

—(1991) *Language and Symbolic Power.* Oxford: Polity Press.

—(1998) *Contre-feux. Propos pour servir à la résistance contre l'invasion néo-libérale.* Paris: Liber-Raisons d'agir.

—(2001) *Contre-feux 2. Pour un mouvement social européen*. Paris: Liber-Raisons d'agir.

Bové, J. (2000) 'Ce n'est qu'un début', *Télérama*, 9 February.

—(2007) *Candidat rebelle*. Paris: Hachette Littératures.

Bové, J. & Dufour, F. (2000) *Le Monde n'est pas une marchandise. Des paysans contre la malbouffe*. Paris: La Découverte.

Bunting, M. (2011) 'Rather than wallow in the boom in gloom, we need to decline gracefully: Politicians may be too nervous to address Britain's increasing irrelevance on the world stage, but they must' *The Guardian*, 24 January.

Braudel, F. (1988) *The Identity of France Vol. 1: History and Environment*. Translated by Siân Reynolds London: Collins.

—(1990) *The Identity of France Vol. 2: People and Production*. Translated by Siân Reynolds, London: Collins.

Brouard, S. & Tiberj, V. (2006) *Le Baromètre politique français 2006–2007*. Paris: Cevipof.

Bruneau, I. (2001) 'La Confédération paysanne', *Regards sur l'actualité*, 269, March.

—(2004) 'La Confédération paysanne et le "mouvement altermondialiste". L'international comme enjeu syndical', *Politix,* 17, 68.

—(2006) *La Confédération paysanne: s'engager à juste distance*. PhD thesis, Université Paris X, November.

Burke, K. (1952) *A Grammar of Motives*. New York: Prentice-Hall.

Cambadélis, J. C. (2002) 'Il faut que les socialistes résistent à l'air du temps', *Libération*, 2 décembre.

Capdevielle, J. (2001) *Modernité du corporatisme*. Paris: Presses de Sciences Po.

Cassen, B. (2003) 'On the Attack', *New Left Review*, 19, Jan–Feb, 41–60.

Chafer, T. (2005) 'Chirac and "la Françafrique": no longer a family affair', *Modern & Contemporary France*, 13(1), 7–23.

Chatterjee, P. (1986) *Nationalist Thought and the Colonial World*. Tokoyo/London: Zed Press.

Chevènement, J.-P. (2011) *La France est-elle finie?* Paris: Fayard.

Chirac, J. (2000) 'Texte de l'allocution prononcée par Jacques Chirac à la télévision et à la radio le 31 décembre 1999', *Le Monde*, 3 janvier.

—(2002a) Discours de M. Jacques Chirac, Président de la République devant l'Assemblée plénière de la conférence internationale sur le financement du développement à Monterrey, Mexique, le 22 mars.

—(2002b) Discours de M. Jacques Chirac Président de la République devant l'Assemblée plénière du Sommet Mondial du Développement Durable à Johannesburg, Afrique du Sud, le 2 septembre.

—(2005) Discours par visio-conférence de M. Jacques Chirac, Président de la République, devant le Forum économique mondial de Davos, Palais de l'Elysée, le 26 janvier.

—(2007) Dernière allocution présidentielle de Jacques Chirac, le 15 mai.

—(2008) Discours du Président Jacques Chirac à l'occasion du lancement de la Fondation Chirac, le 9 juin 2008 au Musée du Quai Branly.

—(2009) Chaque pas doit être un but. Mémoires 1. Paris: Nil.

Cohen, A. P. (1985) *The Symbolic Construction of Community*. London: Tavistock Publications.

Chrisafis, A., Black, I. & Traynor, I. (2009) 'G20: Sarkozy raises the stakes with walkout threat', *The Guardian*, 1 April.

Citron, S. (2008) *Le Mythe national. L'histoire de France revisitée.* Paris: Les Editions de l'Atelier.

Clout, H. & Demossier, M. (2003) 'New countryside, old peasants? Politics, tradition and modernity in rural France', *Modern & Contemporary France*, 11(3), 259–63.

Cogan, C. (2003) *French Negotiating Behavior: Dealing with La Grande Nation.* Washington, DC: United States Institute of Peace Press.

Cohen-Tanugi, L. (2008) *Une Stratégie européenne pour la mondialisation. Rapport en vue de la présidence française du Conseil de l'Union européenne.* Available at: www.euromonde2015.eu.

Cole, A. & Drake, H. (2000) 'The Europeanization of the French polity: continuity, change and adaptation', *Journal of European Public Policy*, 7(1), 26–43.

Confédération paysanne (1989) *Penser globalement, agir localement,* Assemblée générale du 19 et 20 avril 1989. Paris: Confédération paysanne.

—(2006) *Campagnes solidaires,* 212, November.

—(2007a) *Elections chambres* 2007: *Le Programme.* Paris Confédération paysanne.

—(2007b) *Campagnes solidaires,* 221, September.

—(2007c) *Campagnes solidaires,* 214, January.

Conklin, A. L. (1997) *A Mission to Civilize. The Republican Idea of Empire in France and West Africa, 1895–1930.* Stanford, CA: Stanford University Press.

Costantini, D. (2008) *Mission civilisatrice. Le role de l'histoire coloniale dans la construction de l'identité politique française.* Paris: La Découverte.

Coupé, A. (2006) 'A quite extraordinary movement', *International Socialism,* 111, July, 23–9.

Courbage, Y. & Todd, E. (2007) *Le Rendez-vous des civilisations.* Paris: Seuil

Crettiez, X. & Sommier, I. eds. (2002) *La France rebelle.* Paris: Michalon.

Damon, J. (2008) 'Les composantes de l'identité française. Quel modèle social?', *Cahiers français* no. 342 'L'identité nationale', 68–72.

Dardot, P. & Laval, C. (2011) 'Le Retour de la guerre sociale', in C. Aguiton et al. *Tous dans la rue. Le mouvement social de l'automne 2010.* Paris: Seuil, pp. 147–63.

Dauncey, H. (2010) 'L'Exception culturelle', in T. Chafer & E. Godin, eds. *The End of the French Exception? Decline and Revival of the 'French Model'.* Basingstoke: Palgrave Macmillan, pp. 72–84.

Davies, L. (2010) 'Sarkozy under fire after France shelves plans to introduce carbon tax', *The Guardian*, 24 March.

Debray, R. (1992) *Contretemps. Eloges des idéaux perdus.* Paris: Folio.

Demossier, M. (2000) 'Culinary heritage and *produits de terroir* in France: food for thought' in Blowen, Demossier & Picard (eds). op. cit., 141–53.

Desbos, C. (2006) Attac et la taxe Tobin: la gauche plurielle à l'épreuve de l'altermondialisation. PhD thesis, University of Limerick, Ireland.

Detienne, M. (2010) *L'identité nationale, une énigme.* Paris: Gallimard.

Dimitrakopoulos, D. G., Menon, A. & Passas, A. G. (2009) 'France and the EU under Sarkozy: between European ambitions and national objectives?', *Modern & Contemporary France* (special issue: The Sarkozy Presidency), 17(4), 451–65.

Dockès, P. (2007) *L'Enfer, ce n'est pas les autres. Bref essai sur la mondialisation.* Paris: Descartes & Cie.

Dosse, F. (1994) *New History in France. The Triumph of the Annales.* Urbana, IL: University of Illinois Press.

Drake, D. (2002). *Intellectuals and Politics in Post-War France.* Basingstoke: Palgrave.

Drescher, S., Sabean, D. & Sharlin, A., eds. (1982) *Political Symbolism in Modern Europe.* New Brunswick: Transaction.

Durand, G. (1992) 'La vigne et le vin', in P. Nora, ed. *Les Lieux de mémoire.* Tome III, Les France, Vol. 2, 'Traditions', 785–821.

Duval, J., Gaubert, C., Lebaron, F., Marchetti, D. & Pavis, F. (1998) *Le 'décembre' des intellectuels français.* Paris: Raisons d'agir.

Dyson, K. (1999) 'EMU, political discourse and the Fifth French Republic: historical institutionalism, path dependency and "craftsmen" of discourse' *Modern & Contemporary France,* 7(2), 179–96.

Elysée. fr (2009) *Mission sur la dimension sociale de la mondialisation confiée à Mme Christine Boutin.* Available at: www.elysee.fr/president/root/bank/print/1956.htm

Emery, M. (2010) 'Europe, immigration and the Sarkozian concept of fraternité', *French Cultural Studies,* 21(2), 115–29.

Eribon, D. (2007) *D'une Révolution conservatrice et de ses effets sur la gauche française.* Paris: Editions Léo Scheer.

European Commission, Directorate General Communication (2010) *Eurobarometer* 73 'Public Opinion in the European Union', Brussels: TNS Opinion & Social.

Farchy, J. (1999) *La fin de l'exception culturelle.* Paris: CNRS Editions.

Ferrand, E., ed. (2007) 'Pour une République revivifiée', in E. Ferrand, ed. *Quelle République pour le 21ᵉ siècle?* Paris: L'Harmattan, 9–14.

Finkielkraut, A. & Gallo, M. (2007) 'Comment peut-on être français?', *Le Figaro littéraire,* 15 March.

Forrester, V. (1996) *L'Horreur économique.* Paris: Fayard.

—(2000) *Une Etrange dictature.* Paris: Fayard.

Fougier, E. (2001) 'Perceptions de la mondialisation en France et aux Etats-Unis', *Politique étrangère,* 3, 569–87.

Fougier, E. ed. (2006) 'La France face à la mondialisation', *Problèmes politiques et sociaux* (numéro spécial) no. 920, janvier.

—(2008a) *L'Altermondialisme.* Paris: Le Cavalier Bleu.

—(2008b) 'Où en est le mouvement altermondialiste? Réflexions sur l'essoufflement', *La Vie des idées,* 3 mars. Available at: www.laviedesidees.fr/Ou-en-est-le-mouvement.html?

Frémont, A. (1992) 'La Terre', in P. Nora, ed. *Les Lieux de mémoire.* Tome III, Les France, Vol. 2, 'Traditions', 18–55.

George, S. (2002) 'Cette classe qui veut tout', in Attac (2002b), *Attac au Zénith.* Paris: Mille et Une Nuits, 29–31.

—(2007) 'Un nouveau départ pour Attac France' Transnational Institute, February. Available at: www.tni.org/article/un-nouveau-depart-pour-attac-france.

Gollain, F. (1999) 'Des Intellectuels contre l'idéologie économique', *Modern & Contemporary France,* 7(4), 485–97.

Gordon, P. & Meunier, S. (2001) *The French Challenge: Adapting to Globalization.* Washington, DC: Brookings Institution Press.

Grosrichard, F. (1999) 'Le monde agricole, entre surenchères et défis', *Le Monde,* 28 September.

Guichard, O. (2002) quoted by E. Zemmour in *L'homme qui ne s'aimait pas.* Paris: Balland, p. 33.

Guiral, A. & Losson, C. (2002) 'Comment Chirac est venu au monde', *Libération,* 9 September.

Hamilton, D. S. & Quinlan, J. P. (2008) *La France face à la mondialisation.* Washington, DC: Center for Transatlantic Relations.

Hardt, M. & Negri, A. (2000) *Empire.* Cambridge, MA: Harvard University Press.

—(2005) *Multitude.* London: Penguin Books.

Hayward, J. (1973) *The One and Indivisible French Republic.* London: Weidenfeld and Nicolson.

—(2007) *Fragmented France. Two Centuries of Disputed Identity.* Oxford: Oxford University Press.

Hazareesingh, S. (1994) *Political Traditions in Modern France.* Oxford: Oxford University Press.

Hessel, S. (2010) *Indignez-Vous!* Montpellier: Indigène Editions.

Hewlett, N. (2003) *Democracy in Modern France.* London & New York: Continuum.

Hochart, R. (2007) Discours de clôture du Congrès du Mans, 23 and 24 May.

Howarth, D. (2002), 'The European policy of the Jospin government: a new twist to old French games', *Modern & Contemporary France,* 10(3), 353–70.

—(2008) 'Using Europe to keep the world at bay: French policy on EU economic governance', in M. Maclean & J. Szarka, eds. *France on the World Stage. Nation State Strategies in the Global Era.* Basingstoke: Palgrave Macmillan.

Hugeux, V. (2007) 'Le testament de Chirac l'Africain', *L'Express,* le 15 février.

Huntington, S. (1997) *The Clash of Civilisations and the Remaking of the World Order.* New York: Simon & Schuster.

Izraelewicz, E. (1995) 'La première révolte contre la mondialisation', *Le Monde,* 7 décembre.

Jacoby, W. & Meunier, S. (2010) 'Europe and the management of globalization', *Journal of European Public Policy,* 17(3), 299–317.

Johnson, D. (2002) 'Obiturary: Pierre Bourdieu', *The Guardian,* 28 January 2002.

Jospin, L. (1998) 'La position française officielle sur l'AMI' *Déclaration de Lionel Jospin à l'Assemblée nationale, le 14 octobre 1998.* Available at: www.syti. net/AMI_Jospin.html

—(1999), *Modern Socialism.* London: The Fabian Society.

—(2002a) *My Vision of Europe and Globalization.* London: Polity.

—(2002b) *Le temps de répondre.* Paris: Stock.

—(2005) *Le Monde comme je le vois.* Paris: Gallimard.

Julliard, J. (2005) *Le Malheur français.* Paris: Flammarion.

Juvin, H. (2010) *Le Renversement du monde. Politique de la crise.* Paris: Gallimard.

Kaplan, S. (1999) 'Long-run lamentations: Braudel on France', in S. Clark, ed. *The Annales School. Critical Assessments,* vol. III. London & New York: Routledge, pp. 294–308.

Klein, N. (2002) *Fences and Windows*. London: Flamingo.

Kouvélakis, S. (2007) *La France en révolte. Luttes sociales et cycles politiques*. Paris: Textuel.

Kresl, P. & Gallais, S. (2002) *France Encounters Globalization*. Cheltenham: Edward Edgar.

Kuisel, R (1995) 'The France we have lost: social, economic and cultural discontinuities', in G. Flynn, ed. *Remaking the Hexagon. The New France in the New Europe*. Boulder, CO: Westview Press, pp. 31–48.

Latouche, S. (1996) *The Westernization of the World: The Significance, Scope and Limits of the Drive Towards Global Uniformity*. Cambridge: Polity.

Laurent, E. (2010) 'The French Carbon Tax. Autopsy of an ambition', *French Politics, Culture & Society*, 28(3) 114–22.

Laval, G. (1999a) 'Le briseur de McDo reste au frais', *Libération*, 1 September.

—(1999b) 'José Bové préfère la prison aux "chaînes de la mondialisation"', *Libération*, 1 September.

Lebègue, T. (2002) 'Le PS court après les altermondialistes', *Libération*, 1 décembre.

Legrand, T. (2010) *Ce n'est rien qu'un président qui nous fait perdre du temps*. Paris: Stock.

Lemieux, E. (2003) *Pouvoir intellectuel. Les nouveaux réseaux*. Paris: Denoël.

LeParisien. fr (2009) 'Chirac retourne sur ses terres', mis en ligne le 10 juin.

Lepeltier, S. (2004) *Réconcilier la France et la mondialisation*. Paris: Bureau de dialogue et d'initiative.

Levy, J. D. (2008), 'From the dirigiste state to the social anaesthesia state: French economic policy in the longue durée', *Modern & Contemporary France*, 16(4), November, 417–35.

Lichfield, J. (2006) 'Has Jacques Chirac's presidency been a complete disaster for France?', *The Independent*, 28 December.

Lindenberg, D. (2002) *Le Rappel à l'ordre*. Paris: Seuil.

—(2009) *Le Procès des Lumières*. Paris: Seuil.

Lordon, F. (2009) *La Crise de trop. Reconstruction d'un monde failli*. Paris: Fayard.

Losson, C. & Quinio, P. (2002) *Génération Seattle. Les rebelles de la mondialisation*. Paris: Grasset.

Maclean, M. & Szarka, J. eds. (2008) *France on the World Stage. Nation State Strategies in the Global Era*. Basingstoke: Palgrave Macmillan.

Majumdar, M. A. & Chafer, T. (2010) 'Back to the future? Franco-African relations in the shadow of France's colonial past', in T. Chafer & E. Godin, eds. *The End of the French Exception? Decline and Revival of the 'French Model'*. Basingstoke: Palgrave Macmillan, pp. 203–20.

Manifeste d'économistes atterrés (2010) Paris: Les Liens qui libèrent.

Maris, B. (2009) 'Sarko, nouvelle égérie d'Attac?', *Marianne*, 2, 16 juin.

Marlière, P. (2009) 'Sarkozysm as an ideological theme park. Nicolas Sarkozy and Right-wing political thought', *Modern & Contemporary France* (special issue: the Sarkozy Presidency) 17(4), 375–90.

Martigny, V. (2009) 'Le Débat autour de l'identité nationale dans la campagne présidentielle 2007: quelle rupture?', *French Politics, Culture and Society*, 27(1), 23–42.

Martin, J.-P. (2005) *Histoire de la nouvelle gauche paysanne. Des Contestations des années 1960 à la Confédération paysanne*. Paris: La Découverte.

Mattelart, A. (2007) *Diversité culturelle et mondialisation*. Paris: La Découverte.

Mayer, O. (2008) 'Pour les dix ans d'Attac . . . le temps des questions', *L'Humanité*, 22 août.

McNeill, W. H. (2001) 'Fernand Braudel, historian', *Journal of Modern History*, 73(1), March.

Mendras, H. (1967) La Fin des paysans. Innovation et changement dans l'agriculture française. (Paris: Sedeis), translated by J. Lerner, The Vanishing Peasant. Innovation and Change in French Agriculture. Cambridge and London: MIT Press, 1970.

Meunier, S. (2003) 'France's double-talk on globalization', *French Politics, Culture & Society*, 21(1), 98–107.

—(2004) 'Free-falling France or free-trading France?', *French Politics, Culture & Society*, 22(1), 98–107.

Michelet, J. (1881) *Histoire de France I*. Paris: Marpon & Flammarion.

Monnot, C. (2001a) 'La gauche antimondialisation prépare la campagne présidentielle', *Le Monde*, 9 mai.

—(2001b) 'Attac rappellera leurs promesses aux candidats "en temps voulu"', *Le Monde*, 6 novembre.

Mordillat, G. (2011) 'Préface', in C. Aguiton et al. *Tous dans la rue. Le mouvement social de l'automne 2010*. Paris: Seuil, pp. 7–10.

Mouchard, D. (2005) 'Le Creuset de la mobilisation anti-AMI de 1998', in E. Agrikoliansky, O. Fillieule, N. Mayer, *L'Altermondialisme en France. La Longue histoire d'une nouvelle cause*. Paris: Flammarion. pp. 317–37.

Mouffe, C. (1994) *Le Politique et ses enjeux. Pour une démocratie plurielle*. Paris: Découverte/MAUSS.

Naím, M. (2009) 'Globalization', *Foreign Policy*, 171, March/April, 28–34.

Nikonoff, J. (2009) 'L'Altermondialisme en déclin', *Libération*, 7 août 2009.

Noiriel, G. (2005) *Les Fils maudits de la République. L'avenir des intellectuels en France*. Paris: Fayard.

—(2007) *A Quoi sert 'l'identité nationale'*. Marseille: Agone.

Nora, P. ed. (1984) *Les Lieux de mémoire*. Tome I: La République. Paris: Gallimard.

—(1986) *Les Lieux de mémoire*. Tome II: La Nation, vol. 1. Paris: Gallimard.

Nora, P. (2001) *Rethinking France. Les lieux de mémoire*, translated by Mary Trouille. London and Chicago: University of Chicago Press.

Panitch, L. (1996) 'Rethinking the role of the State', in J. H. Mittelman, ed. *Globalization. Critical Reflections*. Boulder, CO and London: Lynne Rienner Publishers, pp. 83–113.

Passet, R. (2000) 'Le Conseil scientifique. Un bilan à fin juin 2000', document published on Attac's website, 3 July 2000. Available at: www.france.attac.org/

Peillon, V. (2008) *La Révolution française n'est pas terminée*. Paris: Seuil.

Pingaud, D. (2000) *La Gauche de la gauche*. Paris: Seuil.

Pleyers, G. (2003) 'Le modèle français: 1995–2000', in M. Wieviorka, ed. *Un Autre monde. Contestations, dérives et surprise dans l'antimondialisation*. Paris: Balland, pp. 141–54.

Poulet, B. (1999). 'A gauche de la gauche', *Le débat*, 103, janvier–février, 39–59.

Puljak, N. (2009) 'Sarkozy défend l'agriculture, et par elle, "l'identité nationale française"' *Le Point*, 27 octobre 2009.

Ramonet, I. (1995) 'La pensée unique', *Le Monde diplomatique*, janvier 1995.

—(1997) 'Désarmer les marchés', *Le Monde diplomatique*, December.

—(1999) *Géopolitique du chaos*. Paris: Gallimard.

—(2001) *Nouveaux pouvoirs, nouveaux maîtres du monde*. Quebec: Les Editions Fides.

—(2002) 'Cela s'appelle l'aurore', *Attac au Zénith*, Paris: Mille et Une Nuits, pp. 13–25.

—(2006) 'Guerre des idées', *Le Monde diplomatique*, 626, mai 2006.

—(2009) *Le Krach parfait. Crise du siècle et refondation de l'avenir*. Paris: Galilée.

RFI (2004) 'Chirac appelle à une fiscalité internationale', le 21 septembre. Available at: www.rfi.fr/actufr/articles/057/article_30614.asp

Rogers, S. C. (1987) 'Good to think; the "peasant" in contemporary France', *Anthropological Quarterly*, 60(2), April, 56, 60.

—(2000) 'Farming visions. Agriculture in French culture', *French Politics, Culture and Society*, 18(1), Spring, 62.

Rouart, J. M. (2003) *Adieu à la France qui s'en va*. Paris: Grasset.

Royal, S. & Touraine, A. (2008) *Si la gauche veut des idées*. Paris: Grasset.

Rozès, S. (2009) 'L'individu, l'imaginaire et la crise', *Le Débat* (155) mai–août, 46–53.

Rudelle, O. (1982) *La République absolue. Aux origines de l'instabilité constitutionnelle de la France républicaine*. Paris: Publications de la Sorbonne.

Said, E. (1991) *Orientalism*. Polity.

Sarkozy, N. (2007a) *Discours à Caen*, 9 mars.

—(2007b) *Discours à Bercy*, 29 avril.

—(2008a) Conférence de presse de M. Le Président de la République au Palais de l'Elysée, 8 janvier.

—(2008b) *Discours à Toulon*, 25 septembre.

—(2009a) *Discours à Nîmes*, 5 mars.

—(2009b) *Discours à Toulon – La Seyne-sur-Mer*, le 1 décembre.

—(2010) Discours au 40ème Forum économique mondial à Davos, 27 janvier.

Schmidt, V. A. (2002) *The Future of European Capitalisms*. Oxford: Oxford University Press.

Schnapper, D. (2008) 'L'identité nationale: quelles réalités?' *Cahiers français*, 342, jan–fev, 3–7.

Schneider, I. (1988) 'Myth and Mythology in the Drama of Botho Strauss' in W. G. Sebald *A Radical Stage: Theatre in Germany in the 1970s and 1980s*. Oxford: Berg, 31–51.

Segerstad A. F. (2006) 'Airline Ticket Taxes: Innovation or Idiocy?', *Institute of Economic Affairs – Economic Viewpoints*. Oxford: Blackwell Publishing.

Sieffert, D. (2006) *Comment peut-on être (vraiment) républicain?* Paris: La Découverte.

Slama, A.-G. (1995) 'Democratic dysfunctions and republican obsolescence: the demise of French exceptionalism', in G. Flynn, *Remaking the Hexagon*. Boulder, CO: Westview Press.

Smith, T. B. (2004) *France in Crisis. Welfare, Inequality and Globalization since 1980*. Cambridge: Cambridge University Press.

Sylvestre, J. M. (2008) *La France piégée'*. Paris: Buchet/Chastel.

Snow, D. A. (1997) 'Frame alignment processes, micromobilization and movement participation', in S. M. Buecheler & F. K. Cylke, eds. *Social Movements, Perspectives and Issues*. California: Mayfield, pp. 211–28.

Sommier, I. (2003) *Les Nouveaux mouvements contestataires à l'heure de la mondialisation*. Paris: Flammarion.

Sonntag, A. (2008) 'The burdensome heritage of prestige politics', in M. Maclean & J. Szarka, *France on the World Stage. Nation State Strategies in the Global Era*. Basingstoke: Palgrave Macmillan. op. cit.

Spitz, J.-F. (2005) *Le Moment républicain en France*. Paris: Gallimard.

Starr, A. (2000) Naming the enemy: anti-corporate movements confront globalization. London: Zed Books.

—(2005) Global Revolt: A Guide to the Movements against Globalization. New York: Pan Books.

Startin, N. (2008) 'The French rejection of the 2005 EU Constitution in a global context: a public opinion perspective', in M. Maclean & J. Szarka, eds. *France on the World Stage. Nation State Strategies in the Global Era*. Basingstoke: Palgrave Macmillan, pp. 91–110.

Suleiman, E. (1999) 'Les Nouveaux habits de l'antiaméricanisme', *Le Monde,* 29 September 1999.

—(2007) 'Les corporatismes, les ressorts cachés de la réussite française, les relations transatlantiques', in K.E. Bitar & R. Fadel, eds. *Les Regards sur la France*. Paris: Seuil.

Szcepanski-Huillery, M. (2003). 'Les Usages militants de la lecture et de l'écriture. L'exemple du Monde diplomatique', paper presented at *'Les mobilisations altermondialistes'* conference, Cevipof, Paris, 3–5 décembre 2003 (published on Cevipof website).

Thiesse, A.-M. (2001) *La Création des identités nationales. Europe XVIIIe–XIXe siècle*. Paris: Seuil.

—(2008) 'L'identité nationale: quelles realités? Crise identitaire, crise de la modernité', *Cahiers français*, 342, jan–fév, 10–15.

Thompson, D. (2003) 'Protest politics and violence in the French countryside in the 1990s: the expression of Euroscepticism?', *Modern & Contemporary France,* 11(3), 293–306.

Todd, E. (1998) *L'Illusion économique*. Paris: Gallimard.

—(2006) 'L'égalité: une passion française', *Problèmes politiques et sociaux,* 920, special issue edited by E. Fougier, 87–9.

—(2008) *Après la démocratie*. Paris: Gallimard.

Touraine, A. (1996) 'L'Ombre d'un mouvement', in A. Touraine et al., eds. *Le Grand Refus. Réflexions sur la grève de décembre 1995*. Paris: Fayard, pp. 11–102.

—(2001) *Beyond Neoliberalism,* translated by David Macey. Cambridge: Polity Press.

—(2010) *Après la crise*. Paris: Seuil.

Trautmann, F. (2001). 'Internet au service de la démocratie? Le cas d'Attac'. *Cahiers du Cevipof,* 30, 1–60.

Turner, B. (1986) *Citizenship and Capitalism. The Debate Over Reformism*. London: Allen & Unwin.

Unesco Press (2001), *Jacques Chirac: Les politiques ont le devoir de civiliser la mondialisation*. Available at: www.unesco.org/bpi/fre/unescopresse/2001/01-105f.shtml.

—(2003) A L'Unesco, Jacques Chirac plaide pour l'adoption de conventions internationales sur la diversité culturelle et la bioéthique (29 septembre–17 octobre 2003). Available at: http://portal.unesco.org/fr/ev.php-URL_ID=16645&URL_DO=DO_TOPIC&UTL_S.

Vandore, E. (2008) 'Leftist France gloats at capitalism's failings', *The Associated Press*, 21 October.

Védrine, H. (2007) Rapport pour le Président de la République sur la France et la mondialisation.

Veseth, M. (2005) *Globaloney: Unraveling the Myths of Globalization*. Oxford: Rowman & Littlefield.

Viard, J. (1999) 'Bonne terre, bonne bouffe, bonne France', *Le Figaro*, 29 September.

Vidal, P. M. (2006) 'ATTAC en perdition', *Acteurs publics*, 28 November.

Vidal, J. (2008) *La Fabrique de l'impuissance 1. La Gauche, les intellectuels et le libéralisme sécuritaire*. Paris: Editions Amsterdam.

Vincent, H. (2007) 'Le testament de Chirac l'Africain,' *L'Express*, 15 février.

Wainwright, M. (2000) 'Review of L'Horreur Economique', *Socialism Today*, 45, February. Available at: www.socialismtoday.org/45/economic_horror.html

Warnier, J.-P. (2004) *La Mondialisation de la culture*. Paris: La Découverte.

The Washington Post (2007) Farewell, Jacques Chirac: A Leader with a Deep Scorn for Democracy, 8 May 2007.

Weber, E. (1976) *Peasants into Frenchmen: The Modernization of Rural France, 1870–1914*. Stanford: Stanford University Press.

Weill, N. (1999) 'Attac entre contre-expertise, action et récuperation', *Le Monde*, 26 octobre.

—(2010) 'Y'a-t-il encore une vie intellectuelle en France?', *Le Monde*, 5 juin.

Wieder, T. (2010) 'Rentrée des essais: un tour d'horizon', *Le Monde*, 27 août.

Wieviorka, M., ed. (2003) *Un Autre monde. Contestations, derives et surprises dans l'antimondialisation*. Paris: Balland.

Williams, G. (2008) *Struggles for an Alternative Globalization. An Ethnography of Counterpower in Southern France*. Aldershot: Ashgate.

Wintour, P. & Black, I. (2002) 'Chirac furious after row with Blair: Chirac cancels summit', *The Guardian*, 29 October.

Wintrebrau, R. (2007) *Attac, la politique autrement? Enquête sur l'histoire et la crise d'une organisation militante*. Paris: La Découverte

Wolfreys, J. (1999) 'Class struggles in France', *International Socialism*, 84, 31–68.

Zappi, S. (2006) 'Attac en perte d'influence chez les altermondialistes', *Le Monde*, 17 junin.

Zemmour, E. (2010) *Mélancolie française*. Paris: Fayard & Denoël.

Index

Note: page numbers in **bold** refer to a whole chapter. 'n.' after a page reference
indicates the number of a note on that page